D1472082

SPORTS STARS

SERIES 4

SPORTS
STARS
S E R I E S 4

Michael A. Paré

AN IMPRINT OF GALE

DETROIT · NEW YORK · LONDON

SPORTS STARS, SERIES 4

Michael A. Paré

Staff

Julie L. Carnagie, *U·X·L Associate Developmental Editor*
Carol DeKane Nagel, *U·X·L Managing Editor*
Thomas L. Romig, *U·X·L Publisher*

Shalice Shah, *Permissions Associate*
Graphix Group, *Typesetting*

Shanna P. Heilveil, *Production Assistant*
Evi Seoud, *Assistant Production Manager*
Mary Beth Trimper, *Production Director*

Michelle DiMercurio, *Art Director*
Cynthia Baldwin, *Product Design Manager*

Library of Congress Cataloging-in-Publication Data

Paré, Michael A.
    Sports stars. Series 4 / Michael A. Paré
        p.   cm.
    Includes bibliographical references and index.
    Summary: Presents thirty biographical sketches of popular athletes active in a variety of sports, including Nicole Bobek, Terrell Davis, Mark McGwire, and Gabrielle Reece.
    ISBN 0-7876-2784-4 (alk. paper)
    1. Athletes—Biography—Juvenile literature.   [1. Athletes.]
I. Title
GV697.A1P323 1998
796'.092'2—dc21
[B]

98-5008
CIP
AC

Cover photographs (clockwise from top left): Curtis Martin, photograph by Winslow Townson. Courtesy of AP/Wide World Photos, Inc.; Steve Yzerman, Courtesy of AP/Wide World Photos, Inc.; Martina Hingis, photograph by Mike Blake. Courtesy of Archive Photos; Annika Sorestam, photograph by Steve Dipaola. Courtesy of Archive Photos.

∞™ This book is printed on acid-free paper that meets the minimum requirements of American National Standard for Information Sciences—Permanence Paper for Printed Library Materials, ANSI Z39.48-1984.

Printed in the United States of America

Contents

Biographical Listings

Athletes by Sport

Italics indicates series. Entries in Series 4 are **bolded.**

FIGURE SKATING

FOOTBALL

GOLF

GYMNASTICS

HOCKEY

HORSE RACING

SKIING

SOCCER

SPEED SKATING

SWIMMING

TENNIS

TRACK AND FIELD

VOLLEYBALL

YACHTING

Reader's Guide

Sports Stars, Series 4, presents biographies of thirty amateur and professional athletes, including Terrell Davis, Kobe Bryant, and Nicole Bobek. Besides offering biographies of baseball, basketball, and football sports figures, *Sports Stars,* Series 4, provides increased coverage of athletes in a greater variety of sports, such as volleyball, horse racing, and figure skating, and features biographies of women, including Ila Borders and Cynthia Cooper, who have broken the sex barrier to participate in the male-dominated sports of baseball and basketball.

Athletes profiled in *Sports Stars,* Series 4, meet one or more of the following criteria. The featured athletes are:

- Currently active in amateur or professional sports

- Considered top performers in their fields

- Role models who have overcome physical obstacles or societal constraints to reach the top of their professions.

Format

The thirty profiles of *Sports Stars,* Series 4, are arranged alphabetically. Each biography opens with the birth date and place of the individual as well as a "Scoreboard" box listing the athlete's top awards. Every essay contains a "Growing Up" section focusing on the early life and motivations of the individual and a "Superstar" section highlighting the featured athlete's career. The profiles also contain portraits and often additional action shots of the individual. A "Where to Write" section listing an address and a list of sources for further reading conclude each profile. Additionally, sidebars containing interesting details about the individuals are sprinkled throughout the text.

Additional Features

Sports Stars, Series 4, includes a listing by sport of all the athletes featured in Series 1, Series 2, Series 3 and Series 4, as well as a cumulative name and subject index covering athletes found in all four series.

Comments and Suggestions

We welcome your comments on this work as well as your suggestions for individuals to be featured in future editions of *Sports Stars.* Please write: Editor, *Sports Stars,* U•X•L, 835 Penobscot Bldg., Detroit, Michigan 48226-4094; call toll-free: 800-877-4253; or fax toll-free: 800-414-5043.

Photo Credits

UPI/Corbis-Bettmann. Reproduced by permission: p. 70; Photograph by Ed Andrieski. AP/Wide World Photos, Inc. Reproduced by permission: p. 78; Photograph by Gary Caskey. Archive Photos. Reproduced by permission: pp. 81, 286; Photograph by Luc Novovitch. AP/Wide World Photos. Reproduced by permission: p. 94; Photograph by Dennis Paquin. AP/Wide World Photos. Reproduced by permission: p. 97; Photograph by John Makely. AP/Wide World Photos. Reproduced by permission: p. 105; Photograph by Craig Fuji. AP/Wide World Photos. Reproduced by permission: p. 108; Photograph by Scott Olson. Archive Photos. Reproduced by permission: p. 120; Photograph by Ruben Sprich. Archive Photos. Reproduced by permission: p. 132; Photograph by Frank Gunn. AP/Wide World Photos, Inc. Reproduced by permission: p. 138; Photograph by Peter Jones. Archive Photos. Reproduced by permission: p. 141; Photograph by Mike Blake. Archive Photos. Reproduced by permission: p. 150; Photograph by Wade Payne. AP/Wide World Photos, Inc. Reproduced by permission: p. 160; Photograph by Beth A. Keiser. AP/Wide World Photos, Inc. Reproduced by permission: p. 168; Photograph by Jerry Lampen. Archive Photos. Reproduced by permission: p. 182; Photograph by Kimimasa Mayama. Archive Photos. Reproduced by permission: p. 195; Photograph by Jim Bourg. Archive Photos. Reproduced by permission: p. 205; Photograph by Winslow Townson. AP/Wide World Photos, Inc. Reproduced by permission: p. 208; Photograph by Kevin J. Larkin. Corbis-Bettmann. Reproduced by permission: p. 215; Photograph by Ray Stubblebine. Archive Photos. Reproduced by permission: pp. 218, 230; Washington Wizards. Reproduced by permission: p. 250; Photograph by Mark J. Terrell. AP/Wide World Photos, Inc. Reproduced by permission: p. 265; Photograph by Steve Marcus. Archive Photos. Reproduced by permission: p. 274; Photograph by Steve Dipaola. Archive Photos. Reproduced by permission: p. 277; Photograph by Pete Fontaine. LPGA. © SportImages. Reproduced by permission: pp. 295, 298; Photograph by Marty Lederhandler. AP/Wide World

Photos. Reproduced by permission: p. 303; **Photograph by Ron Frehm. AP/Wide World Photos. Reproduced by permission:** p. 305; **Photograph by the National Hockey League. AP/Wide World Photos, Inc. Reproduced by permission:** p. 313; **Photograph by Bill Kostroun. AP/Wide World Photos, Inc. Reproduced by permission:** p. 316.

Jeff Bagwell

1968–

A s a child Jeff Bagwell had one dream: to play base-ball for his favorite team, the Boston Red Sox. In 1989 his dream seemed to be coming true when the Red Sox drafted him out of the University of Hartford. A year later, however, Boston traded Bagwell to the Houston Astros. Although he was disappointed, he decided to make the best of a bad situation. Bagwell did so well with his new team that he earned the 1994 National League Most Valuable Player award and has become one of the most feared hitters in the major leagues. Though he would still love to play in Fenway Park (Boston's home field), Bagwell now calls the Astrodome his home.

Growing Up

RED SOX FAMILY. Jeffery Robert Bagwell was born May 27, 1968, in Boston, Massachusetts. When he was two years old the family moved to Killingworth, Connecticut. Despite the

"There ain't nothing gifted about Jeff Bagwell."
—Jeff Bagwell.

SCOREBOARD

WON 1994 NATIONAL LEAGUE
MOST VALUABLE PLAYER AWARD.

WON 1991 NATIONAL LEAGUE
ROOKIE OF THE YEAR AWARD.

HAS BATTED OVER .300
THREE TIMES (1993, 1994 AND
1996) AND HAS DRIVEN IN OVER
100 RUNS THREE TIMES (1994,
1996, AND 1997).

BAGWELL HAS OVERCOME
THREE HAND INJURIES TO
ESTABLISH HIMSELF AS THE BEST-
HITTING FIRST BASEMAN IN THE
NATIONAL LEAGUE.

move, the Bagwell family remained loyal Boston Red Sox fans.

"All my life everything had been Boston," Bagwell told *Sports Illustrated*. "I was born in Boston. My father was from Watertown, my mother was from Newton, both outside Boston. We moved to Connecticut when I was about a year old, but our house was one of those places where you couldn't mention the word [New York] Yankees when you came inside the front door. Every weekend the television would be tuned to channel six. The Red Sox. No other games. My grandmother Alice Hare can tell you anything you want to know about the Red Sox."

Bagwell's hero as a child was Carl Yastrzemski, the Hall-of-Fame left fielder for the Red Sox. "Carl represented all the things that I try to do in life," Bagwell explained in *Sports Illustrated for Kids*. "Get the most out of your ability and work very hard." Bagwell also cheered for Yaz's fellow Red Sox players Dwight Evans and Jim Rice.

DREAM COME TRUE. As a child, Bagwell played basketball and soccer, but his favorite sport was baseball. He was a star Little League player, and he pitched and played shortstop at Xavier High School. "He was one of the hardest workers I've ever coached," his high school manager, Terry Garstka, recalled in *Sports Illustrated for Kids*.

Bagwell's play in high school was good enough to earn him a spot on the University of Hartford baseball team. He batted over .400 his first season, but few major league baseball scouts knew about him. That changed in the summer following his freshman season when Bagwell played in the Cape Cod league.

"I got my chance in the Cape Cod league, during the summer," Bagwell explained in *Sports Illustrated*. "A lot of

the players from the best [college] programs in the country come to play there. You get a job. You play baseball at night. Albert Belle [now of the Chicago White Sox] was playing there. . . . The first year I went I was a last-minute addition to the team in Chatham. I got a job washing dishes at a Friendly's restaurant. The other players on my team, they would come in, eat, then write me notes in ketchup and mustard on their dishes. I hit about .205 that year, but I looked at those guys and decided I could play with them."

Bagwell returned to the Cape Cod league in 1988 and hit .315. The Red Sox made his childhood dream come true when they drafted the young third baseman in the fourth round of the 1989 major league draft. Bagwell learned the news when he returned from playing in a college all-star game at Fenway Park. As he pulled into the driveway his father, Robert, came out of the house carrying a Boston uniform.

DREAM ENDS? Boston sent Bagwell to the minor leagues. He showed promise, but the Red Sox had future hall-of-famer Wade Boggs playing third base and top prospect Scott Cooper was ready to move up to the major leagues. Bagwell hit for a high average, but showed little power. In 205 minor league games he hit only 6 home runs.

Bagwell was having the best season of his career in 1990. He won the Eastern League Most Valuable Player award with a .333 average and 61 RBI (runs-batted-in) as a member of the New Britain Red Sox. On August 31, 1990— the last day major league teams could make a trade—Boston traded Bagwell to the Houston Astros for relief pitcher Larry Andersen.

The Red Sox were in the middle of a tight race for the American League East Division title and hoped Andersen would help them down the stretch. Bagwell learned about the trade from his manager, Butch Hobson, as he prepared to take batting practice. "I was born in Boston," Bagwell told *Sports Illustrated for Kids.* "The Red Sox were my favorite team. Then I'm traded. It was terrible." Boston went on to win the division and Andersen had a 1.23 ERA (earned-run-average) in 15 games for the Red Sox. He left the team the next year, going to the San Diego Padres as a free agent.

TOP ROOKIE. After recovering from the shock of the trade, Bagwell realized the move might be good for his career. "It took about two weeks to realize that, hey, I'm going to get a chance to play in the big leagues more than I would with the Red Sox, and that's what it's all about," Bagwell explained to the *Atlanta Journal-Constitution.*

Bagwell came to spring training in 1991 with little hope of beating out the starting third baseman for the Astros, Ken Caminiti. Despite the fact it might cost him his job, Caminiti helped Bagwell in spring training. "I owe a lot to Caminiti," Bagwell revealed to *Sports Illustrated*. "He was my friend from the beginning, always telling me things that would help. He went about 11 for 11 to start the spring too, just to show how hard it was going to be for me to take his job."

Houston expected to send Bagwell back to the minor leagues. He hit so well in spring training, however, that he earned a spot on the major league roster. To get Bagwell's bat into the lineup, Houston switched him to first base with only ten days left in spring training. He never played third base again.

Bagwell had a great rookie year in 1991. He hit .294 and had 15 home runs and 82 RBI. "What happened was that I had a chance to play from the get-go," he explained to the *Atlanta Journal-Constitution*. "When you get a chance to play and you know you're going to be in the lineup every day, it makes things a lot easier." In a near unanimous decision, 23 of 24 sports writers voted for Bagwell as National League Rookie of the Year. He was the first Astro ever to win the award.

Superstar

MVP. Bagwell continued to improve in his second season [1992]. He hit .273 and had 18 home runs and 96 RBI (sixth in the National League). In 1993 Bagwell was approaching superstar status when Ben Rivera of the Philadelphia Phillies hit him with a pitch, breaking a bone in his left hand. The injury occurred on September 12 and forced him to miss the rest of the season. Bagwell finished the year with a .320 average (sixth in the National League), 20 home runs, and 88 RBI.

Bagwell returned to the Astros lineup in 1994 and had one of the greatest seasons in major league history. He hit .368 (second in the league) and had 39 home runs (second in the National League and a Houston single-season record).

Bagwell also drove in 116 runs (first in the National League) and scored 104 more (led National League). In doing so, he became the first player since his hero Yastrzemski in 1967 to finish first or second in his league in average, RBI, home runs, and runs scored. The last player in the National League to do this was Willie Mays of the New York Giants in 1955.

Bagwell also led the National League in total bases (300), extra-base hits (73), and slugging percentage (.750). In addition he stole 15 bases and won his first Gold Glove award, given to the best fielding player at each position in each league.

Bagwell was the unanimous choice as National League Most Valuable Player, the first Houston player to win this award. Only two other players have won the National League award unanimously since it was established in 1931: Orlando Cepeda of the St. Louis Cardinals in 1967 and Mike Schmidt of the Philadelphia Phillies in 1980. Bagwell became one of only eight players to win both the rookie of the year and MVP trophies in the National League.

"I always compare everything to 1994 because I felt like that was the best I could play," Bagwell explained to the *Houston Chronicle*. "I don't know if I can play better than that. I'd just sit at home and shake my head after some of those games. I was so locked in. For three months I was locked in. Not to toot my own horn or anything, but I was pretty good in 1994. I was about as consistent as anyone could be for three months. It was unbelievable. Wherever we went I knew I was going to get at least two hits."

Bagwell broke his wrist in 1994 when Andy Benes of the San Diego Padres hit him on August 10. The injury knocked him out for the year, and a player's strike ended the season. The strike was caused by a disagreement between the players and baseball team owners over issues like salaries and free agency. The end of the season hurt Houston, since the Astros were only one-half game behind the National League Central Division leading Cincinnati Reds.

SLUMP. Bagwell entered the 1995 season wondering how he could top his MVP season. "I can't believe what I did," he confessed to *Sport*. "I would have been happy with 20 homers, 100 RBI and to hit .300. I've been telling people they shouldn't expect me to put up [1994's] numbers next year—or ever again for that matter."

Bagwell started slowly, batting only .183 through May. "I'd get in the batter's box, and I'd have no idea what I was doing," he explained to *Sports Illustrated*. "The bases would be loaded, and I'd be up there thinking, 'What do I do here?' My hands were all wrong, my feet were messed up. Then self-doubt came in. I started thinking, 'Maybe I'm not as good as last year.' Then I was in big trouble."

The troubles for Bagwell on the field were made worse by a painful divorce from his wife, Shaune. "It's a tough game [baseball] when your mind is right," he admitted to the *Los Angeles Times*. "Mine wasn't. I set certain criteria for myself after '94 and began to think maybe I wasn't that good. I let off-field problems snowball."

NOT AGAIN! Bagwell finally decided to change his outlook. "I was tired of thinking about everything else except what I should be thinking about," he revealed to the *Los Angeles Times*. "I was determined to make [baseball] fun again."

The change in attitude helped turn around Bagwell's season. He batted .339 in June and drove in 31 runs in July. Just as his season was getting on track, Bagwell broke his hand again when Brian Williams of the San Diego Padres hit him. "I got scared. I knew it hurt," Bagwell said.

The injury forced Bagwell to miss a month of the season and the Astros went 9-21 in his absence. He returned in September to bat .313 with five home runs and 21 RBI. Houston came within one game of winning the National League wild-card spot, losing out on the last day of the season to the Colorado Rockies. "It was a very emotional year for me," Bagwell revealed in *Sports Illustrated*. "Up and down, up and down. But I learned a lot about myself. After last year, I know now I can deal with anything." Bagwell finished the season with a .290 average, 22 home runs, and 87 RBI.

FULL SEASON. Bagwell had only one goal in 1996—to play a full season. "My only goal is to get through 162 games with two hands," he told the *Los Angeles Times*. "I'm tired of taking my uniform off with one. We have a tendency to gripe and moan about the schedule and having to come to the park every day, but I don't take anything for granted any more. I can't wait to come out every day."

Bagwell achieved his goal, starting all 162 of Houston's games. "After breaking my hands three years in a row, I'm just happy every day I can be in the lineup," Bagwell explained in the *Houston Chronicle*. "I've told [manager] Terry [Collins] not to ever ask me if I want a day off. Every day that I can wake up and have feeling in my hand, I want to play."

Coming down the stretch Bagwell was in competition for his second National League MVP award. His main competition was his good friend Ken Caminiti, who had been traded to the San Diego Padres after the 1994 season. "I want Cammy to play as well as he can," Bagwell declared to the *Sporting News*. "And if he wins the MVP, that's terrific. I want to win it again, there's no question about that. But, I mean, what could be better than to have one of your best friends win the award? I'm proud of him."

Bagwell finished the 1996 season with a .315 average (eighth in the National League), 120 RBI (tied for sixth in the National League), and 31 home runs. He also set Astros single-season records for doubles (48, first in the National League), extra-base hits (81, fourth in the National League), total bases (324), and RBI. The big slugger also stole 21 bases.

"He means an awful lot to us," Collins told the *Atlanta Journal-Constitution*. "We've got some pretty good players, but Jeff's our go-to guy. He's the guy that wants the big hits for us. He wants to be in a situation where he can come through." Caminiti won the National League MVP award as he led the Padres into the play-offs.

PLAYOFF BOUND. In 1997 Bagwell teamed up with second baseman Craig Biggio and right fielder Derek Bell to form the "Killer Bees." These three players provided the offense to carry the Astros to their first-ever National League Central Division title and a spot in the playoffs for the first time since 1986. Bagwell led the way with a .286 average, 43 home runs, and 135 RBI. "When he gets locked in, he gets locked in for a season," Biggio explained in *Sports Illustrated.* "Then you jump on the train and go for a ride."

STRANGE STANCE

Bagwell has an unorthodox swing. He bats in a crouch, has an uppercut swing, and holds his hands over the plate. Batting coaches have tried to change his stance and swing, but Bagwell knows only one way to hit. "If I try to make big adjustments [in my swing], it would take me too long to learn how to hit again, and I just don't have time for that," he explained to the *Atlanta Journal-Constitution.* Bagwell also likes to swing for the fences. "It's all or nothing," he told the Gannett News Service.

In the playoffs Houston ran into one of the greatest pitching staffs in baseball history. The Atlanta Braves shut down the "Killer Bees" and swept the Divisional Series 3-0. Bagwell was disappointed in his performance, as he had only one hit in twelve at-bats and no RBI against the Braves. "Losing like this doesn't take anything away from our season," Bagwell said. "These three games in the postseason don't wipe out what we did in the regular season."

Bagwell generates great bat speed and has great hand-eye coordination. But the fact that he holds his hands low and near the plate puts him in danger of being hit, explaining his many injuries. Bagwell now wears a plastic protector with an inflatable pad on the back of his left hand.

Despite his strange stance, Bagwell has become one of the most feared hitters in the National League. "Hitting is such an individualistic thing," he explained to the *Atlanta Journal-Constitution.* "If there was one way to hit, everybody would be like that. You've got to do what feels comfortable and for whatever reason, I feel comfortable in that stance. I don't understand why, it doesn't look that comfortable."

OFF THE FIELD. Bagwell lives in Houston, Texas. His nickname is Bags. Bagwell lifts weights. His hobby is collecting autographs from other athletes. During his time off Bagwell likes to play golf and occasionally goes fishing.

Bagwell does not let his success go to his head. "Everyone sees what you've done, so why talk about it," he told *Sport.* "I think success and money should make someone more humble. Anyway, I'm the type of person who always expects the worst. Maybe it's my New England upbringing. But that way, if you expect the worst, it's easier to accept something if it doesn't go your way."

Bagwell would like to play against the Red Sox in the World Series. "It would be a dream come true," he admitted to *Sports Illustrated for Kids.* He also does not discount the idea of one time playing for the Red Sox. "I've thought about it a thousand times," Bagwell revealed to *Sport.* "Don't get me wrong, I love Houston, I love playing for the Astros. But in today's market, it's definitely feasible I might move on. I've wondered what it'd be like to put on that uniform, to play in Fenway, to play where Yaz played. It'd be a wonderful feeling."

Bagwell has some simple advice for children who want to play major league baseball. "When you are a kid growing up, and you have [a dream] and talent, the main thing you can do is play," he said in an interview. "Every chance I got, I played baseball. Don't ever give up or let anyone tell you that you can't do it. If the will, desire, and hard work are there, then you have a chance."

Only hard work will keep Bagwell on top. "I think dangerous hitters are guys who you say, 'He didn't hit that ball too good,' and then you look up and it's gone," he told the *Houston Chronicle.* "I'm 5 [feet], 11 [inches], I have the weirdest stance in baseball and I struggle every day to try to fix it. There ain't nothing gifted about Jeff Bagwell."

WHERE TO WRITE:

C/O HOUSTON ASTROS, ASTRODOME,
8400 KIRBY DRIVE,
HOUSTON, TX 77054.

Sources

Atlanta Journal-Constitution, July 7, 1996.
Baseball Weekly, June 25, 1997.
Houston Chronicle, June 30, 1996.
Los Angeles Times, June 23, 1996.
Sport, May 1995.
Sporting News, October 31, 1994; September 16, 1996.
Sports Illustrated, July 26, 1993; May 29, 1995; June 17, 1996.
Sports Illustrated for Kids, February 1, 1995.
Additional information provided by the Associated Press, the Gannett News
    Service, and the Houston Astros.

Jerome Bettis

1972–

"You can't just take what's given to you in life. You have to earn some things."
—Jerome Bettis.

Jerome Bettis—the star running back of the Pittsburgh Steelers—is an excellent bowler. In a tournament he once rolled a perfect 300 game. On the football field Bettis treats defensive players like bowling pins, knocking them down faster than almost any other runner in the National Football League (NFL). In 1996 he earned the nickname "The Bus" and delivered his Steeler teammates into the American Football Conference (AFC) playoffs. Once a player with a bad reputation, Bettis has proven he is one of the most reliable forms of NFL transportation.

Growing Up

BOWLING BETTIS. Jerome Abrams Bettis was born February 16, 1972, in Detroit, Michigan. He was the youngest of three children of Gladys and Johnnie Bettis. "When Jerome gets on the field, his dad's gruffness comes out," Gladys Bettis explained to *USA Today.* "All the rest of it—the sweetness, the kindness—he gets from his mom."

Bettis's favorite sport as a child was bowling. Gladys Bettis took her son to the Central City Lanes in Detroit when he was seven. "She felt going bowling was a way to keep me out of trouble in the inner city," Bettis told the *Los Angeles Times.* "I learned to love it because it's a sport in which you are in competition with yourself. You can only beat yourself. That's what I love about it."

TWO-WAY THREAT. Bettis dreamed of becoming a professional bowler—like his hero Mark Roth—but he also played basketball and football at McKenzie High School in Detroit. He earned three letters in football, serving as the team's captain in both his junior and senior seasons. In his senior season Bettis gained 1,355 yards and scored 14 touchdowns as a fullback, and also averaged 15 tackles per game as a linebacker. "I loved it," he recalled in *Sports Illustrated,* referring to playing defense. "I just wanted to crack somebody."

Bettis earned the Circle of Champions Michigan Player of the Year award his senior season. *Parade* magazine awarded him a spot on its All-American team and the *Sporting News* and *USA Today* each named him one of the top-100 high school seniors in the country. Bettis also earned one letter in basketball at McKenzie.

NOTRE DAME BOUND. College recruiters flocked around Bettis, trying to convince him to attend their schools. Most of the schools, however, wanted him to play linebacker, not fullback. "So many of the recruiters couldn't understand why I wanted to play fullback," Bettis explained in *Sport.* "They couldn't understand why anyone would actually want to play fullback when he could play linebacker. That's because so many of those schools looked at the fullback position as just another blocker lined up in the backfield. But I knew I could be more."

SCOREBOARD

EARNED ASSOCIATED PRESS NFL OFFENSIVE ROOKIE OF THE YEAR HONORS IN 1993.

RUSHED FOR OVER 1,000 YARDS IN FOUR OF FIVE NFL SEASONS.

NAMED TO PRO BOWL ALL-STAR GAME FOUR TIMES (1993, 1994, 1996, AND 1997).

BETTIS HAS OVERCOME HIS DOUBTERS AND ESTABLISHED HIMSELF AS ONE OF THE MOST FEARED RUNNING BACKS IN THE NFL.

Bettis finally chose Notre Dame because coach Lou Holtz wanted him to play fullback. The Irish were loaded at the running back position in Bettis's first season in 1990. Notre Dame's backfield featured Ricky Watters and Reggie Brooks, both of whom went on to star in the NFL.

Bettis spent most of his freshman year serving as the back-up fullback behind Rodney Culver, also from Detroit. He played in 11 games, but gained only 115 yards on 15 carries. Bettis impressed his coaches with his toughness and ability to block and hold on to the football. "Coach Holtz is about a tough, pound-it-out, don't-fumble-the-football running game," Bettis related to *Sport*. "Positive yardage, stay low and don't fumble under any circumstances. If you fumble, he'll say: 'Do you want to play? Then don't fumble the football. It's that simple.'"

STARTING FULLBACK. In his second season (1991) Bettis took over the starting fullback spot. He earned team co-MVP honors with quarterback Rick Mirer after rushing for 972 yards on 168 carries, an average of 5.8 yards every time he ran with the ball. Bettis also scored 20 touchdowns, breaking the school's single-season record for scoring with 120 points. (Tailback Allen Pinkett scored 110 points in 1983.) He also earned MVP honors in the 1992 Sugar Bowl, as he gained 150 yards and scored three touchdowns in Notre Dame's victory over the University of Florida Gators. His touchdowns all came in the last five minutes of the game.

Bettis had a rare combination of skills. He was a big man, but had speed and deceptive moves. "He has all the strengths of a good fullback, but he can also make these incredible cuts and change directions at a split second and then the speed," Irish offensive coordinator Skip Holtz told *Sport*. "He has tailback speed. Plus, he likes to hit people, which comes from his days as a linebacker." His nickname at Notre Dame was "Big Daddy."

Bettis had a chance to win the Heisman Trophy—given to the best college football player in the nation—in 1992, but an ankle injury slowed him down late in the season. He still

Bettis goes for the touchdown.

ran for 825 yards and 10 touchdowns. Bettis closed out his college career with three touchdowns in Notre Dame's 28-3 Cotton Bowl victory over Texas A&M. The Irish finished the season 10-1-1.

BATTERING RAM. Bettis decided to turn professional following his junior season at Notre Dame. In his college career he gained 1,912 yards on the ground, averaged 5.7 yards per carry, and scored 27 touchdowns. "Big Daddy" also caught 32 passes for 429 yards.

The Los Angeles Rams selected Bettis with the tenth overall pick in the 1993 NFL Draft. He became an instant sensation, gaining 1,429 yards rushing (seventh most ever by a rookie) with an average of 4.9 yards per carry and 7 touchdowns. The Associated Press named Bettis the NFL Offensive Rookie of the Year and his fellow players voted him to the Pro Bowl all-star game. To thank the teammates who blocked for him, Bettis bought them 45-inch color televisions.

TROUBLED TIMES. Bettis struggled in his second season. He gained 1,025 yards rushing, but averaged only 3.2 yards per carry. Teams stacked their lines against Bettis because the team's passing game was below average and Los Angeles suffered injuries in the offensive line. Rams coach Chuck Knox lost faith in his big fullback late in the season, cutting his carries by half. Bettis gained only 211 yards in the last seven games of the season.

His poor season did not discourage Bettis. "You don't lose your ability overnight," he explained in *Sport*. "A lot of people talk about the decline in the second half that year. But nobody brings up the amount of carries I got in the second half. I'm getting 12 carries some games. Nine carries! I can't do anything with nine carries. Instead of running the football, we passed it."

HOLD OUT. The Rams fired Knox following the 1994 season and replaced him with Rich Brooks, a coach who had led the University of Oregon to a Rose Bowl appearance the previous season. Bettis ran into problems with Brooks almost immediately. He held out in a contract dispute before the 1995 season, and the new coach labeled him a troublemaker. "He expected me to come into camp when he said to come into camp," Bettis declared in the *Los Angeles Times*. "When I didn't, he took it personal. He held a grudge."

Bettis eventually gave up his holdout, but when he reported to camp out of shape the damage was done. "I took a beating," he admitted in the *Los Angeles Times*. "They said I was a malcontent [troublemaker], that I was lazy and that I was overweight. A lot of things that were said were untrue."

In 1995 Bettis carried the ball only 183 times and gained a measly 637 yards and scored 3 touchdowns. He suffered from foot and ankle injuries, and Brooks wanted a quicker running back for his more wide-open offense. "I had a bad image, but there was a lot more to it," Bettis revealed to the *Los Angeles Times*. "There were problems with the offensive line. They needed to strengthen it. They needed to commit to the running game. They didn't do enough of it [running the ball] in practice."

Bettis was miserable and considered quitting football and returning to school. He wanted to complete his college degree in business management and expand a computer business he had begun in South Bend, Indiana. "If I would have had to go back there [to the Rams], I would have been miserable," he confessed to the *Los Angeles Times*. "I couldn't go back."

ESCAPE FROM L.A. The Rams and Bettis had reached a parting of the ways. Los Angeles worked to trade their star running back, but also spread rumors that Bettis had a bad attitude. "I'll never forgive the Rams for the way they treated me," Bettis admitted to *Sports Illustrated*. "They had to justify getting rid of me when they knew I could still play, so they labeled me as a bad apple."

The Rams—who had moved their franchise to St. Louis, Missouri—traded Bettis to the Pittsburgh Steelers before the 1996 NFL Draft for second- and fourth-round draft choices.

The Steelers had lost their main running back—Bam Morris—when he was arrested for drug possession. The trade was good news for Bettis. "I couldn't have gone anywhere else that runs the football the way Pittsburgh does and loves the big running back," he explained to *Sport*. "The offensive scheme is great. It's built for me."

The Steelers had heard all the stories about Bettis, but they felt his talent made the trade worth the risk. "I couldn't see where he had lost anything," Pittsburgh running-back coach Dick Hoak told the *Los Angeles Time*. The Steelers were the perfect team for Bettis because their offense emphasized running the ball with a big back and Pittsburgh's offensive line was one of the best in the NFL.

Superstar

THE BUS. Bettis felt he had a lot to prove in the 1996 season. "I was pretty optimistic about the season," he revealed in the *Atlanta Journal-Constitution*. "It was going to give me a chance to get rid of the label I was given: malcontent and all those things. Being in this system, I felt I could really flourish. I wanted to come in with the right attitude. I needed to prove I was a good person. My on-the-field reputation has been proven through time. Off the field, I had to prove I [was undeserving of] the bad label that was given to me."

Bettis earned the nickname "The Bus" during the regular season as he carried the Steelers to the AFC Central Division title. He ran for 1,431 yards, the second most in team history. (Barry Foster once ran for 1,690 yards.) "The Bus" finished third in the NFL in rushing, behind Barry Sanders of the Detroit Lions and **Terrell Davis** (see entry) of the Denver Broncos, and ten times he ran for over 100 yards in a game.

His teammates voted Bettis Pittsburgh's most valuable player and for the third time in his career he earned selection to the Pro Bowl all-star game. "We knew he was a good back, and he fits our offense perfectly," Steelers head coach Bill Cowher explained to the *Atlanta Journal-Constitution*. "He has been nothing but a joy to be around. Hardnosed. Tough. Great worker. He's molded right into this team from Day 1."

BUS TO THE PLAYOFFS. Most importantly for Bettis, he got his first chance to play in the NFL playoffs in 1991. "The postseason is all will and determination," he said. "You're not getting paid what you usually get paid, so it's not the factor of money. That doesn't linger over your head. It's just the will and determination to go out there and want to win. That's what's driving us right now."

Bettis ran for 102 yards and 2 touchdowns in a 42-14 first-round playoff victory over the Indianapolis Colts. Pittsburgh had a chance to go the AFC Championship Game, but fell short against the New England Patriots, 28-3. Bettis finished the New England game with only 43 yards on 13 carries, but a groin injury slowed him down. "I wasn't 100 percent, so it was a rough day out there," he admitted to the *Los Angeles Times* after the game. "I stuck in there and gave it everything I had. I didn't want to lose this game wishing and hoping I had played, but didn't play. I wanted to go out there and give it everything and I did that."

WHY SO GOOD?

Bettis has the size of a big fullback at 5 feet, 11 inches and 243 pounds, but the moves and speed of a tailback. This combination is difficult for defenses to stop. "The thing about Jerome that's so crazy is that he's so deceptive," college teammate and NFL star Ricky Watters told *Sport.* "You look at him and think: 'Oh, this is a big guy. I just gotta slow him up, knock his legs out from under him.' But he has great balance and a lot of speed once he gets going."

Ask Bettis why he is such a good running back and he can give several reasons. "I feel I have a lot to give to a team—positiveness, strength, and consistency on the field," he explained to *Sport.* "That's the biggest thing. If you give me the football the same amount of times every game, I'll be consistent."

STAYS WITH STEELERS. A clause in his contract allowed Bettis to become a free agent following the 1996 season. His mother urged him to stay in Pittsburgh. "My family is going to be a part of my decision," Bettis admitted. "They've been part of every decision I've made to this point, so I'm sure they'll be part of this one, too."

Bettis finally decided to stay with the Steelers in February 1997, agreeing to a four-year, $14.4 million contract. "You want to keep your best people, and they don't come any better than Jerome Bettis," Cowher told *USA Today.* The con-

PERFECT GAME

Bettis still loves to bowl and he once rolled a perfect 300 game in a tournament in Michigan. (A person can only achieve a 300 game by bowling 12 strikes in a row.) "Going into that tenth frame, I was afraid of the choke syndrome," he confessed to the *Los Angeles Times.* "When I took that last shot, I just prayed and hit it. It was something special."

Bettis says that his perfect game was his biggest sports thrill. "It was a feeling like no other," he revealed in *Sport.* "All the accomplishments I've done on the field did not add up to that moment because it was so hard. Put it out there and just beg. Either you get it done or you don't." Bettis carries an average of over 200 and he is the best bowler in the NFL.

tract made Bettis the third-highest paid running back in the NFL behind Barry Sanders of the Detroit Lions and Emmitt Smith of the Dallas Cowboys.

BUS ON SCHEDULE. The Steelers offense entered the 1997 season with a new quarterback. Cowher installed Kordell Stewart—who had played several different positions in his first two seasons in the NFL and earned the nickname "Slash"—as the team's signal caller. Pittsburgh knew they would have to depend on their running game—led by Bettis—and a bruising defense while Stewart gained experience.

Bettis thrives on hard work, and he got plenty of it during the 1997 season. He finished second in the AFC with 1,665 rushing yards, trailing only Terrell Davis of the Denver Broncos. "The Bus" earned team most valuable player honors for the second straight season, the first Steeler to do so since quarterback Terry Bradshaw during the 1977 and 1978 seasons. "We're going to run the football," Bettis said. "Regardless of what you do to us, we're going to try to find a way to run the football."

BUCKING THE BRONCOS. The Steelers finished the season with an 11-5 record, good enough to win the AFC Central Division title. Pittsburgh edged the New England Patriots 7-6 in their first playoff game on a 40-yard scramble by Stewart. Bettis gained 67 tough yards on 25 carries as the Patriots defensive front took away the Steelers' running game. "That's a good defense," he related after the game. "That might be the best run defense in the league."

The Steelers would now host the Denver Broncos in the AFC Championship Game, with the winner earning a trip to the Super Bowl. "If I said this is just another week, I'd be lying," Bettis told *USA Today.* "This is the furthest I've ever been in the playoffs, and it means the most to me. I understand I'm going to be asked to do a lot, and I have to be ready to answer the call."

The game featured a battle between the two top running backs in the AFC—Bettis and Davis of the Broncos. Davis got the better of the matchup—gaining 139 yards to 105 for Bettis—and the Broncos won the game 24-21. Stewart struggled during the game, throwing 3 interceptions and losing a fumble.

OFF THE FIELD. Bettis lives in the Pittsburgh area. He sponsors "The Bus" lines of clothing and food products. "It motivates you to see people wearing your jersey number and calling your name," Bettis said. "It makes you want to do even more to get other people to wear your jersey. There's a lot of pride involved. I actually even like the food myself. I even go to the store and buy my own cookies."

Bettis still relies on his family to help with his business affairs. "Everybody's got a job to do around this place," he explained to *USA Today.* "Sometimes, it can be so overwhelming, and you just need some help. My parents have always been my support group."

"The Bus" loves traveling in Pittsburgh. "I identify with the people of Pittsburgh," he revealed to *USA Today.* "It's a blue-collar town and I'm a blue-collar player. I'm not a flashy guy. I think the fans identify with a back who is going to pound for 4 yards, then get up and pound for 4 more yards. And you know they identify with 'The Bus,' that big, bad, bruising kind of thing that carries people."

To raise money for abused and troubled children, Bettis sponsors a program that sells "Bettis Bus Passes" to and from Three Rivers Stadium for Steeler games.

He feels it is important to complete his college education. "I need to be able to complete my degree so that when my children are older, I can say, 'Hey, don't quit,'" Bettis told the *Beaver (Pennsylvania) County Times.* "You can't just take what's given to you in life. You have to earn some things."

WHERE TO WRITE:

C/O PITTSBURGH STEELERS, THREE RIVERS STADIUM,
300 STADIUM DR.,
PITTSBURGH, PA 15212.

Sources

Atlanta Journal-Constitution, October 26, 1996.

Beaver (Pennsylvania) County Times, February 18, 1997.

Jet, January 31, 1994; March 10, 1997.

Los Angeles Times, January 4, 1997; January 6, 1997; December 8, 1997; January 4, 1998.

Newsday, January 2, 1993; October 13, 1994; January 4, 1997.

Sport, October 1992; December 1994; December 1996.

Sports Illustrated, December 20, 1993; October 7, 1996; November 24, 1997.

USA Today, October 7, 1994; February 18, 1997; October 27, 1997; December 30, 1997; January 9, 1998.

Additional information provided by the Gannett News Service and Notre Dame University.

Nicole Bobek

1977–

Figure skater Nicole Bobek has had her share of ups and downs. In 1995 she won the U.S. Figure Skating Championships, stamping herself as the best female American skater. A series of injuries set her career reeling, but in 1997 Bobek again displayed her talent, earning a bronze medal at the U.S. Figure Skating Championships. A self-described free spirit, she has challenged the figure skating establishment with her clothes, off-ice behavior, and unpredictable skating performances. Bobek has continued to skate for one reason: she loves to entertain.

"I always knew I wanted to skate, and that's it."
—Nicole Bobek.

Growing Up

RAISED BY MOM. Nicole Bobek was born August 23, 1977 in Chicago, Illinois. She was raised by her mother, Jana, after her father left home. Jana Bobek escaped from communist Czechoslovakia in 1968, sneaking away alone on a train as a 21-year-old. (Communism is a governmental system characterized by the common ownership of production methods.) Bobek never knew her father and her parents were never married.

Jana Bobek worked several jobs to support her daughter. She worked as an ice cream vendor, sold hot dogs in a Chicago park, and operated a tanning salon. "She could have been like other moms and sent me off on my own, but she has always been right by my side," Bobek told the *Detroit Free Press*. Jana Bobek's friend—Joyce Barron—also helped in raising Nicole.

STARTS SPINNING. Both Bobek's mother and grandmother were figure skaters in Czechoslovakia. Bobek took her first ice skating classes at the age of three and made her debut in front of a crowd at the age of four. "She was gifted," her first coach, Debbie Stoery, recalled in *People Weekly*. "I loved her to pieces. She was kind and loving and outgoing."

Jana Bobek made her daughter practice her trademark spiral in the living room of their house. "My mom always thought that was such a beautiful move and she'd make me stand in the living room and practice it over and over," Bobek told the *Detroit Free Press*. "I used to hate it. Now, every time I do it, I think of her."

Soon figure skating became the biggest thing in Bobek's life. "The ice was her sandbox," Jana Bobek explained to *People Weekly*. Her idols as a young skater were American superstars Dorothy Hamill, Kristi Yamaguchi, and Nancy Kerrigan.

MOVING UP. Bobek began to get noticed in 1991 when she finished fourth at the World Junior Figure Skating Championships. She took eighth in the senior competition at the 1991 U.S. Figure Skating Championships. The next year Bobek improved to seventh in the same competition and in 1993 she moved up to fifth.

WILD CHILD. Bobek did not fit the mold for a young figure skater. She soon gained a reputation for being wild. Figure skating experts criticized Bobek because she wore a ring on each finger, five earrings, and rhinestone-studded jeans. Rumors also spread that she was more interested in boys and partying late into the night than concentrating on her skating.

Jana Bobek claims her daughter was no different than other teenagers. "As a teenager, Nicole made mistakes, like everyone else," she revealed to the *Detroit Free Press*. "She's a headstrong girl, and that has gotten her into trouble at times. But inside, she has a heart of gold. People have said things about her in the skating world, but as long as it doesn't discourage her, I don't care. You can't please everybody."

Bobek admits she did get into trouble, but feels the conservative leaders of the figure skating world blew her problems out of proportion. "I might have had a discipline problem earlier in my career, but it was never as bad as some people made it out to be," she explained to the *Detroit Free Press*. "People tend to pick on the negative because it makes a better story. I always have to worry about my reputation, what I do, how I act, what I wear, what I say. That's been very hard because I'm just a kid. This is how I like to dress [pointing to her eight rings], but you wouldn't catch me wearing this to a competition. I've learned to tone things down and just get away with as much as I can."

OLYMPIC MISS. Bobek trained hard leading up to the 1994 U.S. Figure Skating Championships. The top three finishers in the women's competition would qualify for the 1994 Winter Olympics in Lillehammer, Norway. Bobek's coach noticed the improvement in her pupil. "There is less flopping around on the ice and a lot more mature skating," Kathy Casey told the *Detroit Free Press*. "She could do all the tricks before, but they're more polished now."

THE BOSS AND BOBEK

At the age of 13 Bobek caught the eye of George Steinbrenner—nicknamed "The Boss"—the owner of the New York Yankees baseball team. She was skating at the 1990 U.S. Olympic Festival in Minneapolis, Minnesota, where she finished seventh. Steinbrenner gave her a check for $15,000 to help with her training. The next year Bobek won the Olympic Festival title.

The 1994 U.S. Figure Skating Championships were held at Joe Louis Arena in Detroit, Michigan. Prior to the beginning of the competition the favorite—Nancy Kerrigan—was assaulted when two men hit her on the knee with a metal rod. The injury knocked her out of the competition and gave Bobek a chance to make the Olympic team.

At the end of the women's competition Bobek finished third. Tonya Harding won the competition and Michelle Kwan came in second. The U.S. Figure Skating Association

(USFSA) now had to decide whether to place Kerrigan on the Olympic team. Most experts felt Kerrigan would have won the competition if she had not been attacked.

Bobek—who would lose her spot if the USFSA named Kerrigan to the team—was willing to step aside. "I would accept it if Nancy gets the spot over me," she explained to the *Detroit Free Press*. "Nancy has been in it much longer than I have and if the judges choose her, I'd understand." Finally, the USFSA did put Kerrigan on the Olympic team and Bobek stayed home.

TAKES ON WORLD. Soon after the U.S. Figure Skating Championships, police determined that friends of Harding had arranged for the attack on Kerrigan. Following the Olympics Harding pled guilty to knowing about the attack after it happened and not informing the authorities. Her guilty plea ended her skating career.

The 1994 World Figure Skating Championships were held in Chiba, Japan. Kerrigan decided not to participate and Harding could not because she had been banned from competing by the USFSA. The U.S. women's team, therefore, would be Kwan and Bobek. "I'm on the team," she told the *Detroit Free Press*. "I'm very excited. . . .I'm going to go out there and give everything I've got."

Bobek did not learn that she would compete at the world championships until the Wednesday before the weekend competition began. She did not skate well and was eliminated in the qualifying phase of the championships. "I wasn't really prepared because of the late notice," Bobek admitted to the *Detroit Free Press*. "The lesson I learned is to be prepared right up to the last minute."

Superstar

CHANGE FOR THE BETTER. Throughout her career Bobek had a difficult time finding a coach who could help bring out her best performance. Always a free spirit, she did not like to train hard and often changed her program in the middle of competitions. Bobek many times got caught up in entertaining the fans and not thinking about what the judges were looking for. Her nerves also got the best of her in many competitions, forcing Bobek to make costly mistakes.

In June 1994 Bobek moved to the Detroit Skating Club to train with coach Richard Callaghan. Callaghan had heard all the stories about his new pupil, but he tried to keep an open mind. "I made sure I didn't have any impression of her when she walked in the door," he revealed to the *Detroit Free Press*. "Unfortunately, media people and gossips like to create stories. I blocked them out, and I'm glad I did because Nicole is the very opposite of her reputation. I was told Nicole had terrible technique, but I don't see anything wrong at all. I like her skating. She has genuine charisma. If she has any problem it's that sometimes she gets carried away entertaining, which is why the fans love her. It's been a trick to try and maintain that but have her programs more structured."

Callaghan forced Bobek to train hard and told her she could not change her program while on the ice. She worked hard and looked at Callaghan's other prize student—two-time U.S. men's national champion Todd Eldredge—for motivation. "When I have bad days, I sit back and watch Todd train and see how hard he works and that gets me fired up," Bobek told the *Detroit Free Press*.

NATIONAL CHAMP. The 1995 U.S. Figure Skating Championships were held in Providence, Rhode Island. The overwhelming favorite in the women's competition was Michelle Kwan, the 14-year-old who finished as runner-up the year before. Bobek—at 17—was the old lady of the competition. "There's Kwan and a whole bunch of little kids behind me," she joked in the *Detroit Free Press*. "I feel old. I know that I can't afford to make mistakes because these girls are right behind me."

Bobek entered the competition with great determination. "My goal is to show everybody that I'm trained and I'm ready," she declared to the *Detroit Free Press*. "Most of all, I have something to prove to myself."

Bobek skated her long program at the championships to music from the movie *Dr. Zhivago*. (In the long program—which counts for two-thirds of the final score—a skater can choose which maneuvers to attempt.) She turned in a solid performance, then had to wait while Kwan took her turn.

Kwan would have won the competition if she had skated cleanly, but she stumbled on one jump and fell on another. When the final marks appeared on the scoreboard, Bobek was stunned to discover that she had won. "The score can't be right," she told Callaghan, according to *Sports Illustrated*. "It can't be right. There must be some mistake." Her training partner Eldredge won the men's competition.

TOUGH TIMES. Bobek arrived at the 1995 World Figure Skating Championships in Birmingham, England under a cloud. A report had surfaced during the U.S. Figure Skating Championships that she had been accused of unlawfully entering a fellow skater's home in October 1994. The press also was full of stories that Jana Bobek had been abusive to her daughter and had taken all the money Nicole had earned from her skating.

The unlawful entry charges against Bobek were eventually dismissed, although she was placed on two years of probation. "It was just a misunderstanding," she explained to the *Detroit Free Press*. "I was in the wrong place at the wrong time. It was just a mistake."

Bobek also defended her mother. "She sold her tanning salon in Colorado to come take care of me in Detroit," she revealed in the *Detroit Free Press*. "She does my hair. She lays out my clothes. I went through a rebelling stage, but things have been really good between us lately."

Despite the controversy Bobek knew what she had to do. "I'm not even concentrating on that [the publicity], I'm thinking about the worlds," she explained in the *Detroit Free Press*. "Everything's over with now. People are going to talk. They always do. But they can say whatever they want, and I can go to the worlds and possibly skate great and win."

WORLD MEDALIST. Unlike the year before, Bobek easily qualified for the finals at the world championships. "This meant a lot to me because last year I didn't qualify," she admitted in the *Detroit Free Press*. "It felt good to go out there. I have not been much on international competitions. The judges all know of me but have not seen me enough to really know what I'm capable of doing. This is my chance to prove myself. This is a dream come true. I had a lot to prove."

Bobek won the short program, placing first on six of the nine judges' cards. (In the short program—which counts for one-third of the final score—the skater must complete required jumps and maneuvers.) "When she's on, she's on," a former coach, Carlo Fassi, declared in the *Detroit Free Press*. "Nicole has a sparkle that's incredible. She's a natural. She's exciting. It's nothing studied. Some have it, some don't." Olga Markova of Russia was in second place and 1994 Olympic bronze-medalist Lu Chen of China came in third.

Unfortunately, Bobek did not skate as well in her long program. She fell two times, but was the only woman in the competition to land a triple lutz-triple toe combination, the toughest jump sequence a woman had ever landed. Chen came through to win the world championships and Surya Bonaly of France finished second.

In spite of her stumbles, Bobek held on to take the bronze medal. She was the first American woman in three years to win a world championship medal. Kwan finished fourth and Eldredge took the silver medal in the men's competition.

Her coach was proud of Bobek. "Nicole has grown up a lot," Callaghan told the *Detroit Free Press*. "For a 17-year-old teenager, she has learned to focus and use some strengths she didn't even know she had. She is changed completely from when I started working with her."

ANOTHER CHANGE. Bobek spent the summer of 1995 skating in the Tom Collins Tour of Champions. She also did a fashion shoot for *Vogue* magazine. "It was so great to have everyone around me, prepping me, putting on my makeup, taking my picture," Bobek said in a television interview. "I love modeling."

Bobek's skating earned her almost half a million dollars, but when she returned to competitive skating she struggled. She finished third and sixth in two events she participated in late in 1995. "Everybody tells you how good you are," Callaghan told the *Detroit Free Press*. "They offer you this and that. You can almost lose your perspective on how you got there. And after two or three months of everyone throwing roses at your feet, you have to go back to work."

With only four weeks left before defending her national title, Bobek changed coaches again. She moved to Las Vegas, Nevada, to work with Barbara Roles Williams—a bronze medal winner at the 1960 Olympics—who had coached Bobek seven years earlier. Bobek felt she could no longer work with Callaghan. "I decided to leave Richard because it didn't seem like it was clicking anymore," she revealed to the *Detroit Free Press*. "We tried to do the same thing as last year, but it wasn't working. I have no hard feelings. We had a good year, but people move on." It was Bobek's ninth coaching change in twelve years.

LEFT OUT. Bobek injured her ankle in December 1995. Instead of letting the injury heal, she decided to skate in the *Nutcracker on Ice* Christmas show. "They told me the only way the ankle would heal was if I stayed off it, but they said it wouldn't get worse by skating on it, it just wouldn't get better," Bobek explained in the *Detroit Free Press*. "I was too busy to take time off."

The ankle still bothered Bobek when she arrived in San Jose, California for the 1996 U.S. Figure Skating Championships. The defending champion did not want to let up. "It hurts when I put pressure on it, but I'm going for everything just as planned," she told the *Detroit Free Press*.

Bobek finished third in the short program. She attempted less difficult jumps than she normally would in an effort not to hurt her ankle. Bobek tried to warm up for the long program, but her ankle was swollen and a doctor advised her to withdraw from the competition. "I'm sad," a crying Bobek said at a press conference. "I just hope people don't give up on me. I wanted to skate, but there was no way I could have made it through the program."

The injury cost Bobek a place on the U.S. team for the 1996 World Figure Skating Championships in Birmingham, England. The USFSA could have named Bobek to the team, but decided instead to send second-place finisher Tonia Kwiatkowski and third-place qualifier Tara Lipinski.

The decision by the USFSA hurt Bobek. Three previous times a defending national champion had been forced to withdraw from the U.S. Figure Skating Championships with an injury and each time that skater had been named to either the U.S. Olympic or world championship team because of their past success. Many experts felt that the USFSA was upset that Bobek had skated in the *Nutcracker on Ice* rather than train. "Of course I was upset, but I realized nothing can be changed," Bobek told *USA Today*. "I also know that I have other chances. It's not like this is the Olympic year."

COMEBACK. The rest of 1996 was difficult for Bobek. She missed three months of training with a back injury she suffered on a rowing machine. Tests showed that a nerve in her back was inflamed and that her discs were injured. At one point Bobek had to use a cane to walk.

Bobek had recovered enough to compete at the 1997 U.S. Figure Skating Championships, held in Nashville, Tennessee. She did not expect to win, but wanted to make sure the figure skating world did not forget about her. "People ask, 'Where have you been?'" Bobek told the *Detroit Free Press*. "I've been around, in my own secret way. I have to prove to a lot of people that I'm not out of this sport, that I'm still in it, still going for it. There have been a lot of questions in people's minds—'Where is Nicole? What's she doing?' That's why I'm here, to show them 'don't forget about me.'"

Bobek finished sixth in the short program after stumbling on one jump and making a major mistake on another. She did much better in her long program, successfully completing five triple-jumps. The performance—skated to the music of *Giselle*—brought the crowd to its feet for a standing ovation. "I had nothing to lose," she admitted to the *Chicago Tribune*. "I wanted to skate great for everyone who has never given up on me."

Bobek earned the second best marks in the long program, good enough for her to capture third place in the competition. "I was thinking 'Whoa. Wow! It's a miracle,'" she revealed to the *Dallas Morning News*. "I thank God—and a lot of other people." Lipinski won the competition, upsetting Kwan, the defending world champion. Lipinski had begun training with Callaghan after Bobek left.

Bobek's performance at the U.S. Figure Skating Championships qualified her for the 1997 World Figure Skating Championships in Lausanne, Switzerland. Before the competition began Bobek's newest coach, Carlo Fassi, died of a heart attack. "I know he is here with all of us, but we just can't see him," she told the *Detroit Free Press*. "He was always here for me, and he always cared. He took the place of being a father for me. From what I heard, one of Carlo's last words were to Christa (his wife), asking her to please be with me for my competition. We all love him, and we will miss him." Bobek finished a disappointing thirteenth at the world championships.

OFF THE ICE. Bobek lives in Rochester Hills, Michigan. She enjoys snowboarding, in-line skating, dancing, drawing, writing poetry, modeling, and designing clothes. After her competitive career is over Bobek would like to become a television commentator and choreograph ice shows. Her nickname is Brass Knuckles, a name she got because she wears rings on each finger.

Bobek is the spokesperson for Raising the Spirit— Touching the Heart. As part of the campaign she visits schools, hospitals, and animal shelters. Bobek always receives

THAT'S ENTERTAINMENT

Bobek has always considered herself more of an entertainer than an athlete. Many times judges have marked her down because they do not feel she takes her skating seriously enough and does not stress the difficult triple jumps that are now so important in figure skating. "I'm more into making eye contact, entertaining the audience and getting their attention," Bobek confessed to the *Detroit Free Press*. "I don't think I have to just jump, jump, jump."

a giant stuffed animal after her performances from a fan in the stands.

Despite the time and energy required to be a world-class figure skater, Bobek likes to do other things as well. "I've always had my space and I've made sure I've had my space," she explained to the Gannett News Service. "I need that. I really do. If I just sat there and eat, drink and sleep ice skating, I'd go crazy."

Bobek continues to compete and won a place on the 1998 U.S. Olympic team that will participate at the Winter Olympics in Nagano, Japan. She still loves to skate. "There never was a time when I was confused at what I was doing," Bobek admitted in *People Weekly*. "I always knew I wanted to skate, and that's it."

WHERE TO WRITE:
C/O U.S. FIGURE SKATING ASSOCIATION,
20 FIRST STREET,
COLORADO SPRINGS, CO 80906-3697.

Sources

Atlanta Journal-Constitution, February 14, 1997.
Chicago Tribune, February 16, 1997.
Dallas Morning News, February 16, 1997.
Detroit Free Press, January 4, 1994; January 8, 1994; March 17, 1994; March 21, 1994; March 22, 1994; July 9, 1994; October 26, 1994; November 1, 1994; February 10, 1995; February 17, 1995; February 18, 1995; March 3, 1995; March 6, 1995; March 7, 1995; March 11, 1995; March 13, 1995; October 25, 1995; October 28, 1995; December 19, 1995; January 15, 1996; January 19, 1996; January 22, 1996; February 14, 1997; February 15, 1997; March 21, 1997.
Oakland Press, February 9, 1997.
People Weekly, March 1995.
San Jose Mercury News, January 21, 1996.
Sports Illustrated, February 20, 1995.
USA Today, January 17, 1996; January 18, 1996; March 15, 1996.
Additional information provided by the Gannett News Service and the U.S. Figure Skating Association.

Ila Borders

1975–

Throughout her baseball career people have told pitcher Ila Borders to give up her dream. First they said she could not pitch for her high school boys team, but she went out and won team Most Valuable Player honors at Whittier Christian High School. Then baseball experts said Borders could never pitch for a men's college team. Again she did not listen, and she became the first woman to earn a scholarship to play for a men's college team and the first woman pitcher to ever to win a college game. In 1997 Borders again proved her doubters wrong when she became the first woman to pitch for a men's minor league team. Despite her success, people still say that Borders will never pitch in the major leagues, but she has learned not to listen to those who doubt her.

"I'm a baseball player. That's all I do."—Ila Borders.

Growing Up

LIKE FATHER, LIKE DAUGHTER. Ila (EYE-la) Borders was born February 18, 1975 in Downey, California, and grew up in nearby La Mirada. Her father, Phil, is a former semi-pro pitcher. As a child Borders went to a Los Angeles Dodgers game with her dad. When the crowd cheered a Dodgers' home run, she told her dad she wanted to play in the major leagues someday.

Borders began playing catch with her father when she was three years old. By the time she was ten years old the young left-hander had a decision to make. Borders could play softball on a girls team and pitch underhand, or she could play baseball on a boy's Little League team and pitch overhand.

The decision was easy for Borders: she wanted to play Little League. "We practiced at Little League ballparks, just the two of us," Phil Borders recalled in *Sports Illustrated for Kids*. "I would pitch to her and she would pitch to me."

Borders was the only girl on her Little League team and one of only two females in the whole league. Her coaches wondered how she would do in her first pitching assignment, but they should not have worried. "At first they thought, 'What's going on here?'" Borders told *Sports Illustrated for Kids*. "But I went out and won my first game."

HIGH SCHOOL HURLER. Borders liked playing all sports, especially basketball, but in high school she concentrated solely on baseball. She starred on the boys team at Whittier Christian High School. Borders compiled a four-year record of 16-7 with a 2.37 earned-run-average (ERA) and 165 strikeouts in 147 innings. Her teammates voted her the team's most valuable player her senior season, and she earned first-team all-league honors.

MAKES HISTORY. Borders made history when she became the first woman ever to receive a college baseball scholarship when she agreed to play for the Southern California College

(SCC) Vanguards, a small Christian school. When she won a spot on the roster, Borders had a chance to make history again by becoming the first woman ever to win a game as a pitcher for a men's college team.

Three women had played men's college baseball before Borders. Susan Perabo played one game at second base for Webster College in Missouri in 1985, and Julie Croteau played first base for St. Mary's in Maryland from 1989 to 1991. The only woman to pitch for a men's college baseball team before Borders was Jodi Haller, who pitched in two games for St. Vincent's College in Pennsylvania in 1990.

Many experts accused SCC of putting Borders on their team as a publicity stunt. Coach Charlie Phillips denied that was the reason for naming her to the team. "People think I took her for the publicity—I don't need all this," Phillips told *Sports Illustrated,* referring to the media that had come to cover Borders' debut. "I took her because she can pitch and she can help this team."

The pressure on Borders was intense, as many people were watching to see how well she would perform. "College has definitely been hard to adjust to," she admitted in *Sports Illustrated.* "Everybody tells me I don't belong out here. Sometimes it gets to me, but no one's going to run me off."

WINS DEBUT. Borders was so nervous before her first start for SCC that she could not sleep the night before. Her nervousness did not show on the mound, however, as she pitched the Vanguards to a 12-1 victory over the team from Claremont-Mudd. Borders threw a complete game and gave up only five hits. She now was the first woman to win a game pitching for a men's college team. "All I can say right now is I'm smiling beyond belief," an excited Borders told the *Orange County Register.* "I feel like I have to win every time because if I do get hit hard people are going to say, 'See, you don't belong out there.'"

Borders impressed the opposition. "You've got to respect her, after today," Gabe Rosenthal of Claremont-Mudd, who hit a home run off Borders, confessed to the *Orange*

Borders shows her winning pitching style.

County Register. "After she was getting everybody out I think people realized she was just another pretty good baseball player and forgot she was a girl."

PROVES SHE BELONGS. Borders went out and won her second start, too, 10-1, over Concordia University. In her first 15 2/3 innings she had given up only one earned run. The young left-hander impressed her coach by beating Concordia despite not pitching her best. "If you cut her hair off and look at her out there, you wouldn't know she was a girl, except the obvious physical differences," Phillips admitted to *Baseball Weekly*. "I'll tell you what, she's as competitive as anyone we have on the team."

Borders compiled a 2-4 record with a 2.92 ERA as a freshman in seven starts and two relief appearances. She succeeded by throwing curveballs, sinker-screwballs, and three types of fastballs. "Everybody said, 'You are not going to make it past Little League,'" Borders told *Sports Illustrated*. "Now I am pitching in college."

Despite her obvious ability, other teams and their fans heckled her because she was female. Because of the mean things opposing team fans yelled at her, Borders pitched primarily at home, where she had a rapidly growing cheering section. Even though she made history as the first female pitcher to win a game in men's college baseball, Borders insisted she was not fighting for a cause. "I'm not here to prove anything about women," she explained in *Sports Illustrated*. "This has nothing to do with women's rights. I love the game, nothing else."

Superstar

TURNS PRO. Borders pitched three seasons at SCC, then transferred to Whittier College for the 1997 season. She left SCC because the team's new manager let her pitch only 24 innings in her junior year. "I don't want to say anything [bad] because they [SCC] helped me out, but I've never had as much support as I have at Whittier," Borders told the *Los Angeles Times*. Her three-year record at SCC was 4-12 with a 5.09 ERA.

At Whittier, Borders was one of the team's three main starters and the only left-handed hurler on the team. "We [can]

HALL OF FAMER

Borders got another thrill following her freshman collegiate season. She was notified that information about her would be included in the "Women in Baseball" exhibit at the Baseball Hall of Fame in Cooperstown, New York. "I began saving money when I was 12 just to be able to go and see [the Hall of Fame]," Borders explained to the Knight-Ridder/Tribune News Service. "Now to be displayed there blows my mind. I don't think words can describe how happy I am. When I got the letter during the summer I thought someone was playing a joke on me. I thought it was odd because I'm still only a sophomore in college. I thought if I had a chance it wouldn't be until further down the road. When my father and I found out it was true, I was on cloud nine for at least a week." Borders was asked to send the Hall of Fame a glove, hat, jersey, baseball, baseball shoes, autobiography, and photograph for display.

use an experienced college left-handed pitcher," Whittier coach Jim Pigot explained to the *Los Angeles Times*. "I told her, 'I can't make any promises as far as playing time, that's all up to you.'" In her senior season Borders compiled a 4-5 record with a 5.22 ERA in 81 innings. With the end of her college career, most people thought her baseball playing days were over.

Borders, however, did not want to give up the game she loved. She decided she did not want to play for the Colorado Silver Bullets, the all-female team playing male minor league teams. Her only other option was to try to earn a roster spot with an all-male professional team. "[Pitching in the big leagues] is still my number 1 goal," Borders told *Baseball Weekly*. "I would like to play with the guys, though. I've been doing that since I was 10."

Outfielder Kendra Hanes played several games in 1994 for the Kentucky Rifles of the independent Frontier League. Other women had played in exhibition games, winter league games, and the Negro Leagues. No women had ever pitched for a men's professional team.

MAKES HISTORY, AGAIN. In 1997 Borders tried out for the St. Paul (Minnesota) Saints of the Northern League. She impressed her new manager, Marty Scott, with her fielding, sound fundamentals, and willingness to work hard. When Scott announced the final roster, Borders had made the team. "I told her that on the basis of physical ability it would be easy to let her go," Scott explained to his new pitcher, according to *Sports Illustrated*. "But I said that because of her work ethic and the way she played the game I was keeping her."

Her new teammates accepted Borders. "Actually, I was quite surprised," she confessed to the *St. Paul Pioneer Press*.

"The guys treated me with respect. They didn't point and laugh. I expected a hard time, but nobody did that. It shows this is a classy organization."

MAKES HER PITCH. Borders made her minor league debut May 21, 1997, in an exhibition game against Duluth-Superior. She pitched a scoreless seventh inning, striking out the first batter she faced, but gave up five runs in the eighth, being tagged with the loss in a 9-6 St. Paul defeat. Borders did demonstrate an ability to get left-handed batters out, a skill needed by the Saints. "I felt good both innings, but I got away from my game plan in the second inning," Borders admitted in the *St. Paul Pioneer Press*. "I got three strikeouts, which is definitely exciting."

The fans supported Borders, chanting "Ila, Ila, Ila," and her teammates thought she pitched well. "She did a whale of a job," her catcher, Sean Delaney, told the *St. Paul Pioneer Press*. "She kept the ball down for the most part. It was exciting catching her. The fans got into it. If she stays around, it will be like that all the time."

Borders made her regular season debut on May 31, 1997, against the Sioux Falls Canaries. The Canaries roughed her up, and she allowed three runs without getting a batter out. Borders pitched better the next day, striking out the side in the eighth inning against the same team, then giving up only one run in two innings in her third outing, again against Sioux Falls.

FITTING IN. Her teammates accepted Borders, but other teams were not as nice. One manager called her "that thing." Talk like that bothered her manager. "She doesn't deserve that," Scott told *Sports Illustrated*. "She's an aggressive ballplayer who can help the team. For us there's not special treatment. If she gets the job done she stays with the club. If not, she's gone. Just like any other player."

TRADED. The Saints decided to trade Borders to the Duluth-Superior Dukes on June 25 for infielder Keith English. She was disappointed by the trade because after her disastrous first outing she had an ERA of 3.00. "I truly enjoyed having Ila here, but the fact is that we have four left-handed relievers on our staff and that is simply too many," Scott explained to the *Los Angeles Times*. "She'll get the chance to pitch in Duluth and that is what this league is all about."

Borders spent most of the rest of the season in the bullpen, getting into 11 games as a reliever. The highlight of her time with the Dukes was pitching a scoreless inning in the Northern League Championship Series against the Winnipeg Goldeyes, a series Duluth-Superior won. "It was a dream, basically," Borders said after the series.

Borders finished the season with a record of 0-0 and an ERA of 7.53. She pitched 14.1 innings, gave up 22 hits, and struck out 12 batters. Those numbers were good enough for the Dukes to invite her back for the 1998 season. "I think striking out as many people as she did . . . that tells me she's got the ability," her father, Phil, observed. "She needs to work on some things to get ready for next year."

THE FUTURE. Despite Borders being invited back, the Dukes manager—former big league catcher George Mitterwald—doubted her ability. The main criticism of Borders is that the hardest she can throw is in the upper 70-mile-an-hour range. During the off-season before the 1998 season Borders planned to lift weights in order to add four to five miles-an-hour to her fastball. "I believe my fastball does the job," she explained. "I'm an offspeed pitcher. But I want to get [an extra] five percent on it [her fastball] so I can say, 'Hey, this is what I do throw now. This is fast enough.' [T]hat'll put the critics to rest."

Despite not having the complete support of her manager, Borders enjoyed her first season of professional baseball. "I told myself going there [to the minor leagues] that I was going to enjoy this, because you never know how life's going to turn," Borders said after the season. "I honestly enjoyed it, but it was stressful for me every day."

OFF THE FIELD. Borders re-enrolled at SCC after the baseball season. She is studying physical education. Borders is a devout Christian and says that her faith has helped her when times were tough.

Borders plans to keep playing the game she loves until she runs out of opportunities. "I'm a baseball player," she told *Baseball Weekly*. "That's all I do."

WHERE TO WRITE:
C/O DULUTH-SUPERIOR DUKES,
P.O. BOX 205,
DULUTH, MN 55801.

Sources

Baseball Weekly, February 23, 1994; March 2, 1994; April 24, 1996.
Los Angeles Times, October 30, 1996; February 6, 1997; April 11, 1997; June 26, 1997; July 5, 1997; September 20, 1997.
Orange County Register, February 15, 1994.
Saint Paul Pioneer Press, May 15, 1997; May 23, 1997.
Sporting News, April 4, 1994.
Sports Illustrated, March 7, 1994; June 16, 1997; July 7, 1997.
Sports Illustrated for Kids, August 1994.
USA Today, April 18, 1996.
Additional information provided by the Associated Press and the Duluth-Superior Dukes.

Mark Brunell

1970–

The quarterback is the most important player on a football team. His job is to direct the team's offense and make big plays. One of the best playmakers in the National Football League (NFL) is Mark Brunell of the Jacksonville Jaguars. Brunell is an accurate passer with a rifle arm, and his speed and running ability add a dimension that very few quarterbacks can match. During the 1996 season he led the NFL in passing yardage with 4,637 yards and earned most valuable player honors at the Pro Bowl all-star game. Brunell has overcome two serious knee injuries in his career to become one of the most dangerous offensive threats in professional football.

Growing Up

"RUN IT." Mark Allen Brunell was born September 17, 1970, in Los Angeles, California. He grew up in Santa Maria, California. Brunell starred at St. Joseph High School where his father, Dave, was the athletic director. His father taught his son how to scramble, telling him: "If it's not there, son, run it." "I think he said that because he didn't want me getting killed in the pocket," Brunell explained to *Sports Illustrated*.

Brunell earned letters in football as quarterback and free safety his last three years at St. Joseph. He passed for 5,893 yards and 41 touchdowns during his high school career and earned All-League and All-Desert Mountain Conference honors two times. An all-around athlete, Brunell also played basketball and baseball, a sport in which he earned All-League honors for four straight years. During his senior year he won league most valuable player honors in both football and basketball.

MVP. The *Sporting News* named Brunell one of the top 100 senior high school football players in 1988. He decided to continue his football career at the University of Washington—a traditional powerhouse in the Pacific-10 Conference (Pac-10)—where Brunell played for legendary coach Don James. The Huskies redshirted [sat out] Brunell during the 1988 season, and he saw only limited playing time during the 1989 campaign.

Brunell had a breakthrough season as the starting quarterback in 1990. He earned second-team All-Pac 10 honors as he led Washington to the conference title and a berth in the Rose Bowl. At the Rose Bowl he threw for two touchdowns and ran for two more in the Huskies' 46-34 victory over the University of Iowa Hawkeyes. His performance earned Brunell the game's most valuable player (MVP) award.

END OF CAREER? Three months after his Rose Bowl MVP performance, Brunell injured his right knee during a spring practice. The injury required reconstructive surgery, and he knew his football career could be over. "I had to realize football might've been over at that point," Brunell admitted to

SCOREBOARD

LED NFL IN PASSING YARDAGE DURING THE 1996 SEASON WITH 4,637 YARDS.

IN 1996 BECAME FIRST PLAYER IN 23 YEARS TO LEAD NFL QUARTERBACKS IN BOTH PASSING AND RUSHING YARDS.

WON MOST VALUABLE PLAYER HONORS AT 1997 PRO BOWL ALL-STAR GAME.

BRUNELL CAN MOVE HIS TEAM ON THE GROUND AND THROUGH THE AIR.

Sports Illustrated. "I thought of some other options—going into education, playing baseball. Then I decided, I'm going to fight this thing and get back."

Brunell made a miraculous recovery and returned for the Huskies' third game of the 1991 season. He served as the backup for Billy Joe Hobert, who had led the Huskies to three straight victories. Washington won the Pac-10 title for the second consecutive season and defeated the University of Michigan, 34-14, in the Rose Bowl. Brunell played in eight games during the regular season and directed two scoring drives against Michigan. Washington finished with a 12-0 record and shared the national championship with the University of Miami.

Brunell and Hobert split time at quarterback during the 1992 season, and the duo led Washington to their third straight Pac-10 title. At one point during the season the Huskies owned a 22-game winning streak. Brunell was a finalist for the Johnny Unitas Award, given annually to the nation's best collegiate quarterback.

PACKER PICK. Brunell graduated from Washington in 1993 with a degree in history. During his football career with the Huskies he threw for 3,423 yards and 23 touchdowns. Despite his collegiate success, Brunell was not highly regarded by NFL scouts. "He didn't have all the measurables you want in a franchise quarterback," Michael Huyghue, Jacksonville Jaguars' senior vice president for football operations, explained in the *Sporting News.* "If they don't fit into that category, chances are they will go in later rounds. People didn't know how to measure what kind of leader he was or how heady he was." Many teams thought that at 6 feet, 1 inch Brunell was too short to be an NFL quarterback.

The Green Bay Packers selected Brunell in the fifth round (one-eighteenth pick overall) of the 1993 NFL Draft. The Los Angeles Raiders chose his Washington teammate, Billy Joe Hobert, in the third round. Brunell was the fourth quarterback taken in the draft, after Hobert, Drew Bledsoe of Washington State and Rick Mirer of Notre Dame. "Coming out of college, I certainly wasn't ready for the NFL," Brunell admitted in *USA Today*.

BACKUP. Brunell was frustrated that he lasted so long in the draft, but he knew he would have to work hard to make the Packers' roster. "I just was hoping to make the team my first camp," he confessed to the *Sporting News*. "I never dared think beyond that."

Brunell spent most of his time in Green Bay on the sidelines, watching superstar Brett Favre direct the Packers' offense. He did not play in his rookie season (1993), but beat out Ty Detmer for the backup job in 1994, his second year. Brunell played in only two games in 1994, during which he completed 12 of 27 passes. He used the time on the bench to learn about playing in the NFL. "I wasn't unhappy," Brunell told *USA Today*. "I felt very fortunate to be at Green Bay. I learned a lot about the game from coach [Mike] Holmgren and playing behind Brett [Favre]."

FRANCHISE QUARTERBACK. The Jacksonville Jaguars—one of two new expansion teams—would begin play in the 1995 season. (The other new team was the Carolina Panthers.) The Jaguars hired Boston College coach Tom Coughlin to lead their team, and he had 19 months to put together his first squad. One of Coughlin's main tasks was to find a quarterback for his team. "I looked at everybody, every quarterback available, college and pro," he explained to *USA Today*.

Coughlin soon decided that Brunell was his man. In April 1995 Jacksonville traded third- and fifth-round draft picks to the Packers for the young signal-caller. Brunell joined the Jaguars as the backup for veteran Steve Beuerlein. "Even when I got here [to Jacksonville], Steve [Beuerlein] was the quarterback," he related to *USA Today*. "I thought it would be a couple of years before I got a chance to start."

TAKES OVER TEAM. Brunell's chance to be a starting quarterback came sooner than he expected when Beuerlein suffered an injury in the sixth game of the 1995 season. "I thought I'd get my shot sooner or later," Brunell explained. "To be honest, it came a lot earlier than I thought it would. I thought I'd be in Green Bay maybe three or four years, and even when I got here [to Jacksonville], it looked like it might take a couple of years before I'd even start. So things had certainly sped up."

Brunell started 10 games for Jacksonville and led them to all 4 of their victories in their inaugural season. He threw for 2,168 yards and 15 touchdowns, and led all NFL quarterbacks with 480 yards rushing. Brunell threw 2 touchdown passes in his second career start, a game against the Packers, and had 302 yards passing and three touchdown tosses in a contest against the Chicago Bears.

Superstar

ALL-PRO. Entering his second season as a starting quarterback, Brunell realized he still had a lot to learn. "I have had a kind of wild-man-on-the-field routine in the past," he revealed to *Sports Illustrated*. "I took chances both throwing and running the ball. And my recklessness hurt the team."

The Jaguars traded Beuerlein to the Carolina Panthers prior to the 1996 season, leaving Brunell as the unchallenged starting quarterback. He made the most of his opportunity, leading NFL quarterbacks in both passing yardage (4367, the thirteenth highest total in league history) and rushing (396). Brunell was the first quarterback to lead NFL quarterbacks in both of these categories since Johnny Unitas of the Baltimore Colts in accomplished this feat in 1963.

Brunell was the only quarterback in the NFL to take every snap for his team. He completed 63.4 percent of his passes (third in the NFL), led the league with 7.84 yards per passing attempt, and had 19 touchdown throws. Fans, coaches, and fellow players voted Brunell to the American Football Conference (AFC) team for the Pro Bowl all-star game. He earned most valuable player honors in the game, a 26-23 overtime victory for the AFC. The Jacksonville star passed for 236 yards and a touchdown and directed his team on a 66-yard drive that resulted in the game-winning field goal by Cary Blanchard of the Indianapolis Colts.

CINDERELLA SEASON. Jacksonville began the 1996 season 4-7 and seemed out of playoff contention. It was at this point that the Jaguars' fortunes turned around. The offensive line began to provide Brunell with protection and opened holes for running back Natrone Means. "I'm much more patient now," Brunell explained to *USA Today*. "At times, I was trying to be too precise, make too many big plays. Now, with Natrone running so well, I don't have to force things."

The team's balanced offensive attack—ranked second in the NFL—helped Jacksonville to win four straight games, each by less than a touchdown. The Jaguars now needed only to win their final game of the season against the Atlanta Falcons to make the playoffs for the first time in their history. Morten Andersen—one of the most accurate field goal kickers in NFL history—missed a 30-yard field goal for the Falcons with time running out to give Jacksonville a 19-17 victory, a 9-7 final record, and an AFC wild-card playoff berth in only their second season of existence.

Brunell—who led the AFC with 20 interceptions—did not throw one during the team's final playoff run. "This is an incredible opportunity for us," he told *USA Today*. "We really turned our season around. We're on an emotional roll. The playoffs didn't seem within reach, but we're here, and I feel really good about this team right now."

ROAD WARRIORS. In their first-ever playoff game the Jaguars traveled to Buffalo to face the Bills. Buffalo's great defensive end Bruce Smith knew Brunell would be tough to stop. "He gets the job done," Smith said. "We have to make sure he doesn't scramble outside the pocket because that's when he makes the majority of his big plays. He's very effective once he starts scrambling. He can do a couple of things, like pull it down and take off, or he can fake like he's going to run, take a step or two back, and throw the bomb."

The Bills had never lost a playoff game at Rich Stadium, their home field. Playing in Buffalo did not scare Brunell. "I think we're a team right now that feels pretty good about ourselves," he declared to *Newsday*. "We're going in there to win. We're going to be very disappointed and frustrated if we do lose."

The game was tied 27-27 when Jacksonville kicker Mike Hollis attempted a 45-yard field goal. The kick traveled through the air, hit the top of the right goal post, and bounced through the uprights, providing the winning margin in a 30-27 Jaguar victory. Brunell struggled in the face of a furious pass rush, but led his team to 10 fourth-quarter points after Jacksonville fell behind 27-20.

UPSET. Next up for Jacksonville were the powerful Denver Broncos. Denver finished the 1996 regular season with a 13-3 record, the best in the NFL. The Broncos were led by superstar quarterback John Elway—Brunell's favorite quarterback as a child—and halfback **Terrell Davis** (see entry), the league's second-leading rusher.

The Jaguars entered the game at Mile High Stadium in Denver as underdogs, but Brunell lifted his team to a new level. He completed 18 of 29 passes for 245 yards and 2 touchdowns, including a 16-yard strike to wide receiver Jimmy Smith with only 3:39 left in the game. "He was putting the ball on the money," John Elway told *Sports Illustrated.* "He just made huge plays all day. You don't see a lot of guys who can make things happen like he can."

Brunell also ran seven times for 44 yards, including scrambles of 12 and 29 yards in a fourth-quarter drive that led to Jacksonville's final touchdown in a 30-27 upset win. "A big compliment to Mark Brunell," Broncos head coach Mike Shanahan said after the game. "Being able to improvise the way he did, they came up with big plays and we didn't. He's very impressive, but unfortunately, I was on the wrong side of the football field. He's a great athlete, a great competitor. He showed a lot of poise, he avoided a lot of tackles and threw some pinpoint passes. To me, he's the reason they're having the success that they are."

JUST SHORT OF SUPER. The Jaguars now faced the New England Patriots in the AFC Championship Game for the right to play in the Super Bowl. The two teams had met earlier in the year, with New England taking a 28-25 overtime victory. For the third straight game Jacksonville would play on the road. "It's all a matter of confidence," Brunell explained to *USA Today*. "Our team has changed so much. Now we expect to put points on the board. We've won two playoff games on the road. We think we can win another."

The Jaguars' storybook season came to an end against the Patriots. New England dominated the game, winning 20-6. Brunell threw a costly interception in the Patriots' end zone that killed one scoring drive with Jacksonville trailing 13-6. "To miss an opportunity like that, stop the drive and come away with nothing, that's what's going to bother me, I'm sure, for a while," he admitted to the *Los Angeles Times*. "It didn't work out today, and that's OK, because before every game we pray that God's will be done. We're gonna fight on. Next year is a new year."

SEASON ENDING INJURY? Brunell now felt like he had arrived as an NFL starting quarterback. "I've always had confidence in my ability and I thought I'd get a chance sometime, I just didn't know when," he explained. "Coming out of college, I certainly wasn't ready to be thrown into the fire and compete at this level. It took a while to learn some things and I still have a lot to learn. I have some things to work on, but myself and this football team are headed in the right direction." Before the 1997 season Brunell signed a five-year, $31 million contract extension.

FRIENDS AND RIVALS

Brunell and New England Patriots' quarterback Drew Bledsoe first met when Brunell was at the University of Washington. Bledsoe—a high school senior—paid a visit to Washington. "[Brunell] was a great host, we had a good time," Bledsoe, who chose to attend Washington State University, recalled. "But at the time, they had Mark and then they had Billy Joe Hobert and both guys ended up being drafted in the NFL."

The two players faced each other three times in college, with Washington winning 55-10 in 1990 and 56-21 in 1991, while Washington State captured the 1992 contest, 42-23. Bledsoe was the first player selected in the 1993 NFL Draft, the same draft in which Green Bay selected Brunell.

Though the two are rivals on the field, they are friends in their personal lives. "It is great for me to see Mark having the success that he is because he is a great guy, a very classy individual and he deserves all the credit that he is getting," Bledsoe told *Newsday*. "[What] would I give to have that kind of athletic ability and be able to run around like he does. He just does some things for his team with his feet. I don't know if there is a quarterback in the league that runs and makes plays on the run as well as he does. And he doesn't make mistakes."

In an exhibition game against the New York Giants, linebacker Jessie Armstead tackled Brunell, twisting the quarterback's knee. After the game doctors told Brunell his knee would require reconstructive surgery to repair torn tendons and he would miss the entire 1997 season. "I think everyone was in shock for a couple of days," Coughlin confessed to *Sports Illustrated*. "We, the coaches, were in shock, too. You don't prepare for something like this, losing your starting quarterback. You might think about it every now and then, but when you're preparing for a season, you're preparing to play with the players you have in your lineup. When you lose someone like Mark, well, that's when you have to think about it."

Brunell disagreed with the doctor's diagnosis. He insisted that the knee would heal without surgery and that he would return during the 1997 season. After only six weeks of rehabilitation, Brunell returned to the lineup. The quarterback claimed that God helped him return so quickly. "The Lord has a plan for me and my life," Brunell admitted to the *Sporting News*. "I do believe that God healed my knee."

SOLID SEASON. Brunell made a dramatic return to the line-up—only 44 days after his injury—when the Jaguars made their debut on Monday Night Football against the Pittsburgh Steelers. He passed for 306 yards and a touchdown in leading Jacksonville to a 23-21 victory. "The knee was solid, no pain, and I didn't get hit on it," Brunell told the *Los Angeles Times*.

Despite his return, Brunell's mobility was limited. It took several games for his scrambling ability to return. "Instinctively, you have to be careful about running with the knee," he explained to the *Sporting News*. "I am telling myself, 'Let's not run around like some madman. Stay in the pocket and don't put yourself in a position to get injured.' Whenever I want to take off, I remind myself I am not as fast as I was a couple of months ago."

Brunell finished the season with 3,281 yards passing and 18 touchdown passes, and cut his interceptions down to 7. He tied with Jeff George of the Los Angeles Raiders for first in the AFC with a 91.2 rating in the league's complicated system for measuring a quarterback's efficiency. "I don't think there's a tougher quarterback to defend," Coughlin told *Newsday*. "He's an outstanding competitor."

NO SURPRISE. Jacksonville finished the season with an 11-5 record, tied with the Steelers for the AFC Central Division lead. Pittsburgh won the division because of the NFL's tiebreaker system, so the Jaguars traveled to Denver for the second year in a row. Brunell knew the Broncos wanted revenge. "I think there's a possibility they overlooked us [last year]," he confessed to *Newsday*. "We were a young expansion team that hadn't accomplished a lot. No one gave us a chance. Beating Denver was the biggest win this franchise had ever had."

The Broncos wanted revenge against Jacksonville and this time made no mistakes. Denver rolled to a 42-17 victory behind 310 yards rushing, 184 by Terrell Davis. Brunell threw for 203 yards, but the Broncos defense held Natrone Means to only 40 yards. "[P]ersonally this is a difficult [loss] to take because we're a better football team this year than we were last year," Brunell admitted to the *Los Angeles Times*.

OFF THE FIELD. Brunell lives in Ponte Vedre Beach, Florida, with his wife, Stacy, and their two children, Caitlin and Jacob. He met his wife at Washington, where she ran track and made the finals of the Pacific-10 women's track and field championships in the 800-meter run. The two were married while still in college and Brunell worked construction and roofing jobs to support them.

Brunell is a devout Christian. He leads a Bible study for some members of the Jaguars. "A lot of people are looking for fulfillment," Brunell explained to the *Atlanta Journal-Constitution*. "A lot of people are looking for focus. From my own

YOUNG GUN?

The player with whom Brunell is most often compared is Steve Young, the superstar quarterback of the San Francisco 49ers. Both players wear number 8, throw the football left-handed, and are threats to make big plays running. Brunell appreciates being compared to one of the great quarterbacks in NFL history, but he wants to make his own mark. "I really respect Steve Young and the way he plays, he's one of the best in the league, and I take that kind of talk as a compliment," Brunell admitted. "We're both left-handed, we're both mobile, and we wear the same number, but I don't try to be Steve Young."

personal experience, I don't think there's anything better than Jesus Christ and a relationship with Him to fulfill what people are looking for in life. The way things have worked out, I feel very blessed. I don't think it could be any better."

Brunell hosts the Mark Brunell Charity Golf Tournament that benefits Wolfson Children's Hospital in Jacksonville. He also visits hospitals to see sick children and is a local spokesperson for the Leukemia Society of America. "It's tough because some of them are in really bad shape," Brunell told the *Sporting News*. "But I have to realize that for a lot of them, you may be their hero or the guy they are cheering for. You can't do everything that is asked of you and it's difficult to say no. But I think a lot of players are doing the best they can to serve the community and help others."

In his spare time Brunell enjoys hunting, fishing, and playing golf. He hosts weekly radio and television shows. Brunell has one goal in football: to win the Super Bowl. "I'd give up all the stats in a second for more wins," he revealed to *Sports Illustrated*. "Winning is the ultimate measure of a quarterback."

WHERE TO WRITE:
C/O JACKSONVILLE JAGUARS,
ONE ALLTELL STADIUM PLACE,
JACKSONVILLE, FL 32202.

Sources

Atlanta Journal-Constitution, January 5, 1997; January 11, 1997; January 12, 1997; January 13, 1997.
Detroit Free Press, February 3, 1997.
Los Angeles Times, December 29, 1996; January 12, 1997; January 13, 1997; September 23, 1997; December 28, 1997.
Newsday, December 23, 1996; December 27, 1996; December 29, 1996; January 10, 1997; December 27, 1997.
Sporting News, October 13, 1997.
Sports Illustrated, September 30, 1991; December 30, 1991; January 13, 1992; November 16, 1992; January 11, 1993; December 9, 1996; August 25, 1997; September 1, 1997.
USA Today. December 27, 1996; January 1, 1997; January 10, 1997; September 22, 1997.
Additional Information provided by the Gannett News Service and the Jacksonville Jaguars.

Kobe Bryant

1978–

In 1996 basketball player Kobe Bryant decided to move directly from high school to the National Basketball Association (NBA). When he entered his first game for the Los Angeles Lakers he became the youngest player in NBA history. Skipping college did not mean that Bryant did not value education. His decision meant he wanted to learn about his chosen profession—basketball—from the best teachers in the world.

Growing Up

FATHER'S FOOTSTEPS. Kobe (pronounced KO-bee) Bryant was born on August 23, 1978. He was one of three children of Joe and Pam Bryant. Bryant's first name comes from a type of steak his parents saw on a restaurant menu prior to his birth.

Bryant's father—Joe (Jellybean) Bryant—was a professional basketball player. He played eight seasons in the NBA

"I always tried to hold a basketball, watch basketball, think about basketball. People told me to get away from basketball, but I can't. It's in my blood."
—Kobe Bryant.

with the Philadelphia 76ers, San Diego (now Los Angeles) Clippers, and Houston Rockets. Joe Bryant averaged 8.7 points and 4.0 rebounds per game during his career.

Bryant first showed an interest in basketball at the age of three, playing with a mini-basketball set in front of the television during professional games. "Right away he started dunking," Pam Bryant recalled in the *Los Angeles Times*. "I said, 'Sweetheart, you'll break it. Don't dunk. Just shoot jump shots and layups.' The whole time they were on TV he would play too. He'd have his little cup of Gatorade and his towel and he'd say, 'Mom, I'm sweating.' Everything he does, he puts his heart into. He took karate lessons and he was pretty good at that, too."

WORLD TRAVELER. When Bryant was six years old his family moved to Italy. Joe Bryant played professional basketball there for eight seasons after his NBA career had ended. Living in a new country helped bring the Bryant family close together.

"Traveling made us close," Joe Bryant explained in the *Los Angeles Times*. "When we went over to Europe we had to depend on each other because we couldn't speak the language, so we communicated with each other probably more than we would have in America, where we have TV and radio and so many other distractions. The travel helped [my children] see different people, different religions. I think [my children] look at people as human beings, not as a color or religion, so they don't feel trapped in any kind of stereotypical situation. They're more confident and relaxed in dealing with people."

Not knowing the language forced Bryant and his sisters—Sharia and Shaya—to be friends. "When we went over there, nobody in the family spoke Italian and we couldn't communicate with anybody except members of the family,"

Bryant recalled in the *Los Angeles Times*. "So when we went out, we went out as a group. I had my sisters' back and they had mine." Bryant learned to speak Italian and is now fluent in the language.

RETURN TO AMERICA. The family returned to live in Wynnewood, Pennsylvania—a suburb of Philadelphia—when Bryant was 14. He and his sisters had a hard time adjusting to attending school in the United States. The Bryant children did not know about locking up their possessions—they did not use lockers in Italy—and they were shocked when someone stole their valuables.

Bryant also missed having his sisters by his side—they were now in high school and he was in middle school. "I didn't have anybody to lean on," he admitted to the *Los Angeles Times*. "It was kind of strange because, being away, I didn't know a lot of the slang that kids used. Kids would come up to me and say whatever, and I'd just nod."

BASKETBALL EDUCATION. Bryant played his first organized basketball in Italy. He feels learning the game overseas gave him an advantage. "I started playing basketball over there [in Italy], which was great, because I learned fundamentals first," Bryant told *Newsday*. "I think most kids who grow up here in America learn all the fancy dribbling. In Italy, they teach you true fundamentals and leave out all the nonsense."

Bryant began to play in the Sonny Hill League in Philadelphia at the age of 10. College and professional players from all around the area played in the league, providing tough competition. Joe Bryant learned his basketball in the Sonny Hill League, and he brought his son there to get his hardcourt education. "I believe Kobe is out here most summers, not because I started a trend or anything, but he really wanted to play this game at a young age," Joe Bryant explained in the *Philadelphia Tribune*. "We see it [shaping Kobe's career] as educational."

HIGH SCHOOL PHENOM. Bryant attended Lower Merion High School in Ardmore, Pennsylvania, a suburb of Philadelphia.

Bryant leaps for a slam dunk.

He earned a spot on the varsity team as a freshman. As a junior Bryant averaged 31.1 points, 10.4 rebounds, 5.2 assists, 3.8 blocks, and 2 steals. Lower Merion advanced to the state semifinals.

"He's blessed with a lot of natural ability and great genes, but the work ethic is his and it's very strong," Bryant's high school coach, Gregg Downer, told the *Los Angeles Times*. "Kobe has the skills and the maturity and everything you could want. When I first met him, at age 13, and I saw him play, after five minutes I said, 'This kid is going to be a pro.' Never was there one moment I doubted that."

BIG DECISION. Following his junior high school campaign Bryant played in the Sonny Hill League and at national camps for promising senior players. "I enjoy playing against great competition," Bryant declared in *YSB*. "That's how you get better. I knew that playing for Lower Merion I would be facing the best players from the suburban area. I knew that the Sonny Hill League would give me a chance to face the top players from the city. The ABCD All-American camp put me up against the best players in the country."

Bryant's success gave him great confidence. He also impressed his opponents. "He blended with the rest of us, and if you can blend with us as a high school player, that says something right there," NBA veteran power forward Rick Mahorn explained to *Newsday*. "That says you belong. Dude even tried to [dunk on] me."

In 1995 **Kevin Garnett** (see entry) from Farragutt Academy in Chicago decided to skip college and move directly from high school to the NBA. His decision was influenced by the fact that he could not achieve high enough scores on college entrance exams to earn a college scholarship. Basketball experts predicted disaster for Garnett, but he succeeded in his first professional season with the Minnesota Timberwolves.

Garnett's success opened the way for Bryant to consider turning professional. "I felt real comfortable all summer with the guys [professional players]," he explained to *Newsday* in the summer following his junior season. "I had no butterflies, no nothing. Never felt intimidated. I could get to the hole, I could hit the jumper, I could score, although not at will, but I could get some shots. I was able to create for my teammates and rebound. Plus the guys respected me, and when they respect you, that must mean something. After a while, it kind of popped in my mind that I can play with these guys."

Bryant felt he had the ability to move directly from high school to the professional ranks, but he decided to wait to make his final decision. "I can't give an answer [about joining the NBA] now," he told *Newsday*. "Maybe later on this year. Then I'll look back to see what I've learned as a player. That's when I'll decide. And if I make the decision to go, I'm going. I'm not going to change my mind."

SENIOR SENSATION. In his senior year Bryant led the Aces to the Pennsylvania AAAA state championship. He averaged 31 points, 12 rebounds, 7 assists, 4 blocks, and 5 steals. *USA Today* and *Parade* magazine named him national high school player of the year and Bryant broke the Philadelphia high-school scoring record of basketball legend Wilt Chamberlain. At 6 feet, 6 inches the young point-guard had all the tools: he could pass, shoot, dribble, rebound, and defend.

Bryant's play brought numerous college recruiters to his school. College basketball powerhouses like Duke, North Carolina, Arkansas, and Michigan tried to convince him to attend their universities. Joe Bryant held an assistant coach position at LaSalle University and some experts felt he would pressure his son to attend his school. "Quite naturally, Kobe has attracted a lot of national attention," Joe Bryant explained in *YSB*. "This is a big year for him, but he hasn't let the recruiting and all the publicity change him as a person. He's been able to handle things quite well. I'm really happy for him."

GOING PRO. Bryant considered all his options when the time came to make his final decision. "I don't think there's a wrong choice, either way you look at it," he revealed to the *Los Angeles Times*. "If you go to college and play basketball there, you meet people and on top of that, you get a good education. In the NBA, you're learning from the professionals and maturing as a person and as a basketball player, so the education factor is still there." Unlike Kevin Garnett, Bryant easily earned high enough grades and scores on the Scholastic Aptitude Test (SAT) to earn a college scholarship.

Joe Bryant admitted that he wanted his son to attend college, but would support him no matter what his decision. "Kobe has choices," Joe Bryant told *Newsday.* "He can do whatever he wants. Our family will support Kobe with whatever he decides to do. Talking to Kobe is like talking to a 23-year-old, not a high school kid. If Kobe feels he's ready, then he goes with my blessing."

Bryant finally made the decision to declare himself eligible for the 1996 NBA Draft. He made his announcement at a press conference held in his high school's gym. "It's been my goal [to play in the NBA] ever since I started high school," Bryant told the gathered crowd. "I always wanted the option of going to the NBA. My father played, but that's not the reason. My decision has nothing to do with him. And I'm not studying Kevin Garnett. I wish him the best and hope he exceeds expectations, but what he does really doesn't have any effect on me."

Superstar

LANDS WITH LAKERS. The Charlotte Hornets used the thirteenth overall pick in the 1996 NBA Draft to select Bryant. They then traded the young player to the Los Angeles Lakers for center Vlade Divac. Bryant signed a three-year, $3.5 million contract. "I've heard a lot of people say I don't have the maturity yet for the NBA," he explained to *Newsday.* "Well, I've seen things in my lifetime that ordinary kids my age haven't seen or experienced. I've been all through Europe, to France, Germany, lived in Italy, been around professional basketball players my whole life. Growing up the way I have, I think I've matured faster than the ordinary person my age."

Lakers' head coach Del Harris—who had been Joe Bryant's last NBA head coach during the 1982–83 season for the Houston Rockets—was excited by Bryant's potential. "It's not just [his athleticism]," Harris declared to the *Los Angeles Times*. "I guess you would say it's the athleticism combined with so many skills. You get so many athletes who excite you with potential, but they don't have the ballhandling or shooting skills. And here's a guy that actually has got all these things. It's just that it's in this young body. It's just a matter of how soon will that be able to work against the bigger, older players. We think he's going to reduce the expected time that would be normal for an 18-year-old because he's obviously unique."

Bryant also signed endorsement contracts with Adidas and Sprite. He had to be careful not to let the attention distract him. "It's crazy," Bryant admitted in the *Los Angeles Times*. "If you sit back and start thinking about it, maybe you could be overwhelmed by the situation. You've just got to keep going slowly and keep working hard on your basketball skills. Then, I don't think your head can swell because you won't have time to think about it."

SLOW START. Bryant impressed his coaches and fellow players with his play in summer leagues. In four games he averaged 25 points and 5.3 rebounds. Bryant's progress was interrupted when he broke his wrist in a pick-up basketball game in September 1996. The injury forced him to miss five weeks of training camp and the exhibition schedule.

Missing training camp set back Bryant's NBA education. "[He's] an 18-year-old player and the first training camp is very important," Lakers' general manager Mitch Kupchak explained in the *Los Angeles Times*. "This will set him back. This will certainly ensure that we will bring him along slowly, that's for sure. If you're looking for a silver lining, it's that we won't rush him along."

Sitting out was hard on Bryant because he could not wait to start his NBA career. "I've been waiting to go out and compete with guys like [teammates] Nick Van Exel, Eddie Jones and Cedric Ceballos," he confessed to the *Los Angeles Times*. "But, I'm really excited to have a chance and learn from them."

YOUNGEST EVER. Bryant got his first taste of NBA regular season action in the Lakers second game, against the Minnesota Timberwolves. When he entered the game he became the youngest player in NBA history at 18 years, 2 months and 11 days. He beat the record of 18 years, 4 months set by Philadelphia's Stanley Brown in 1947. (Brown played parts of two NBA seasons for Philadelphia and averaged 3.1 points per game.)

"I guess [the record is] pretty nice because a lot of guys come into the NBA," Bryant explained in the *Los Angeles Times*. "It's pretty cool. It'll be neat one day to sit with my grandkids and tell them I was the youngest player in NBA history. By then, somebody may be coming out of middle school." Later in the year Jermaine O'Neal of the Portland Trailblazers—who is seven weeks younger than Bryant—once again broke the record.

ALL-STAR. The highlight of Bryant's first season came at the 1997 NBA All-Star Game in Cleveland, Ohio. He scored a record 31 points and grabbed 8 rebounds in the Schick Rookie Game. Later that same night Bryant became the youngest-ever winner of the league's slam-dunk competition. He earned 49 of a possible 50 points with a "through the legs" dunk. "When you are out there slam-dunking, your stomach goes a little bit, and you're worried you're going to miss the dunk," Bryant admitted to *USA Today*. "I had a lot of butterflies."

His success at one of the NBA's glamour events was a thrill for Bryant. "This is something I dreamed about doing since I was a little kid," he told *USA Today*. "This has been a great experience since I first got here [to Cleveland] and got the opportunity to see all the great players and having people congratulate me on the first half of the season. It has given me a chance to meet face-to-face with a lot of people. I've really enjoyed it."

PATIENCE. During his first season Bryant played point guard, shooting guard, and small forward. The Lakers brought him along slowly and some games he did not play at all. His role sometimes frustrated Bryant, but he tried not to let his lack of playing time discourage him. "I just have to be real patient," he confessed to the *Los Angeles Times*. "Just keep working on my game. That's what I'm trying to do."

During the season Bryant played in 71 games and started in 6. He averaged 7.6 points, 1.9 rebounds, and 1.3 assists in 15.5 minutes per game. On April 8, 1997 Bryant scored a season-high 24 points in a game against the Golden State Warriors. He earned recognition on the NBA All-Rookie Second Team.

"It was everything I expected and more," Bryant said about his rookie season. "Every night was something new. The whole season was just an ongoing learning process. Being so young and coming in, I really had to focus in on working hard and staying prepared. You have to keep working on your jump shot, your physical preparation. At this level, you always have to be working to improve your game or you'll get left behind."

Bryant took advantage of his opportunity to learn more about the game. "My decision-making has improved," he explained in the *Los Angeles Times*. "The more I would go through, the more I would see, the more I improved. I trust my decisions now. When I first started playing point guard, I didn't know how to run the offense all that well. I feel a lot better now."

AIR BALL. Bryant took his two biggest shots of the season in a game the Lakers had to win. On the brink of elimination in the Western Conference semifinals against the Utah Jazz, Harris made an important decision. He picked Bryant to take the Lakers' final shot, one that would decide if they would win the game or go to overtime. The rookie got his shot off from 14 feet, but missed the basket entirely.

The game progressed through overtime. With 11.3 seconds left, the Lakers needed to make a three-point shot to tie the game. Once again Harris chose Bryant to take this big shot, and once again the rookie shot an air ball. The Jazz won the game 98-93 and captured the series. "Tonight, I just didn't come through," a disappointed Bryant told *USA Today*. "But play the game again, and I want the ball again."

Some experts questioned why the Lakers asked their 18-year-old rookie to take such a big shot, but Harris had confidence in Bryant's ability. "I will run that play any time," Harris declared to *USA Today*. "Kobe can get his shot any time he wants. He's 18, but you can't guard him. Believe me, he's a great shooter, and he's going to be a great, great player." Bryant averaged 8.2 points in nine playoff games.

OFF THE COURT. Bryant lives in Pacific Palisades, California, in a house overlooking the Pacific Ocean. His family is still very close, and his parents and sister, Shaya, live with him. Bryant's other sister, Sharia, played volleyball at Temple University in Philadelphia. His flashy play earned Bryant the nickname "Showboat." "I'm not trying to be flashy," Bryant told *People*. "I just do what comes naturally."

Bryant's favorite television shows are *Living Single* and *Jamie Foxx*. He likes listening to rap music and his favorite artists are Biggie Smalls, the Fugees, and Wu-tang Clan. Bryant has considered taking college courses on the Internet. In his spare time he enjoys reading and playing video games.

The son now has gained the advantage over the father in the Bryant household. "When he [Bryant's father] plays me he always seems to want to play half court," Bryant explained in *Newsday*. "He's a little older than me, you know. Can't move quick like he used to. He knows that in full court, I always beat him."

Bryant works hard at his game. "I always tried to hold a basketball, watch basketball, think about basketball," he told the *Los Angeles Times*. "People told me to get away from basketball, but I can't. It's in my blood."

GET BACK UP

Bryant has a philosophy about life and basketball that helped him survive his first season in the NBA. "Basketball is kind of like life," he told the *Los Angeles Times*. "It can get rough at times. You can get knocked on your butt a couple of times. But what you have to do is get up and hold your head high and try again. That's how I'm going to be. I'm sure there are going to be times guys are knocking me on my back and pushing me and I might start bleeding, but I have to get back up and keep going."

WHERE TO WRITE:

C/O LOS ANGELES LAKERS, GREAT WESTERN FORUM,
3900 W. MANCHESTER BLVD.,
INGLEWOOD, CA 90306.

Sources

Los Angeles Times, October 15, 1996; October 18, 1996; November 4, 1996;
    December 8, 1996; December 12, 1996; December 17, 1996; February 9,
    1997; February 14, 1997; March 10, 1997; May 6, 1997.

Newsday, December 17, 1995; April 30, 1996; September 4, 1996; October 15,
    1996.

People Weekly, March 31, 1997.

Philadelphia Tribune, July 26, 1994.

Sports Illustrated, March 3, 1997.

USA Today, February 10, 1997; May 14, 1997; November 4, 1997.

YSB, October 31, 1995.

Additional information provided by the Los Angeles Lakers and the Gannett
    News Service.

Cynthia Cooper

1963–

Cynthia Cooper is a great basketball player. For years she could not make money playing the game she loved in the United States. Finally, in 1997, her dream came true when the Women's National Basketball Association (WNBA) was formed. Cooper's return to the United States was successful, as she led the WNBA in scoring and earned regular season Most Valuable Player (MVP) honors. Just when she thought her season could not get any better, her Houston Comets won the first-ever WNBA Championship with Cooper earning the championship game MVP award. For all these reasons, basketball experts dubbed the sharp-shooting guard the "Michael Jordan of the WNBA."

"She's not the Michael Jordan of the league. She's the Cynthia Cooper of the league."
—Michelle Timms, player for the Phoenix Mercury.

Growing Up

INTELLIGENT, STRONG BLACK WOMAN. Cynthia Lynne Cooper was born April 14, 1963. Her mother, Mary Cobbs, sacrificed to raise Cooper and her seven siblings. "When I was growing up, my family had it tough," Cooper told the *Los Angeles Times*. "And I never dreamed of being a pro sports athlete. I didn't know for sure what I wanted. But I knew what I didn't want to be. I didn't want to be a drug addict, or get pregnant, or get into gangs. I wanted to be viewed as an intelligent, strong black woman, successful at something."

Cooper grew up in the Watts section of Los Angeles, one of the poorest areas in the United States. Crime and drugs ruled her neighborhood. Her experiences growing up helped make Cooper stronger. "I grew up in a rather rough neighborhood, Watts to be exact," she recalled. "You have to grow up fast in that kind of environment, if you don't it could be detrimental [harmful] to your health. I think my experience has helped me to be mentally as well as physically tough and be able to meet some major challenges and demands that I have been faced with."

LATE DRIBBLER. Cooper played many sports, including tennis and volleyball, and ran the 400 meters in track. Despite her interest in athletics, she did not start playing basketball until she was 16. "I just happened to be in the gym...and saw this older girl come down the court, put the ball behind her back from her left to her right hand and then make a layup," Cooper recalled in *Sports Illustrated*. "Up until then I had run track. But just like that I said, 'Oooh. Wow. I want to play like that someday.'"

Since she did not start playing basketball until tenth grade, Cooper had a lot of ground to make up. "By that time I knew I wanted to play college ball, so I had to work hard," she explained. "That's what it's all about—working hard."

By the time Cooper was a senior at Locke High School she had become a star. She averaged 31 points per game and led her team to a state championship. Cooper's play earned her recognition as the Los Angeles city player of the year and a scholarship to play at the University of Southern California (USC). During her four seasons at USC, the Trojans won National Collegiate Athletic Association (NCAA) national championships in 1983 and 1984 and made the Final Four in 1986.

Cooper played a supporting role on the championship teams, which were led by the great Cheryl Miller and the McGee twins, Pam and Paula. She became a team leader in 1986, averaging 17.2 points. Cooper earned Final Four All-Tournament Team honors in 1986. During her career at USC Cooper averaged 12.9 points and 3.9 rebounds per game.

Cooper's lively personality helped to keep her team loose. "Cynthia is either singing, dancing or entertaining her teammates or whoever will take time to watch when she's not playing basketball," Trojans coach Linda Sharp explained. "She keeps the team up and adds that special dimension which keeps the team cohesive. In all honesty she is a great player and a sweet person."

WORLD TRAVELER. Like most female basketball players in the United States, Cooper had to go overseas to play professionally when her college career ended. For eleven years she played in Europe for three different teams. Cooper played for Segovia in Spain (1986–87), and Parma (1987–94) and Alcamo (1994–96) in Italy. During those years she led her team in scoring eight times and finished second twice. In both 1988 and 1992 she won the three-point shooting contest for the European League, and in 1987 Cooper won the Most Valuable Player award at the European League All-Star Game. During the 1995–96 season she averaged 35.5 points per game for Alcamo.

Twice Cooper returned home to play for the U.S. Olympic women's basketball team. She was the third-leading scorer (14.2 points per game) on the team that won the gold medal in 1988 in Seoul, South Korea, and she also played on the bronze-medal-winning squad at the 1992 Games in Barcelona, Spain. Cooper's proudest moment came when she

Cooper goes for a basket during the 1988 Olympics in Seoul, South Korea.

gave her gold medal to her mother on her birthday, September 29, 1988.

Superstar

COMING HOME. Cooper had experienced great success as a professional basketball player, but still she felt something was missing. "I never felt like I had given all I was capable of giving to one of my teams," she explained in *Sports Illustrated*. "I was always the sort of player who was asked to pass the ball to the marquee players and set picks, run the fast break. My role might be to come into the game to be a defensive stopper, or a spark plug. But all along, I told myself, 'This is not my game. This is not who I am as a basketball player. And this is not all I can do.' I wanted to be one of those people who took the clutch shots and carried teams on their shoulders."

Cooper also wanted to have a chance to play at home. Because she played in Europe, her mother never had a chance to see her perform. So the news that the Women's National Basketball Association (WNBA)—one of the first professional basketball leagues in the United States for women—planned to begin play in the summer of 1997 thrilled Cooper. "I've been in Europe 11 years [and] this is the first year I've been able to share my pro basketball life with my mom," a happy Cooper told the *Los Angeles Times*.

CLOSE TO MOM. During the first-ever WNBA Draft Cooper was assigned to play for the Houston Comets. She wanted to play for Houston because her mother now lived in that city. Cooper's happiness turned to sadness when her mother was diagnosed as having breast cancer before the WNBA season began. Being in Houston allowed Cooper to take her mother to her doctor appointments. "It was unbelievable how it's all worked out," Cooper told *Sports Illustrated*.

Cooper called her mom after every game during the WNBA season, and sometimes the Comets delayed practice so she could take her mother to the doctor. "The thing I always tell her is, 'Coop, when I put myself in your place, I don't know how you do it all,'" Kim Perrot, Cooper's friend and road roommate revealed to *Sports Illustrated*. Cooper also has helped raise a niece and nephew and is in the process of adopting another nephew.

COMET'S TALE. The star of the Comets was expected to be Sheryl Swoopes. She was a great former Texas Tech University superstar who also played on the 1996 U.S. Women's Olympic "Dream Team" that won the gold medal in Atlanta, Georgia. Swoopes, however, missed most of the season because she was pregnant. Without their superstar, most basketball experts did not figure the Comets would be able to compete for the WNBA title.

The experts seemed to be right when Houston lost to the New York Liberty—led by "Dream Team" member Rebecca Lobo—three times in the first two weeks of the season. "There was doubt in everyone's mind but ours," Cooper admitted to *Newsday*. "When we lost to New York, we went back to the drawing board. We defined our roles."

COACH CALLS ON COOPER. Houston coach Van Chancellor—who had previously spent 19 years as the women's basketball coach at the University of Mississippi—knew his team needed a spark. His wife, Betty, told him that Cooper was the player who could lead the Comets. "She [Betty] said, 'Van, you've just not done a very good job of coaching Cynthia,'" Chancellor explained in *USA Today*. "'You need to go meet with her and get her motivated and get her to understand the things you want her to do.' So, I just sat down with Cynthia and told her that I thought she needed to lighten up a little bit on the court, and just go get the ball and play her game."

Cooper and the Comets took off after Chancellor talked to his star player. "It was something I needed to hear from him and the rest of the coaching staff," Cooper revealed in *Sports*

Illustrated. In one three-game stretch she scored 30 points against Sacramento, 32 against Phoenix, and 44 against Sacramento, setting one-game WNBA scoring marks each time. In seven of the thirteen games after her meeting with Chancellor, Cooper scored over 30 points. "Since my meeting with coach, I've felt very relaxed on the court," she told *USA Today.* 'He just wanted to put me at ease and [help me] play more relaxed."

CONFERENCE CHAMPS. Swoopes gave birth to her son, Jordan, June 25, and joined the team in early August. The return of Swoopes—in addition to the outstanding play of Cooper—helped Houston move to the top of the standings. When the Comets defeated the Liberty, 70-55, they won the Eastern Conference title.

SUPER COOP. Houston's opponents recognized how well Cooper was playing. "She's the best all-around player I've ever faced," Liberty guard Vickie Johnson confessed in *Sports Illustrated.* "She can go left if you stop her from going right, and she goes right if you stop her from going left. She can shoot the three, she can drive and score or pass off. After seeing her for four games now, nothing she does surprises me. She always seems to have something up her sleeve."

Success did not come easily for Cooper. She had to work hard. When Cooper suffered through a shooting slump, she listened to advice from her brother, Eric. "He said, 'You just need to get in the gym and shoot 500 jumpers a day,'" Cooper told *USA Today.* "So I stay after practice and come in early before practice and get those things done on my own. Now I feel more confident and comfortable with the ball."

Cooper led the WNBA with a 22.2 points per game average. She hit 47 percent of her field goals and dished out 4.7 assists and had 2.11 steals per game. Her play earned Cooper the nickname "Super Coop." "Coop can shoot, rebound, pass, lead and guard the other team's best player," Chancellor explained to the *Los Angeles Times.* "That's about all of it, isn't it? She's one of the hardest-working players I've ever been around." Cooper also played through pain for much of the season, suffering from a thigh bruise and badly sprained ankle.

MVP. When the WNBA announced the winner of its first Most Valuable Player award, no one was surprised that Cooper was the unanimous choice. She received all 37 first-place votes to finish far ahead of Lisa Leslie, the center for the Los Angeles Sparks. Cooper dedicated the award to her mother. "I've been tucked away in Europe for 11 years, and my mom hasn't been able to share any of the special moments," she revealed to *Sports Illustrated.* "She's my MVP."

ROAD TO THE TITLE. As Eastern Conference champion, Houston had the homecourt advantage in the WNBA semifinals against the Charlotte Sting. Charlotte took a 33-29 lead at halftime, but with eight minutes left in the second half the Comets tied the game, 48-48. It was then that the Comets' Wanda Guyton collided with teammate Tina Thompson. Guyton fell hard and suffered a mild concussion.

With her teammate injured, Cooper knew she would have to lift her team. "I didn't tell her [Guyton] we'd win the game for her because I was just concerned about Wanda at the time," she recalled in *Newsday.* "I prayed over her and told her that she would be all right and that she would be with us." Houston went on a 10-0 run after Guyton's injury to take command of the game. "We wanted to step it up," Cooper told *USA Today.* "We each picked up our games and then played tough, tough basketball after she went out."

Cooper scored 31 points, including 8 down the stretch, as the Comets earned a place in the first-ever WNBA Championship Game with a 70-54 win. She also pulled down 5 rebounds and dished out 5 assists. "She had one of those quiet nights tonight," Chancellor explained to *USA Today.* "That 31 tonight was quiet, but I'm glad she had them. She had them when they counted. She's just a gamer."

TITLE MATCH. The Comets faced the Liberty and Lobo—who defeated Phoenix, 59-41 in the other semifinal—in the WNBA Championship Game. New York did a good job keeping Cooper in check during the regular season, holding her to 17.3 points per game. The Liberty defeated the Comets both times they faced them on Houston's home court, the Summit, where the championship game would be played.

Winning the championship was important to Cooper. "I gave up a lot to win," she confessed to *Sports Illustrated.* "It'd make up for all the hard work, the sweat, the elbows received."

Houston led by four at halftime of the championship game, and then opened up a twelve-point lead in the first five minutes of the second half. New York double-teamed Cooper, but they could not stop her from scoring a game-high twenty-five points. "Super Coop" was too much for the Liberty. Cynthia controlled the ball," Liberty coach Nancy Darsch told *Newsday.* "She has size. She has quickness. She made some passes that I don't even know how she knew there was a teammate there."

The Comets won the inaugural WNBA Championship by a 65-51 margin, and Cooper earned game most valuable player honors. When the final buzzer sounded, Houston began to celebrate their achievement. "I was looking for my mom, and just joy," Cooper recalled. "I was overwhelmed. Words can't express the way I was feeling. I was overjoyed. I couldn't believe we had accomplished what we had accomplished. If I had just one word, it would be joy."

Cooper also thanked her coach after the game. "Cynthia hugged me and said, 'Coach, I couldn't have done it without you,'" Chancellor related to the *Los Angeles Times.* "I feel for her, to say something like that to me at that moment. Well, she's a special person. Cynthia is all about grit, desire, determination. She can guard, she can shoot, rebound and she can pass." Chancellor earned WNBA Coach of the Year honors.

LOVES TO PLAY. Cooper played for a team in Brazil during the off-season, then planned to return for the 1998 WNBA season. She says the competition is tougher in the WNBA than what she faced in Europe. "The WNBA is more challenging,"

MICHAEL JORDAN OF THE WNBA

Because Cooper is the best player in the WNBA, basketball experts naturally compare her to the best player in the National Basketball Association (NBA)—Michael Jordan of the Chicago Bulls. Cooper enjoys being compared to Jordan. "I love being called the Michael Jordan of the WNBA," Cooper said. "To be affiliated with such a great player, to have my name in the same sentence is something special. It says a lot about my game. I feel very honored. I met Michael [at] the 1992 Olympics in Barcelona [Spain]."

Cooper said. "In Italy, the only real competition is the other foreign players. In the WNBA you have 10 talented players day in and day out, very quick, agile and tough. It is more difficult to play in the WNBA than it is to play overseas."

Cooper feels that—despite her success—she can still become a better basketball player. "I am still learning this game," she explained to the *Los Angeles Times*. "I learn something new every day. I'll be a much better player three years from now and a much better player three years after that."

Even after playing ten years of professional basketball, Cooper still loves the game. "Are you kidding me?" she said to a reporter, who asked if she still liked playing basketball, according to the *Los Angeles Times*. "I love it. I have never loved playing this game more than I do right now. I've wanted this most of my life—to play pro ball in my own country. I played 10 years in Italy and enjoyed it, but this tops everything."

OFF THE COURT. Cooper is engaged to marry Gianluca Castaldini, who plays for Dolce Parma in the men's Italian League. She has three brothers, Kenneth, Everett, and Charles, and four sisters, Joanne, Drena, Stephanie, and Lisa. Cooper majored in physical education at USC. She is fluent in Italian and also speaks Spanish.

Following the WNBA Championship Game, Cooper's picture appeared on a Kellogg's cereal box. "I look good on this box," she admitted to *Newsday*. Cooper also made appearances on *The Late Show with David Letterman* and *The Rosie O'Donnell Show*.

Cooper says that coaches and teachers have been the biggest influences on her, and she wants to be a role model for children. "The advice I would have is to work hard at whatever you do, to hang tough in the tough moments," she said.

"You might not be as good as you would like to be. And try and be consistent. I've always worked hard, so that's the one thing I would say. And take care of your body."

With her play and determination, Cooper has earned the respect of her opponents. "She's not the Michael Jordan of the league," Michelle Timms of the Phoenix Mercury told *USA Today.* "She's the Cynthia Cooper of the league."

 WHERE TO WRITE:

C/O HOUSTON COMETS,
TWO GREENWAY PLAZA, SUITE 400,
HOUSTON, TX 77046.

Sources

Los Angeles Times, August 1, 1997; August 2, 1997; August 19, 1997; August 31, 1997.
Newsday, June 22, 1997; August 29, 1997; August 30, 1997; August 31, 1997.
Sports Illustrated, August 18, 1997; August 28, 1997.
USA Today, June 20, 1997; July 31, 1997; August 8, 1997; August 28, 1997; August 29, 1997.
Additional information provided by the University of Southern California and the Houston Comets.

Terrell Davis

1972–

In January 1998 running back Terrell Davis of the Denver Broncos achieved a feat that only few football players have ever accomplished when he won the Most Valuable Player award for Super Bowl XXXII. Overcoming a migraine headache that forced him to sit out the second quarter, he returned to the game, gained 157 yards, and scored a Super Bowl record 3 rushing touchdowns as the Broncos defeated the defending champion Green Bay Packers 31-24. Conquering difficulties was nothing new for Davis, who had already proved to doubters that he could compete with the best football players in the world.

Growing Up

SCARY PAIN. Terrell Davis was born October 28, 1972, in San Diego, California. He and his five brothers were raised by his mother, Kateree, and father, Joe. Davis grew up in the Lincoln Park area of San Diego, a neighborhood ruled by gangs, drugs, and crime.

When Davis was 7 years old he suffered the first episode of a very painful headache. He did not have another until he was 13, but then they began to occur every three weeks. The headaches caused intense pain, nausea, and blurred vision. They arrived with flashes of light, like a thousand flashbulbs going off at the same time. "I'd rather be dead," Davis would scream to himself, according to the *Sporting News*. "I don't want to live. I can't stand the pain. It hurts so bad."

Davis looked to his mother for help, but she could do nothing to stop the pain. "There wasn't any medication or anything we could give him, just the tea," Kateree Davis explained to the *Sporting News*. "I knew he was strong, but he was so brave, too. After a while, he learned he just had to be patient until the pain went away."

Davis learned that the best thing he could do to deal with the pain was to find a dark room and sit very still, with his head and back against the wall and a cold washcloth on his forehead. The only thing that he could do to make the pain in his head go away was to sleep. When Davis did doze off, however, he would soon wake up and have to vomit into a bucket he kept close by. The lingering effects of the headaches could last days.

What Davis suffered from were migraine headaches. Neither he or his parents knew that millions of people suffered from this ailment and that their were treatments that could help ease the pain. Growing up, Davis felt he was a freak and was afraid to tell his family and friends about how bad the pain really was. "Probably my biggest worry was not having a name for it, not knowing what it was," Davis admitted to *People Weekly*. "At the time I thought everyone who had headaches felt like I did, so I didn't think a doctor would help. I just had to deal with it. I tried to keep everything about my headaches to myself. I thought people would think I was crazy if I told them what it was like."

CHARGER FAN. Davis was a big fan of the hometown San Diego Chargers football team of the National Football League (NFL). He made his bedroom into a shrine to his favorite team, and he cried when they lost. "I was a Charger fanatic," Davis recalled in the *Los Angeles Times*. "I had all the [souvenirs] in my room."

Davis starred on his Pop Warner youth football team. He earned the nickname "Boss Hog." The league had a weight limit, so Davis exercised wearing plastic bags on his legs. The young player hoped training in this way would enable him to maintain his weight at a low enough level to keep playing.

LOSES FATHER. As Davis entered high school he was faced with a difficult personal crisis. His father, Joe Davis, had suffered from lupus, an illness that attacks the immune system, the part of the body that helps fight off diseases. Joe Davis died when his son was in ninth grade. "That was definitely something to deal with," Davis admitted to *USA Today.*

The running back did not play football during his first two years at Morse High School because his father's death caused him to lose interest in sports. The loss saddened Davis so much that he let his school work fall apart. He even flunked physical education. "I was a little disobedient at that stage," Davis confessed to *USA Today.* "It took me a while to get my life straight."

WANTS TO PLAY. Prior to his junior year in high school Davis transferred to Lincoln Academy in San Diego, the same school that produced the legendary running back Marcus Allen. Attending a new school and playing football helped him overcome his father's death. "It was a new atmosphere, a new environment," Davis explained to *USA Today.* "It was the best thing that ever happened to me."

In order to play as much as he could, Davis volunteered to play six different positions—including nose guard

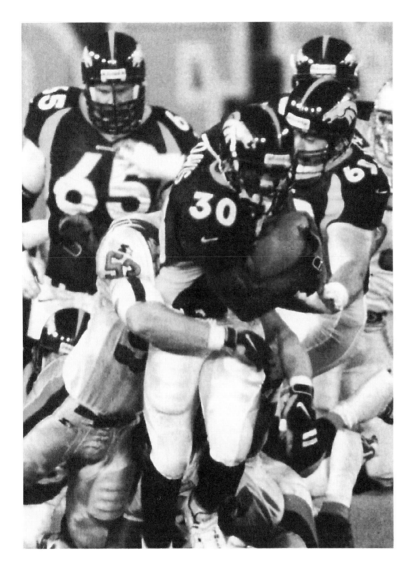

on defense—his first year. "He was a beautiful kid," Lincoln Prep's trainer, John White, said. "He didn't care where he played. He gave 100 percent. He just wanted to play football."

Davis begged his coach for more playing time before his senior season. "His senior year, he came up to me again and said, 'Give me a shot,'" his high school coach, Vic Player, told *USA Today*. "'If I don't make it, I won't bother you no more. If I do well, then I deserve to play. But just give me a

shot.' When a kid comes to you with that type of mature attitude, how in the world can you say no?"

As a senior Davis became the team's starting fullback
because of his blocking ability. He earned All-San Diego Section second-team honors in football and also starred on the
school's track team. Davis still holds the Lincoln Prep record
in the discus throw. Sports helped Davis concentrate on his
classroom work, and by the end of his senior year in high
school he had become an honor student.

Because Davis did not have great natural ability, he
knew he had to work hard to succeed. "I knew that because of
my lack of speed, I had to compensate one way or another,"
he explained in *Sport*. "And catching the ball and blocking
were two things I needed to do in order to play. I'm glad I did-
n't have the speed because I probably wouldn't have worked
as hard on catching and blocking at that early age."

GEORGIA BOUND. College recruiters did not show much
interest in Davis following his graduation from high school,
especially since he missed part of his senior season with a
shoulder injury. His brother Terry played tailback for Long
Beach State University, and he convinced the team's coach,
George Allen, to give his sibling a chance. Allen had previously coached the Los Angeles Rams and the Washington
Redskins in the NFL and he was trying to make the struggling
Long Beach program successful. Before Allen arrived the
school had considered eliminating the football program
because of lack of interest.

Davis starred on the freshmen team in 1990, attracting
his head coach's attention and earning the starting halfback
spot for his sophomore season. Unfortunately, Allen died on
December 31, 1990, and the program stumbled without its
leader. Long Beach State finished 2-9 in 1991, and the school
decided to close down the football program.

The players from the Long Beach program were now free
to transfer to other schools to continue their career. Davis had
gained only 262 yards in 1991, but two major universities—

UCLA and Georgia—showed interest in the running back. He eventually accepted an offer to join the Georgia Bulldogs, even though he did not know where the state was located.

"If you'd have given me a puzzle of the 50 states, I wouldn't have known where to put Georgia," he admitted to *Sports Illustrated*. "But it was a free trip, so I went [to visit the Georgia campus]. They took me through this big old museum-looking building with all these trophies and video screens. When you touched the screens, they showed famous plays. Downstairs, in the locker room, it's all red and pretty. They give you cleats and gloves—at Long Beach State we had to pay for those things. You get a game helmet and a practice helmet. They had my jersey with my name already on it. I was like, 'I'm here!'"

NEXT IN LINE? Georgia had a history of producing fine running backs. Herschel Walker had won the Heisman Trophy—awarded to the nation's best college football player—and both Rodney Hampton and Garrison Hearst went on to successful careers in the NFL. Davis hoped he could be the next in line of great Bulldog rushers.

Davis spent his first year at Georgia serving as the backup for Hearst. Hearst left Georgia for the NFL the next season (1993) and Davis got his chance to start. To his surprise the coaching staff decided to change the team's offense. The Bulldogs became a passing team, relying on the strong arm of quarterback Eric Zeier. Despite the coaching staff's decision, Davis still rushed for 824 yards, averaged 4.9 yards per carry, and scored 8 touchdowns.

GETS RELIEF. When Davis arrived at Georgia he discovered that he suffered from migraine headaches. "During football practice I got a headache, and one of the doctors told me, 'You have classic migraines,'" Davis recalled in *People Weekly*. "Migraines—it's a harsh word. But at least now I finally had a name for it. Some people said to me, 'Oh yeah, I get migraines, too.' That gave me a sense of security. I figured if this many people have them, and they aren't dead, obviously these things aren't life-threatening."

Davis began to take an anti-inflammatory medication. His headaches came less frequently. Instead of suffering three or four migraines every month, Davis had only one.

DISAPPOINTING YEAR. Despite producing solid numbers during his junior season, Georgia head coach Ray Goff was disappointed with Davis's play. When Davis suffered a tear in his hamstring muscle during camp before his senior season, Goff accused him of not wanting to play. Under pressure Davis returned to action too soon and more seriously injured his leg in a game against the University of Tennessee. "You almost feel like you're being forced to play," Davis revealed to the *Atlanta Journal-Constitution*. "[The muscle] just got worse and worse, and eventually it tore. When I missed some games, I figured my career was over."

The hamstring injury helped limit Davis to only 445 yards rushing on 97 carries in his senior season (1994) at Georgia. Professional scouts had rated him as a top prospect after his junior year, but his fall-off in production led many to doubt whether he could play in the NFL. "You know, at the end of my junior year, I was projected as the third back to be taken in the draft," Davis explained to *Sport*. "So how can you go from being someone who's projected third in the draft to what happened in my senior season? What, do you just lose skill? What happened? I mean, my stock dropped because I missed a few games, but that means I can't play anymore?"

Davis also suffered a personal loss in 1994 when an assailant shot his cousin, Jemaul Pennington, to death in San Diego. The two relatives had been friends for many years and Pennington was one of the few people Davis trusted enough to tell about his headaches. "We were the same age, and we were very close," Davis recalled in *People Weekly*. "He didn't know what was wrong with me; he just knew that I would get sick sometimes and he would have to take care of me; get me some hot tea, shut off the lights and make sure nobody bothered me. We had big plans for our futures, how we were going to have all this money and drive nice cars and open up a club.

Then, in 1994, he was shot and killed in San Diego. I still don't know why."

DENVER DRAFTEE. Davis thought his football career might be over after his final season at Georgia and he considered beginning a career in accounting. He just wanted a chance to go to training camp with a professional team. The NFL invited Davis to the scouting combine, where professional prospects are gathered to be tested by talent evaluators. He performed poorly and was convinced he would go unselected in the 1995 NFL Draft.

"I have always been in these situations where things didn't look good, where I couldn't see a light at the end of the tunnel," Davis related to the *Sporting News*. "I figured football was over for me when I finished high school. Same with college. I was never a blue-chipper, I was never the guy everyone knew to be the best. I can't explain what has happened. But maybe for the first time, I realized there were no more levels in football for me to try. If I didn't make the NFL, there wasn't a higher league waiting that I could move to."

As the 1995 NFL Draft progressed, name after name was called, but not Terrell Davis. He waited patiently at his girlfriend's house playing board games while 21 running backs and 195 players overall were chosen ahead of him. Finally, the Denver Broncos used their sixth-round pick—number 196 in the draft—to take Davis. Denver had liked his play at the Blue-Gray college all-star game and thought he might be a third-down back and special teams player.

PROVES HE BELONGS. Davis took the fact that so many teams passed him by in the draft as a challenge. "Being drafted in the sixth round was really a slap in the face for me," he admitted to the *Atlanta Journal-Constitution*. "But deep down inside I knew I wasn't a sixth-round pick. I came in here [to training camp] with something to prove."

Denver coaches did not give Davis much of a chance to win a job in training camp. "If there had been 20 backs, he would have been 20th," Broncos running backs coach Bobby

Turner confessed to the *Sporting News*. Davis impressed the coaching staff with his ability to quickly learn the Broncos' complicated offense and he worked hard on the punt and kick-off teams.

By the end of training camp Davis was challenging to be the team's starting tailback. "[Davis] has surprised me," Broncos coach Mike Shanahan admitted in the *Atlanta Journal-Constitution*. "He's really competing right now for a starting job, and that doesn't happen very often with a sixth-round draft choice and a guy that really didn't carry the ball a lot his senior year."

ROOKIE RUNNER. Davis beat out Glynn Milburn to earn the starting tailback job with the Broncos. He was the lowest paid player on the team, making only the league minimum of $119,000. "I am not afraid of this," Davis explained to the *Atlanta Journal-Constitution*. "I feel like I have nothing to lose."

The rookie running back stepped in and gave Denver's offense a boost. Despite missing two games with a hamstring injury, Davis finished the 1995 season with 1,117 yards on the ground, third in the American Football Conference (AFC) and a 4.7 yards per carry average. He was the first Denver running back to gain 1,000 yards since Gaston Green turned the trick in 1991, and he was the lowest drafted running back in NFL history ever to gain over 1,000 yards in his first year. His Bronco teammates named Davis—who also caught 49 passes—the team's most valuable offensive player, giving him the nod over legendary quarterback John Elway.

The best performance of Davis's rookie season came when he gained 176 yards against the Chargers, his favorite team as a child. Denver rewarded Davis for his outstanding rookie campaign with a five-year, $6.8 million contract after his first year. "I've come from nowhere," he declared in *Atlanta Journal-Constitution*. "That's a big motivation. I've never been pampered. I've never been on a team where everybody looked to me as one of their weapons."

Davis felt that he could improve on his rookie season during his second year. "I looked at last year's season and analyzed every game and situation and felt that, yeah, with the low standards that people put on me, that was a great year," he explained in *Sport*. "But I looked at it as a mediocre year that anyone could have had. And I felt that having that one year under my belt, having played with the offense for a full season, my knowledge of the game had increased a great deal, so I knew that I'd have a better year."

HEADACHES RETURN. Not once during his rookie season did a migraine headache affect Davis during a game. On September 15, 1996, linebacker Lonnie Marts of the Tampa Bay Buccaneers hit Davis hard. The Denver star left the game and soon realized a migraine headache had begun. "It got to the point where I couldn't see anything," David recalled in *Sports Illustrated*. "It was a blur out there." The light flashes began, but he did not have a full-fledged headache.

Davis returned to the game after halftime to rush for 94 of his 137 yards and scored the winning touchdown in a 27-23 Denver victory. "This is the first time ever that I have felt wanted, where I have been an integral part of an offense, of a team," he told the *Sporting News,* explaining why he played in the second half. "A lot of people on the team count on me. When I am not out there, I am thinking I am letting them down. It is not fun or comfortable at all to keep playing. But I know that if I don't go back in, the next day I will be sitting at home and the migraine will be gone and I will be really mad at myself for not giving it a shot."

Three weeks later Davis suffered another headache, this time during a game against the Chargers. Once again the Broncos' training staff gave him an anti-inflammatory medication called Lidocaine and had the running back breathe oxygen. The treatment helped prevent the most severe symptoms of the headaches, and Davis played the remainder of the season without another incident.

Superstar

BEST RECORD. The Broncos got off to a 10-1 start during the 1996 season and boasted the top rated offense and running

PLAYING WITH FEAR

Doctors have been able to develop a treatment plan to help prevent the headaches Davis suffers from. He changed his diet and doctors widened the spaces between his teeth and fit him with a brace to straighten out his jaw.

Despite having the ailment under control, the Bronco star knows that migraine headaches cannot be cured. "At least we have made some progress," Davis declared to the Sporting News. "If I take the anti-inflammatory medicine before every workout, it helps. And if I feel a headache starting and we take the Lidocaine and breathe (extra) oxygen, I haven't had the full migraine anymore. So now we are dealing only with the aura. I don't get the rest of the headache."

Davis realizes he cannot play football if he is worried about his migraine headaches. "I can't wake up every day thinking something might happen," Davis admitted to the Sporting News. "If they got so bad that I was getting them every game, I'd have to deal with it. Maybe I would have to stop playing. That's why I can't get too excited about what is happening to me now. It could end tomorrow."

attack in the league. In a big regular season game, Denver routed the AFC East Division leading New England Patriots, 34-8. Davis rushed for 154 yards and scored 3 touchdowns against the Patriots. Denver finished the season with a 13-3 record, the best in the AFC.

Davis finished the 1996 season with 1,538 yards rushing. He became the fourteenth player in NFL history to rush for 1,000 yards in each of his first two seasons and only the second Bronco. (Bobby Humphrey was the other.) In a game against the Baltimore Ravens he broke the team's single-game record with a 194-yard performance. The Associated Press named Davis the NFL Offensive Player of the Year. "Davis right now may be the best back in the National Football League," Kansas City Chiefs coach Marty Schottenheimer told Sport. "He's got the entire package. He's got the power, he's got the vision, he's got the toughness."

Following Denver's last game Davis led the NFL in rushing. He then had to wait to see if Barry Sanders of the Detroit Lions could pass him in the season's final Monday night game against the San Francisco 49ers. Sanders needed 161 yards to win the rushing title. He finished with 175, edging out Davis.

UPSETTING GAME. Davis looked forward to leading the Broncos into the playoffs. "Without a doubt, I think I could be the difference between past Bronco Super Bowl teams and this team," he explained to Sport. "We have a well-rounded team. This is the type of team I look at and compare to past Super Bowl champions. They have a pretty good running game, they have an excellent quarter-back, they have good receivers and a great defense, and I think we possess all those things right now."

Denver held home-field (Mile High Stadium) advantage throughout the AFC playoffs. In their first game they faced the Jacksonville Jaguars, a team playing in only their second NFL season. The Jaguars had already won a playoff game, defeating the Buffalo Bills 30-27. In a stunning upset, Jacksonville defeated the Broncos in the game at Mile High Stadium by an identical 30-27 score. Davis carried the ball only 14 times, but gained 91 yards. He had to leave the game in the first half with a knee injury.

2,000 YARDS? Davis had the best season of his career in 1997. Once again he and Sanders battled down the stretch for the NFL rushing title. Both backs also had another milestone in view: 2,000 rushing yards in one season. The 2,000 yard mark had only been reached twice in NFL history—in 1973 O.J. Simpson of the Buffalo Bills ran for 2,003 yards and Eric Dickerson of the Los Angeles Rams set the NFL record with 2,105 yards in 1984.

"Really, I can't imagine anyone gaining 2,000 yards in a season," Davis revealed to the *Sporting News*. "But even if I could, I won't let myself think in those terms. My dreams are career dreams. If I start thinking of season goals, I will limit myself. What if I want 2,000 and don't make it? Does that mean I have had a disappointing season?"

Davis partially separated his shoulder in Denver's second-to-last game against the San Francisco 49ers. He missed half of that game and the season finale. The missed playing time meant that Davis finished the season with 1,750 rushing yards, second again to Sanders in the NFL. (Sanders finished the season with 2,053 rushing yards, the second-highest single-season total in league history.) He set a Broncos' single-game record with 215 yards rushing against the Cincinnati Bengals and tied the Denver record with 15 touchdowns.

GRUDGE MATCH. Denver finished the season 12-4 in 1997, good enough for second place in the AFC West Division behind the Kansas City Chiefs. In a much-anticipated re-match, the Jaguars once again traveled to Mile High Stadium for a first-round playoff game. Davis returned to the Broncos' lineup for the first time since separating his shoulder.

This time Denver was ready for the Jaguars. Davis ran for 184 yards and scored 2 touchdowns as the Broncos defeated Jacksonville 42-17. The Broncos finished the game with 310 yards rushing. Davis had to leave the game with bruised ribs after carrying the ball on a 59-yard run. "I thought I had the wind knocked out of me, but when I got back to the bench and sat down, that's when I noticed it," he revealed in the *Los Angeles Times*. "It's painful; it's the type of injury that when you breathe, you feel it."

SUPER BOWL BOUND. After gaining revenge against the Jaguars, Denver traveled to Kansas City to meet their fierce rivals the Chiefs, who had not lost at home during the 1997 season. The game was a tough defensive struggle, but in the end the Broncos prevailed 14-10. Davis—playing with painful ribs—was the star for Denver, rushing for 101 yards against the tough Kansas City defense and scoring both of his team's touchdowns.

Now Denver was in the AFC Championship Game for the first time since 1992. The Pittsburgh Steelers stood between the Broncos and the Super Bowl. On his first carry against the Steelers, Davis broke a 43-yard gain. "It gave us the confidence early in the game to let us know we can run the ball against this defense," he explained to *USA Today*.

The Broncos fell behind early, 14-7, but then ripped off 17 unanswered second-quarter points to hold a 24-14 halftime lead. Denver made that lead hold up in the second half, winning the game 24-21. Davis ran for 139 yards and a touchdown against a Pittsburgh defense that ranked first in the NFL in stopping the run and had not allowed an 100-yard rushing performance in 19 games. "I'm going home," Davis said after the game, referring to the fact that Super Bowl XXII was to be played in his hometown, San Diego.

MIGRAINES TO MVP. Denver had appeared in the Super Bowl four times in their history before 1997, losing every time by a lop-sided score. The Broncos entered Super Bowl XXXII as 12-point underdogs to the defending champion Green Bay Packers. The Packers were a powerful team led by three-time NFL most valuable player Brett Favre. If Denver lost again they would be the first team in league history to lose five Super Bowl games, and they would extend the losing streak for the AFC to 14 in the NFL's biggest contest.

Green Bay began Super Bowl XXXII by driving down the field and scoring a touchdown. Denver answered with a 58-yard drive of their own, with Davis gaining 38 of those yards and scoring the team's first touchdown. Late in the first quarter a Green Bay defensive player hit Davis hard in his head. He felt dizzy and came to the sideline. Soon Davis and the team's trainers realized that the tackle had trig-gered a migraine headache. The running back began to have the aura that blurred his vision. "I kind of blacked out for about two seconds," Davis explained. "My equilibrium was out of kilter. That's when I had aura problems."

With Davis out of the game the Broncos' offense sput-tered. Denver could not earn a first down in the second quar-ter, but held a slim 17-14 lead at halftime. Davis took his medication and rested in the locker room during the entire second quarter and the Super Bowl's extended halftime. "I wasn't in much pain," he revealed after the game. "I just had to go to the sideline and take my medication."

The medication helped Davis return to the lineup for the second half. He fumbled the ball on his first carry, but then proceeded to destroy Green Bay's hopes of a Super Bowl repeat. Davis gained 93 yards in the second half and scored 2 of his Super Bowl record 3 rushing touchdowns, including the

NEVER GIVE UP

Davis visited his old high school—Lincoln Prep—during Super Bowl week. The school held a "Terrell Davis Day" and retired his former jersey number, 7. Davis had a simple message to pass along to the students at his former school. "I just want the kids to have a sense of hope," he told *USA Today.* "I remember when I went to Lincoln Prep, a lot of kids in my circle, they were just living day to day. A lot of people didn't have aspirations for anything different. If you think your dreams are dashed early, you just never give up. You never know what's going to happen."

game winner with only 1:42 left in the game in a 31-24 Denver victory. "I'm numb right now," he confessed. "I can't reflect on my game. It is going to take a while for this to set in."

Writers covering the game voted Davis the game's most valuable player. He finished the game with 157 yards rushing and helped Denver control the ball. Davis's teammates appreciated his effort. "Without him, we couldn't have done it," right tackle Tony Jones said. "I am so impressed with him."

Davis's performance helped him set NFL records for total carries (481) and total rushing yards (2,369) in one season, including playoff games. "Man, I've seen a lot of great running backs, and to come up with those kinds of numbers, that's kind of wild," he told *USA Today*. "It doesn't seem like I have that many yards."

OFF THE FIELD. Davis lives in an apartment in Denver with his oldest brother, Tyrone, and his mother lives nearby. His girlfriend lives in Atlanta, Georgia. In his free time Davis likes to play computer games, bowl, and ride jet skis. He owns a four-wheel-drive vehicle and bought his mother a mini-van. "I wouldn't want to go through what is happening to me without her sharing in it," Davis explained to the *Sporting News,* referring to his mother.

Davis has reached the top of his profession, but he always tries to remember how hard he had to work. "For me, it's just gratifying that I'm able to excel at this level," he expressed in *Sport*. "You know, I really didn't have any success in college or high school, so it amazes me that I'm at the highest level possible and I'm doing as well as I can."

WHERE TO WRITE:

C/O DENVER BRONCOS,
13655 E. DOVE VALLEY PKWY.,
ENGLEWOOD, CO 80112.

Sources

Atlanta Journal-Constitution, August 17, 1995; October 5, 1995; November 26, 1995; November 16, 1996; January 12, 1998; January 15, 1998.

Los Angeles Times, November 20, 1995; December 27, 1996; January 5, 1997; December 17, 1997; December 28, 1997; January 12, 1998; January 21, 1998.

Newsday, October 5, 1996; December 7, 1997; December 28, 1997.

People Weekly, December 23, 1996.

Sport, February 1997.

Sporting News, November 25, 1996; November 17, 1997.

Sports Illustrated, November 1, 1993; October 28, 1996; November 25, 1996.

USA Today, December 24, 1996; August 22, 1997; December 29, 1997; January 5, 1998; January 12, 1998; January 13, 1998; January 19, 1998; January 21, 1998.

Additional information provided by the Gannett News Service.

Pat Day

1953–

"Pat is a world-class rider, but, more important, he is a world-class human being."
—Horse racing trainer D. Wayne Lukas.

Pat Day is built to be a horse racing jockey. He weighs 100 pounds and stands 4-feet-11-inches tall, but has as big a heart as any athlete in any sport. Five times Day has ridden his horse to victory at the Preakness Stakes—one of horse racing's Triple Crown—and four times he has won the Eclipse Award, given annually to the best jockey in the United States. Six times he has won more races in a year than any other jockey, and he stands fifth on the all-time win list. Day has achieved all of these accomplishments after overcoming alcohol and drug addictions that almost ended his career and his life.

Growing Up

COWBOY DREAM. Pat Alan Day was born October 13, 1953, in Brush, Colorado. His father was an auto repairman, and the family lived in several towns in Colorado. Day credits his father with his love of horses. "I came from a ranching community—and I believe I inherited my father's uncanny knack of understanding animals," he revealed in the *Chicago Tribune*. "My father was a tremendous horseman in his own right, taught me basic horsemanship that has been my foundation. That has helped me tremendously in a roundabout way—being able to understand the temperament of the horse, and adjusting to get along with that."

Day was a successful wrestler at Eagle High School, but he had only one dream: to be a rodeo cowboy. "My childhood dream was to become a professional rodeo cowboy," Day recalled. "I was involved in the Little Britches Rodeo in the summer and was on the high school rodeo team. After graduating from high school in 1971, I continued to pursue my dream. I worked Monday through Friday at a gas station and then was going to rodeos on the weekends. It wasn't a money-making proposition in that I was having a very limited amount of success, but I was having a good time." Day roped steers and rode bulls.

CAREER MOVE. Being only 4 feet, 11 inches tall and under 100 pounds, Day had a hard time surviving in the rodeo without getting bumps and bruises. "I bit the dust a lot more times than I stayed on," he admitted in *Sports Illustrated*. "I didn't show much promise."

Day participated in the rodeo for a year. At that point he listened to friends who advised him to explore becoming a jockey. He first worked at a horse farm, then moved to a track in Las Vegas, Nevada, operating the starting gate and working out horses. Day took advantage of his position by asking the jockeys for tips on how to win races.

In July 1973 Day won the first race of his career—aboard a horse named Foreblunged—at Prescott Downs, a

---

SCOREBOARD

WINNER OF EIGHT HORSE RACING TRIPLE CROWN RACES, INCLUDING FIVE PREAKNESS STAKES (1985, 1990, 1994, 1995, AND 1996), TWO BELMONT STAKES (1989 AND 1994), AND ONE KENTUCKY DERBY (1992).

FOUR-TIME WINNER OF THE ECLIPSE AWARD, GIVEN TO THE BEST JOCKEY IN THE UNITED STATES (1984, 1986, 1987, AND 1991).

WINNER OF OVER 7,000 RACES IN HIS CAREER.

DAY HAS A CHANCE TO BECOME THE WINNINGEST JOCKEY OF ALL TIME.

small track in Arizona. By the winter of 1973 he was the leading rider at Turf Paradise, the biggest track in Arizona. Before long Day was winning races in Massachusetts, Chicago, and New Orleans, and his reputation began to grow. "Knowledgeable people who saw me claimed they knew right off that I had something," he told *Sports Illustrated*. "I didn't have to be taught—it was just there."

LIFE IN THE FAST LANE. A jockey has to be confident in order to succeed, but Day soon became cocky. "I was cocky before I got on the racetrack," he confessed to *Sports Illustrated*. "When I did good immediately, I started to think I was the center around which the racetrack revolved."

Day also started to live his life off the track in the fast lane. "I was running the streets all night, working horses all morning, and riding horses all afternoon, and I was doing good," he told *Sports Illustrated*. Day admits to drinking heavily and taking drugs.

In 1976 Day married Deborah Bailey—the daughter of a former jockey—and moved to New York to ride. The move was a mistake. "I started riding terrible," he recalled in *Sport*. "Being the kind of person I was, I put the blame on everybody at the track. The more I blamed them, the worse my business got. I got to messing with drugs and went on a self-destruction kick." Day got into locker-room fights with two other well-known jockeys, Angel Cordero and Jorge Velasquez.

Day decided New York was not the place for him. "I'm a country boy from a little-bitty town," he explained in *Horse Player*. "I just couldn't adjust to the lifestyle in New York. And I had some personal problems at the time."

OUT OF CONTROL. Day's on- and off-track problems soon tore his life apart. He and his wife were divorced in 1978, and he moved to Miami, Florida. "I was a real basket case after my marriage fell apart," Day admitted in the *Chicago Tribune*. "I was wanting to blame the race track for my personal crisis, and the race track was not to blame. It was my immaturity and inability to handle my personal affairs."

Day angered other riders, and his agent quit. He could not ride, had no money, and was drinking and taking drugs. "I rode for maybe 10 days, but it just wasn't there," he told *Sports Illustrated*. "I turned my back on the racetrack." A friend named Steve Rowan helped Day get himself together. Rowan took the jockey to New Orleans and convinced trainers to give him another chance.

LEADS NATION. Day pulled himself together enough to begin riding again. Soon he was one of the best jockeys in the country. On New Year's Eve of 1993, Day and Cordero were tied for the most wins by a jockey during the preceding year.

Day took extreme measures to try to win his first-ever national riding title. "Day didn't want a tie, so he took a plane ride which could only be described as horrendous to Delta Downs in Vinton, Louisiana, about 250 miles west of New Orleans, to compete that night," the *Daily Racing Form* reported. "After dodging rainstorms, lightning and absolutely horrible weather, most passengers would be grateful to be alive, but Day was not to be denied in his bid for national laurels. He rode two winners that night to capture the title."

In 1984 Day won his first major race. He captured the inaugural Breeder's Cup Classic, the richest race in the sport with a $3 million purse. For three straight years (1982–84) Day won more races than any other jockey in the United States. During those years he had 399, 454, and 339 victories respectively. Day became only the second rider in history to win three straight championships. (Bill Hartack was the first jockey to accomplish this feat when he led the country from 1955–57.) In 1984 Day won the Eclipse Award—given every year to the best jockey in the United States—for the first time.

CHANGES LIFE. Day had reached the top of his sport, but his personal life was still unstable. He continued to drink and abuse drugs, and his body began to show the strain. Day had remarried and once again his behavior placed his relationship in danger. "When Pat did the drugs and the drinking he was a different person," his second wife, Sheila Johnson, told *Sports Illustrated*. "When we were first together I used to pray, God we need help." One time Day jumped off a second floor balcony after he and his wife argued.

In January 1984 Day claims he had an experience in a hotel room in Miami, Florida, that changed his life. After watching a preacher on television, he fell asleep. When he woke up Day was convinced that the spirit of Jesus Christ was in the room with him. He decided at that moment to dedicate his life to Christianity. "There was an immediate transformation within me," Day revealed in *Sports Illustrated*. "I fell on my face in front of the TV and wept."

Before this episode Day said he had been a nonpracticing Christian. Since that moment, however, he gave up alcohol and drugs. Day also considered retiring from horse racing and becoming a minister. "I felt I was being hypocritical, making a stand for Christ and being involved in an industry that revolves around gambling," he explained in the *Chicago Tribune*. "I really struggled with that. Finally, the Lord revealed to me he had saved me to work within the industry, not to leave it—to use the God-given talent I had."

PREAKNESS NO. 1. In 1985 Day came to the Preakness Stakes—one of horse racing's Triple Crown—to ride Tank's Prospect. (The Triple Crown consists of the Kentucky Derby, the Preakness Stakes, and the Belmont Stakes. The races are for three-year-old horses only.) Two weeks earlier at the Kentucky Derby, Tank's Prospect had finished seventh. The first and second place finishers at the Derby—Spend a Buck and Stephan's Odyssey—decided to skip the Preakness Stakes.

Chief's Crown—the third-place finisher at the Kentucky Derby—was the favorite to win the race. Tank's Prospect was bumped coming out of the gate, but soon Day had his horse in contention. "I was sitting on a lot of horse," he explained to *Sports Illustrated*. "[If] we didn't run out of room, I knew that I was going to beat Chief's Crown." The two horses came down the homestretch neck and neck. At the wire Tank's Prospect broke the finish line first in a race record time of 1:53-2/5. Day had his first Triple Crown victory.

Superstar

BEST OF THE DECADE. By the end of the 1980s Day had established himself as the winningest jockey in the United States. He won the Eclipse Award two more times—in 1986 and 1987—and led all riders in wins for the decade with 3,270. In 1986 he won the national riding title with 429 wins. On September 14, 1989, Day set a one-day record when he rode eight winners in nine races at Arlington Race Track, the top winning percentage ever for one day's work.

In 1989 Day had his best chance to win the Triple Crown. He was the jockey for Easy Goer, a horse many experts compared to the greatest champions of all-time. "This is not only the best horse I have ever sat on," Day declared to *Sports Illustrated*. "This could be the best I've ever seen. There's something this horse has—I can't put my hands on it. I've never found it with any other horse."

Easy Goer was favored to win the Kentucky Derby, but finished 2 1/2 lengths behind Sunday Silence. "Sunday Silence was up in front of me and I tried to stay in contact with him," Day explained in *Sports Illustrated*. "When he started drawing away from us on the backside, I nudged my horse a little bit and I got no response."

Two weeks later at the Preakness Stakes the race was closer, but the result was the same. Sunday Silence edged Easy Goer in a photo-finish. It was now Sunday Silence that had the chance to make history at the Belmont Stakes. A victory would make the horse only the twelfth Triple Crown champion. "In the Belmont, you've got a horse that's going to try and win the Triple Crown," Easy Goer's trainer, Shug McGaughey, told *Sports Illustrated*. "And a horse that's going to try to stop him."

Day and Easy Goer would not be denied at the Belmont Stakes. In the second-fastest time in race history—2:26—Easy Goer crushed Sunday Silence and the rest of the nine-horse field. The two horses once again were neck and neck at the top of the stretch, but this time it was Easy Goer who had more strength. "Easy Goer just outran him," Charlie Whittingham, the trainer of Sunday Silence, told *Sports Illustrated*. "Maybe that was one of the great mile-and-a-halfs [the length of the Belmont] of all time."

DERBY DISAPPOINTMENT. During the 1980s Day made the legendary Churchill Downs race track in Louisville, Kentucky, his home base. He is the winningest jockey ever at the famous track, but in his first nine tries he could not win the most important race of the year at Churchill Downs: the Kentucky Derby. In three straight years—1989 to 1991—he finished second.

Several times Day had the chance to ride what would become a Derby winner but passed up the ride for another horse. In 1987 he could have ridden Alysheba but opted for a horse that pulled out during the race because he was bleeding from his nose. In 1990 he was invited to ride Unbridled, but chose Summer Squall instead. Unbridled won and Summer Squall finished a close second. For some reason Day never could win. "Time and time again, I thought there was a Derby with my name on it somewhere," he confessed to *Sports Illustrated.*

DAY'S DAY. Day visited the Kosair's Children Hospital the day before the 1992 Kentucky Derby. He predicted he would win the race while talking to a young boy recovering from a bone marrow transplant. Day told the youngster that he would wear a Kosair's Children Hospital cap in the winner's circle.

At the 1992 Derby Day was aboard Lil E. Tee, a 17 to 1 long-shot. At one point the horse had been unable to compete because of physical problems. The favorite in the race was Arazi, a French horse that had won the Breeder's Cup Juvenile race the previous year.

Arazi held the lead on the final turn, but he used up all of his energy trying to stay in front. Day realized his horse was also tiring, but he took the lead. Coming down the stretch Lil E. Tee had just enough speed to hold off Casual Lies by a length to win the Kentucky Derby. The winning time of 2:04 was the slowest for the race in 18 years.

As he rode Lil E. Tee into the winner's circle, Day took off his riding cap and put on the hat he had promised to wear. "Boy, does this feel good," he declared to *Sports Illustrated.* "All in God's good time. It feels so good. I think I'll do it again. The longer you wait, the sweeter it tastes!"

RECORD BREAKER. Day continued to win the big races in the 1990s. In 1990 he won the Preakness Stakes for the second time in his career aboard Summer Squall. Then Day set a new record by winning the Preakness for three straight years (1994–96).

In 1991 he became only the sixth jockey to win over $100 million in prize money in his career. In 1994 Day won both the Preakness Stakes and Belmont on Tabasco Cat, the only time in his career he had won two Triple Crown races in the same year. That same year he became only the seventh rider in history to win 6,000 career races.

SUBSTITUTE RIDER. In 1996 Day rode Prince of Thieves to a third-place finish in the Kentucky Derby. A week before the Preakness, trainer D. Wayne Lukas replaced Day with Jerry Bailey, the hottest jockey in the United States. Bailey had ridden Grindstone to the Kentucky Derby title, but that horse could not run in the Preakness because of bone chips in his right front knee.

The decision to replace Day surprised many observers. The jockey had won the Preakness the last two years on horses trained by Lukas and had won the race four times in the prior ten races and finished second three other times. "Wayne said it was a coaching move," Day said. "Jerry was riding as good or better than anybody in the world. You can't blame him for that."

Day signed on to ride Louis Quatorze, a horse that had finished sixteenth at the Kentucky Derby. When the gates opened he took his horse straight to the lead. Day stayed there the entire race, urging Louis Quatorze to hold off a late-charging Skip Away. "I kept expecting someone to make a run at us," Day said. "I was surprised they weren't."

Louis Quatorze won the race with a record-tying time of 1:532/5. He was the first horse to win wire-to-wire (leading a race from start to finish) since Aloma's Ruler in 1982. "If somebody else had ridden this horse, he would have won today," Day said. "I'm not saying anybody could have won on him today, but a number of riders could have. I feel fortunate I was the one." As he crossed the finish line Day pumped his fist and yelled "five, five, five," signifying his fifth Preakness win.

He now trailed only the legendary Eddie Arcaro, who won the race a record six times.

Bailey and Prince of Thieves finished seventh. The defeat ended the streak of six straight Triple Crown race victories by horses trained by Lukas. Day's win gave him a record-tying third straight Preakness win. He tipped his cap to Lukas, an act of good sportsmanship. "I'm sorry his streak ended, but I was happy my streak continued," Day said after the race.

ONE OF THE BEST. Day took his place with the great jockeys in history when he was inducted in the Racing Hall of Fame in 1991. That same year he won his fourth Eclipse Award. On August 25, 1997, Day became a member of a select group of jockeys when he won his seven-thousandth race. Only four other jockeys had ever won that many. "All the milestones are special, but this one is doubly so because the number is so big," Day told the *Daily Racing Form.* " He has led the nation in races won six times.

WHY SO GOOD? Day has a unique ability to analyze his horse. Trainers trust his opinion, even if he does not like their horse. "Pat has a sixth sense of knowing where he is in a race and how much horse he has and what he can do with that horse," trainer D. Wayne Lukas told *Sports Illustrated.*

Because he knows his horse so well, Day can often wait well into a race before making his move. "He's a very patient rider," trainer Shug McGaughey explained in *Sports Illustrated.* "He'll stay and he'll wait and wait to make a move, and sometimes you wonder how in the world he can wait as long as he does."

Day has shed his bad reputation and now is one of the most respected jockeys in racing. "Pat is a world-class rider, but, more important, he is a world-class human being," Lukas told the *Chicago Tribune.*

EDDIE ARCARO

Eddie Arcaro—who died in November 1997—was the only jockey ever to win the Triple Crown twice. He swept the Kentucky Derby, Preakness Stakes, and Belmont Stakes on Whirlaway in 1941 and on Citation in 1948. Arcaro also holds the record for most wins in Triple Crown races with seventeen. He won the Kentucky Derby five times, the Preakness a record six times, and the Belmont Stakes six times.

BIG WINNERS

The following chart lists the top five winningest jockeys in U.S. history as of August 1997.

Bill Shoemaker	8,833
Laffit Pincay Jr.	8,545
David Gall	7,134
Angel Cordero Jr.	7,057
Pat Day	7,000

OFF THE TRACK. Day lives in Crestwood, Kentucky—a suburb of Louisville—with his wife, Sheila, and their 10-year-old adopted daughter, Irene Elizabeth. Day reads the Bible every day and his favorite passage is from Romans 8:28: "All things work together for the good of those who love Jesus and are called according to his purpose."

At only 44 years old in 1997, Day has a chance to become the winningest jockey of all-time. He plans to keep racing as long as he can. "As for the future, the sky's the limit," Day told the *Daily Racing Form.* "I don't have the problems other riders have like weight, and my health is good. I'll just take it one day at a time, and keep going as long as the Lord permits."

WHERE TO WRITE:
C/O CHURCHILL DOWNS,
700 CENTER AVE.,
LOUISVILLE, KY 80208-1200.

Sources

Chicago Tribune, July 14, 1991; August 8, 1991.
Daily Racing Form, August 27, 1997.
Detroit Free Press, May 5, 1989.
Horse Player, Fall 1994.
New York Times, May 19, 1996.
Philadelphia Daily News, May 16, 1992.
Sport, May 1985.
Sporting News, May 11, 1992.
Sports Illustrated, August 22, 1983; May 27, 1985; May 1, 1989; May 15, 1989; May 29, 1989; June 19, 1989; November 13, 1989; March 26, 1990; June 18, 1990; May 11, 1992; May 27, 1996.
USA Today, May 20, 1996.
Washington Post, May 3, 1992.
Additional information provided by the National Museum of Racing and Hall of Fame.

Rudy Galindo

1969–

Figure skater Rudy Galindo never quit. He did not give up when his skating partner—Kristi Yamaguchi—broke up their partnership just two years before the 1992 Winter Olympics. Galindo kept going when his father, older brother, and two skating coaches died. He also continued working when no one gave him a chance to win the men's competition at the 1996 U.S. Figure Skating Championships. In front of a home town crowd, Galindo turned in the performance of his life, winning the national championship and making his dream come true.

"Rudy Galindo is the [best example] of never, ever, ever quit."
—Galindo's agent, Michael Rosenberg.

Growing Up

TRUCK DRIVER'S SON. Rudy Galindo was born September 7, 1969, in San Jose, California. His grandparents on his father's side came to the United States from Mexico. Galindo's father, Jess, drove a truck for the United Technologies Corporation. He carried rocket fuel from Gilroy, California, to Carson City, Nevada.

The Galindo family lived in a trailer park in East San Jose, California. "I thought our trailer was just fine," Galindo wrote in his book *Icebreaker: The Autobiography of Rudy Galindo.* "There wasn't any reason for me to think otherwise. The whole neighborhood was a trailer park, so that's how all my neighbors lived."

Galindo did not see his parents very often. His father was on the road much of the time and his mother—Margaret—suffered from a mental illness. Several times she had to be taken from home to a hospital. Because of his parents' problems, Galindo was raised for much of his childhood by his older sister, Laura. Since her father could barely read or write, Laura also kept track of the family's finances.

FAMILY AFFAIR. Drugs and gangs were all around the trailer park. Jess Galindo did not allow his children to play outside and looked for a way to keep them from getting in trouble. He encouraged his children to spend their time at the Eastridge Ice Arena—only five minutes from home.

Laura Galindo began skating at the age of 10—after falling in love with the sport at a birthday party—and her brother came along with her. "We were in bed by 7:30 almost every night, then up at 4:45 to do our figures [a type of figure skating] before school," Laura Galindo recalled in *Sports Illustrated.* "All the extra money went to skating." Galindo also took ballet to work on the artistic part of his skating.

The cost of paying for skating lessons for two children meant that the Galindo family had to pass up opportunities to move from the trailer park. "Sometimes I'd hear arguments at home about the bills, but Dad never asked me to stop [skating]," Galindo explained to *Sports Illustrated.* "And Laura paid for some of my lessons when she worked at Taco Bell in high school." Galindo and his mother moved the furniture in the trailer's living room so he could practice his skating moves at home.

TEAMMATES. Galindo's skating quickly earned him international recognition. He finished third at the World Junior Figure Skating Championships at the age of 15 and won the title two years later in 1987. Galindo also enjoyed pairs skating, and soon he decided to participate in this form of figure skating full-time.

In 1983 Galindo began skating with Kristi Yamaguchi. Together the two skaters won the pairs title at both the 1989 and 1990 U.S. Figure Skating Championships and finished fifth at the 1990 World Figure Skating Championships. With continued improvement the couple figured to be medal favorites at the 1992 Winter Olympics in Albertville, France.

The two young skaters were also close off the ice. Galindo lived with the Yamaguchi family for two years. In order to better promote their partnership, Galindo changed the spelling of his first name from Rudy to Rudi. In this way his name would be a better match with Kristi.

BIG BREAK-UP. Being so close to Yamaguchi, Galindo was shocked when she announced that she was giving up pairs skating to work only at women's singles. "April 26, 1990," he recalled the date in *Sports Illustrated*. "I guess I knew it would happen. You hear comments from other skaters. But Kristi had never said anything. We were like brother and sister, then we just went our separate ways."

After the split Yamaguchi's career took off. She won the gold medal in the women's competition at the 1992 Winter Olympics. Galindo returned to men's singles skating because he could not find another partner as good as Yamaguchi. His career faltered as he finished eleventh at the U.S. Figure Skating Championships in 1991 and eighth in 1992.

Galindo's career was now in severe jeopardy. He completely missed the 1992 Winter Olympics, but he never blamed Yamaguchi openly for her decision. "He never said one bad word about Kristi," Laura Galindo revealed in *Sports*

Galindo giving his first-place performance during the 1996 U.S. Figure Skating Championships.

Illustrated. "He just bottled it up." Yamaguchi explained what happened to *People Weekly:* "It's not a perfect world. Our lives went in different directions."

DIFFICULT TIMES. For the next few years Galindo's career and personal life suffered many setbacks. The decline of his career was a blow to his family. Because Galindo did not participate in the Olympics his ability to make money skating was severely damaged.

More importantly, Jess Galindo was seriously ill and told Galindo he was trying to stay alive so that he could see his son in the Olympics. "A half-hour after I told him [Kristi and I] had broken up, I saw him sitting there with a tear running down from his eye," Galindo recalled in *Time*. "That's what made me angry."

PERSONAL TRAGEDIES. Jess Galindo died of a heart attack in 1993. His death hit Galindo very hard. "I wish I could have given something back to him: a vacation, a new car," he confessed to *Sports Illustrated*. "All the things he couldn't afford so I could skate."

Galindo's older brother, George, contracted the AIDS virus and moved back in with his mother in 1992. Galindo moved home to help care for him. In 1989 he had lost his skating coach, Jim Hullick, to the disease.

Caring for George was very hard work. "I gave my brother baths," he explained in *Sports Illustrated*. "I'd take him to the hospital for his treatments, and he would barely be able to walk. I was angry that I was the one who had to take care of him. Then near the end, he didn't recognize me. AIDS patients often suffer from dementia, and he'd go, 'Who are you?' He'd hide from me under the bed. I had to leave for a competition in Vienna, and I had a feeling he wouldn't make it. I kissed him and told him I loved him, and he kissed me and told me he loved me. Then he died the same time I was doing my long program. I came right home. That was hard. I went from the ice to the funeral."

Then in 1995 Galindo's second coach, Rick Inglesi, also died from AIDS. The tragedies he suffered led Galindo to begin drinking too much and experimenting with drugs. He also did not train as hard as he should have and began suffering from exercise-induced asthma. "I got numb—to all the suffering around me, numb even to death itself," Galindo admitted to *Time*. "Nothing got through to me except skating in the morning. It was my only release."

Superstar

THE BLAME GAME. Galindo escaped from his personal tragedies by skating, but he continued to struggle during competitions. He finished eighth at the 1995 U.S. Figure Skating Championships and blamed the judges for his low finish. Galindo felt that he did not get top scores because his skating was more artistic and involved fewer jumps than his competitors. "American judges tend not to be as receptive to the artistic style of skating as European judges," he complained to *Sports Illustrated*. "Maybe they didn't like it when I did ballet moves, or held my arms a certain way. Though when you're angry you tend to blame your losses on anything."

Galindo always made a costly mistake that caused him to do poorly in competitions. "He was blaming everyone else—Dad for dying, George for going to the hospital, the judging—but I knew he had to hit his program," Laura Galindo said in *Sports Illustrated*. "We've gone through hell, but we're not the only people who've had tragedy. Everything happens for a reason. By passing away, those loved ones may have given us something they wouldn't have been able to give us while they were alive: the toughness, the bravery to stay in this sport."

LAST CHANCE. Galindo took some time off from skating after his disappointing performance at the 1995 U.S. Figure Skating Championships. He needed to decide whether to continue competing or begin coaching other skaters. During his break from training he worked for his sister Laura at the San Jose Ice Center, teaching seven- and eight-year-old skaters.

After considerable soul searching, Galindo decided he would compete one last time at the 1996 U.S. Figure Skating Championships. His decision was influenced by the fact that the championships were being held in San Jose on his home ice at the San Jose Ice Center. His mother—who no longer liked to travel—could come see him skate. "I knew he'd come back," Laura Galindo confessed in *USA Today*. "But he had to make that decision."

NEW ATTITUDE. When Galindo began training again—in September 1995—he was a changed man."I got it into my head that no matter what, my friends would still like me, and my sister would still love me," he explained to *Sports Illustrated*. "So just skate and enjoy it."

Galindo worked hard for what he thought would be his farewell performance. He lifted weights and lost 25 pounds. On the ice Galindo skated his programs over and over again to build up his stamina and eliminate mistakes. Laura—now his coach—insisted that he tone down his costumes, which were usually very flamboyant. Galindo's costume for the upcoming competition would be plain black.

To save money and keep his mother company, Galindo continued to live in the family trailer. His only car—a 1982 Honda—had been driven 208,000 miles. Galindo rode his bike 3½ miles to the rink, then to the gym, then 8 miles back home.

Galindo tried to help his mother as much as he could. She suffered emotional problems after the death of her husband. "Once my dad passed away, she kind of hung up her gloves," Galindo told *Sports Illustrated*. He shopped for his mother, cleaned the trailer, and kept track of her bills.

The change in her brother was obvious to Laura Galindo. "Rudy became a whole person this year," she explained to *Sports Illustrated*. "He confronted all the issues in his life and stopped putting the blame on everyone else. There was a different kind of fight in Rudy this year. He had so little, and he wanted to give something to Mom."

ONCE IN A LIFETIME. Entering the 1996 U.S. Figure Skating Championships, Galindo hoped to finish in the top six in the men's competition. The main contenders for the championship were three-time national champion Todd Eldredge and two-time U.S. champion Scott Davis. Galindo was such a long-shot that the media guide for the competition did not even mention his name.

Knowing that this was his last competition eased Galindo's nerves. He skated a mistake-free short program, but ended up in third place behind Eldredge and Davis. (The short program consists of skaters performing required maneuvers and counts for one-third of the final score.) "I was thinking about all my friends and family that passed away," Galindo revealed in the *Atlanta Constitution*. "I know that they're watching me. Before I skated tonight, I was like, 'Please help me.'"

STANDING OVATION. The long program was held January 20, 1996. Galindo skated his long program to music of Tchaikovsky's *Swan Lake*. (The long program allows the skater to choose which maneuvers to attempt and counts for two-thirds of the final score.) He decided to go all out, including eight triple jumps in his program and two triple jump combinations—two more than any other competitor tried. "Before each jump, I would say, 'OK, land it, because I want to hear the applause,'" Galindo explained in the *Los Angeles Times*.

The sell-out crowd of 10,869 rose to their feet cheering with 15 seconds left in Galindo's program. "My jumps seemed so light and easy, like I didn't have to try hard at all,' Galindo recalled in the *Atlanta Journal-Constitution*. Leaving the ice he shouted, "Thank you, Dad. Thank you, George, Jim, Rick." "I'd like to tell them I did it all for them," Galindo explained to *People Weekly*.

Galindo and Laura hugged and cried after he came off the ice. He received two perfect marks of 6.0 for artistic merit—the first perfect marks he had ever received and the first awarded to a man at the national championships since Paul Wylie received perfect marks in 1990. More importantly, seven judges placed Galindo in first place and only two favored Eldredge. Galindo had won the national championship.

The sell-out crowd chanted "Rudy, Rudy, Rudy" after the public address announcer reported the final results. "It's almost like a dream," Galindo confessed to the Gannett News Service. "I just had this feeling all week—I must have been psychic—I would visualize coming off the ice and the crowd would be standing."

With the victory the 26-year-old Galindo became the oldest U.S. men's figure skating champion in 70 years. (Chris Christenson won in 1926 at the age of 51.) Galindo also was the first Hispanic winner in the history of the event. "I wanted to skate well for my family—and to help out my mom and me financially," Galindo explained to *People Weekly.* "Right away I thought, 'Now I don't have to worry about how I'm going to pay for my skating.'"

TAKES ON THE WORLD. Galindo was thrilled to have won the national title, but he had a hard time dealing with all the attention being paid to him. "Sometimes, it's hard for me to deal with," he admitted to *USA Today.* "I always liked when no one paid any attention to me. I've been trying not to let everything get to me, but it's getting harder to block out. Everywhere I go, people say, 'Just do a program like you did at nationals, and you'll be world champion.'" Galindo began to see a sports psychologist to help him deal with the pressure.

Galindo's victory at the U.S. Figure Skating Championships qualified him for his first-ever World Figure Skating Championships, held in 1996 in Edmonton, Alberta, Canada. He entered the competition hoping to finish in the top ten. "I'm not even thinking about a medal," Galindo confessed to *USA Today.* "I'm just glad to be here." The favorites for the 1996 men's world championship competition were Eldredge,

REUNION

Galindo and Yamaguchi did not talk much since their split in 1990. The two finally spoke on the phone after Galindo won the U.S. championship when Yamaguchi called him. "It was so incredible," Galindo admitted to *USA Today.* "It was so nice. It was the first time since we split up that we talked one-on-one on the phone."

Yamaguchi told Galindo she was proud of him. "Rudy has such an incredible talent," she told *People Weekly.* "I knew that if he could channel it and work through all his struggles, he could really do well."

DREAM COME TRUE

Galindo had always dreamed of owning a Corvette automobile. After winning the U.S. title, Galindo went to a local Chevrolet dealership in San Jose and test-drove his dream car. "It was so funny when we went to the dealership, because they asked for my insurance card," Galindo wrote in his book *Icebreaker: The Autobiography of Rudy Galindo.* "I didn't need insurance to drive my bicycle. So Laura took care of that by giving the dealer her insurance card, and he handed me the keys to a forest-green T-top Corvette. That's the kind where you can remove the roof panels, so it's like a convertible."

1994 Olympic gold medalist Alexei Urmanov of Russia, and defending former champion and home-country hero Elvis Stojko of Canada.

Leading up to the world championships Galindo sprained his ankle. He worried about his injury and battled his nerves the first time he took the ice in Edmonton, participating in a qualifying competition. "I was gasping for air that wasn't there," Galindo explained in *USA Today.* "I thought there's no way I can do this program. That was the most nerve-racking warm-up I've ever had. I don't know if it was doing so well at nationals and having something to prove here—that that wasn't a once in a lifetime performance."

ONE OF THE BEST. To help quiet his nerves Galindo went to the West Edmonton Mall and took several turns on the amusement park rides located there. "I had an all-day pass," he explained to *USA Today.* "I don't skate well if I stay in the hotel room all day. If I go out with my family and friends, then I don't think about my skating so much."

Eldredge and Ilia Kulik of Russia finished one and two in the short program. Galindo came in fourth. He did not make any mistakes, but his failure to attempt a triple jump combination cost him points. Stojko eliminated himself from contention when he fell during his program and finished seventh.

Galindo skated the same long program he performed at the U.S. Figure Skating Championships. He landed all eight of his triple jumps, but did not show the same emotion he had in San Jose. "Nationals was more magical, but I proved here I can be consistent," Galindo told *Sports Illustrated.* "The memories of winning in San Jose will always be there, but I've discovered there's more within me to give."

Eldredge put on the best performance of his life in the long program. He skated a near-perfect program to win the world title. Galindo ranked fourth in the long program, a finish that was good enough to earn him third place and a bronze medal. "I thought of everything that's gone on in my life when I was up on the podium," Galindo revealed in *USA Today*. "I wished my dad and brother were there." Kulik captured the silver medal.

The last time two American men had finished with medals at the world championships was in 1981 when Scott Hamilton won the gold and David Santee took the silver. "I have to thank Rudy for beating me at this year's nationals," Eldredge told *Sports Illustrated*. "It made me go back and train and get my act together."

TURNS PRO. After the world championships Galindo signed to skate in the Campbell's Tour of Olympic and World Figure Skating Champions for $200,000, more money than he had ever made before. He did not go crazy with his newfound wealth. Galindo wanted to buy his mom a new house, but she did not want to leave the family trailer. Instead, he bought her new furniture.

Galindo also wanted to repay his sister—whom he jokingly called "the Bank of Laura"—for all of her financial and emotional support. The grateful Galindo bought her a new dress and a leather jacket. "I'd like to save all my money for Laura's future," he said in *Sports Illustrated*. "The way I look at it, I made it without money. Why do I need all this stuff now?"

In September 1996 Galindo announced that he was giving up his chance to defend his U.S. Figure Skating Championship title by turning professional. He had already signed deals for an autobiography, a made-for-television movie, and skating tours and exhibitions. Galindo's life story, *Icebreaker: The Autobiography of Rudy Galindo,* was published in 1997. "It was hard to open your heart," Galindo told *USA Today*. "But I like telling the story. It was good therapy."

OFF THE ICE. Galindo continued to live with his mother after his U.S. championship, but planned to move out and get a place of his own. Despite his Mexican heritage, Galindo cannot speak Spanish. He has Laura's name tattooed on his right shoulder. Galindo owns two cats, Sky and Trucker (named after his father). He lifts weights and enjoys designing skating costumes.

Galindo's agent, Michael Rosenberg, summed up his client's career in *USA Today:* "Rudy Galindo is the [best example] of never, ever, ever quit."

 WHERE TO WRITE:
C/O U.S. FIGURE SKATING ASSOCIATION,
20 FIRST STREET,
COLORADO SPRINGS, CO 80906-3697.

Sources

Atlanta Journal-Constitution, January 1, 1996; January 21, 1996.
Los Angeles Times, January 21, 1996; March 18, 1996; March 22, 1996;
    September 11, 1996.
People Weekly, February 5, 1996; March 18, 1996.
Sports Illustrated, March 11, 1996; April 1, 1996.
Time, March 18, 1996.
USA Today, January 20, 1996; March 1, 1996; March 18, 1996; March 21, 1996;
    March 22, 1996; May 2, 1997.
Additional information provided by the Gannett News Service.

Kevin Garnett

1976–

When Kevin Garnett declared himself eligible for the 1995 National Basketball Association (NBA) Draft, most experts said he had made a big mistake. A senior in high school, most people felt he was too young to succeed in professional basketball. After becoming an All-Star in only his second season with the Minnesota Timberwolves, Garnett has proved the critics wrong. Only the fourth American-born player to go directly from high school to the NBA, Garnett has taken his place as the foundation on which the Timberwolves hope to build a championship team.

"He can be as good as he wants to be,"
—Houston Rockets forward Charles Barkley.

Growing Up

HOOP DREAMS. Kevin Garnett was born May 19, 1976. His father left the family when Garnett was only a small child and his mother, Shirley Irby, remarried when her son was only five years old. Irby worked as a hair stylist to help support her family.

Garnett never got along very well with his stepfather, and he missed not having a relationship with his father. When Garnett was in sixth grade, he, his mother and stepfather, and two sisters moved to the middle-class city of Mauldin, South Carolina, a suburb of Greenville.

Garnett used basketball as an escape. He studied tapes of NBA games, focusing on his hero, Magic Johnson of the Los Angeles Lakers. He then tried out his moves on his friend Jaime Peters, whose nickname is "Bug." Garnett earned a spot on the high-school team in Mauldin. There he played for Duke Fisher, a coach who stressed fundamentals.

Fisher remembers that Garnett had a natural feel for the game and did what he needed to do to win. "He didn't care who scored," Fisher recalled in the *Sporting News*. "That is the truth. The only thing he hated was to lose."

Garnett soon established himself as the team's best player. Mauldin went 22-7 during his junior season, and he averaged 27 points, 17 rebounds, and 7 blocks per game. This performance earned Garnett "Mr. Basketball" honors in the state of South Carolina, and he began to attract recruiters from major colleges. Garnett's future seemed bright.

THE INCIDENT. Garnett did not work as hard in the classroom as he did on his game. He played basketball during his free time and did not concentrate on his homework. Worse still, Garnett began to hang out with a bad group of friends. He would sneak out of the house in the middle of the night and began to commit petty crimes.

His lifestyle finally caught up with Garnett in May of his junior year. Police arrested him after a fight broke out at school, leaving a student badly beaten. Garnett claimed he did not participate in the fight, but he was in the wrong place at the wrong time. Charges were filed against the teenager and suddenly his future did not seem so promising.

CHANGE OF SCENERY. Because he had never been arrested before, police dropped the charges against Garnett. He worried that his arrest would scare off the college recruiters who had been interested in him. Garnett used the incident to change his life. "I'm a wiser Kevin, a smarter Kevin, a more mature Kevin," he admitted in the *Sporting News*. "After the incident happened, I calmed myself, I settled myself. It was a wake-up call."

> ### RUBBERBAND MAN
>
> Garnett has attracted attention in the NBA by wearing rubber bands on his wrist. He says it is a habit he picked up as a kid. "When I was young I couldn't afford jewelry, and I saw some of the guys in the neighborhood wearing nice jewelry on their wrists," Garnett explained. "So, I started wearing rubber bands to have something that I knew was mine."

Garnett and his mother did not feel that school administrators in Mauldin treated him fairly following the incident. When the coaches at Farragut Academy in Chicago recruited him during a summer basketball camp to play his senior season at their school, Garnett jumped at the chance to start a new life. "I knew Kevin had to leave Mauldin," his mother told *Sports Illustrated*. "And I knew we didn't have much time."

The neighborhood in Chicago to which Garnett, his mother, and sister Ashley moved had far more dangers than anything he had experienced in South Carolina. Gangs ruled the area and drugs and crime were everywhere. "I had to deal with a gang leader named Seven-Gun Marcello," Garnett revealed to *Newsweek*. "No fun."

Garnett used his new neighborhood as motivation to succeed. He averaged 25.2 points, 17.9 rebounds, 6.7 assists, and 6.5 blocked shots per game during his senior season at Farragut. These numbers were good enough to earn Garnett "Mr. Basketball" honors in the state of Illinois and many national player of the year awards.

Garnett went to the McDonald's All-America high school basketball game in St. Louis, Missouri, to prove himself against the best seniors in the United States. He scored 18

Garnett slam dunks over Chicago Bull's Luc Longley.

points and pulled down 11 rebounds in the game, earning most valuable player honors. As one of the top high-school seniors in the United States, Garnett was recruited by college basketball powers like Maryland, Michigan, North Carolina, and South Carolina.

TESTING TIMES. Garnett worked hard in the classroom at his new school, earning a 3.8 grade point average, but still had trouble in courses that required extensive reading. In order to accept a basketball scholarship he needed to meet the minimum National Collegiate Athletic Association (NCAA) score on one of the two college entrance exams. The two exams are the American College Testing (ACT) exam and the Scholastic Aptitude Test (SAT).

Unfortunately, Garnett could not achieve a high enough score on either test to qualify for a college scholarship. Because he was such a well-known player, his inability to get adequate scores on these tests became national news and embarrassed the young man. "That hurt Kevin," his mother explained in the *Sporting News*. "That hurt him deeply."

TURNS PRO. His inability to qualify for a basketball scholarship disappointed Garnett. "Man, I wanted to go to college," he told *Sport*. "I went to class. I took the ACT classes. I wanted to have options." Under NCAA rules, Garnett could have accepted a scholarship to attend college, but he would have been forced to sit out his first season and prove he could succeed academically.

Unlike most high-school players, Garnett had another option. He could declare himself eligible for the National Basketball Association (NBA) Draft. NBA scouts liked Garnett's ability to run the floor, shoot from the outside, and pass the ball. Most experts, however, doubted whether a player could move directly from high school to the best professional league in the world. They worried that he would not be able to handle the pressure and the fame that came with playing in the NBA.

Superstar

DRAFT DAY. Garnett entered the 1995 NBA Draft, becoming the first player in over 20 years to attempt to move directly from high school to the NBA. (The other players to move directly from high school to the NBA or the former American Basketball Association [ABA] are Darryl Dawkins, Moses Malone, and Bill Willoughby.) Most experts expected one of the new expansion teams—Toronto or Vancouver—to pick Garnett, but he did not care which team drafted him. "Wherever I go, it'll be an opportunity," he said in *Sports Illustrated*. "Millions of kids want to play pro basketball, and here I am getting the chance early. I learned one thing—never hate a positive option." Garnett received the news on the day of the draft that he had earned a qualifying score on the ACT exam in his last attempt.

In a surprising move, the Minnesota Timberwolves used the fifth overall pick to choose Garnett. The young player had impressed the Timberwolves in a private workout. Minnesota had never made the playoffs in its four years of existence and had never even won 30 games in an 82-game season. Making the Timberwolves a winner was a big challenge, but Garnett was ready. "I figured this was a place that wanted me, needed me, to make an impact," he explained in *Newsweek*. Garnett signed a three-year, $5.6 million contract.

T-WOLF PUPPY. Garnett was excited about reaching his goal of playing in the NBA. "I was always on the outside looking in wondering what it would be like, now I'm on the inside and I'm about to find out,' he declared to *Jet*. His new Minnesota teammates gave him the nickname "Da Kid."

Garnett played only a few minutes per game early in his first season because Minnesota wanted to give him time to get used to life in the NBA. At the All-Star break, he had averaged only 21 minutes, 6.4 points, and 4.2 rebounds per game. Garnett shared an apartment with his old friend Bug Peters. "I don't drink or smoke or go out much at all," he told the *Sporting News*. "I've done all that, and it got me in trouble. I have an image to uphold. People are watching; kids are watching. I prefer staying home with Bug, playing CDs and Sega."

TURNING POINT. Garnett got along well with his new teammates, except for the Timberworlves' star, Christian Laettner. Laettner criticized the rookie in what many people saw as a selfish attack. Garnett showed his maturity by not lashing out at Laettner. Instead, he talked privately with his teammate and tried to work out their differences.

Minnesota made the decision that Garnett, not Laettner, was the future star for the Timberwolves. The team traded Laettner to the Atlanta Hawks, making Garnett a starter. He was ready for more playing time. "I'm stepping up my workload for these final months," he explained to *Sports Illustrated*. "That's how I operate. If it kills me, it kills me."

Garnett started the last 42 games of his rookie season and averaged 14 points, 8.4 rebounds, and two blocked shots per game in that stretch. He also shot 53 percent from the floor. For the season he averaged 10.4 points and 6.3 rebounds and he led all rookies with 1.64 blocks per game. "He's a leader," coach Flip Saunders told *Sport*. "He earned that starting role. He's worked tremendously hard all year."

Experts watched Garnett carefully, expecting him to fall apart under the pressure. Instead, they discovered that he was a very mature and polite person. "I know people were watching me," Garnett admitted to *Sport*. "I know people wanted me to fail. But you've got to want to get better, and that's what really keeps me going. I want to get better every game I play. I want to show the world. I want to beat the odds."

FRIENDS AND TEAMMATES. Even though he was an outgoing person with his teammates, Garnett had a hard time making friends. When the fighting incident occurred in Mauldin, he felt that many people he thought were his friends turned their backs on him. "At the time I thought I had [lots] of friends," Garnett recalled in the *Sporting News*. "I thought everybody was my boy. When you get in trouble, or you go broke, that's

> ### OOPS!
> Garnett had one embarrassing moment his rookie season. He jumped off the bench to come into a game, but the referee noticed something strange. "Where's your jersey?" he asked. Garnett looked down and realized he was still wearing a t-shirt from practice.

when you find out who your boys are. When you get in trouble, you see all the masks come off. You've got something like basketball or a nice job, people always want to be around you. Once you mess up? They're gone."

His old friend Bug was one person who stood by Garnett during his problems. The other person whom he knew he could count on was Stephon Marbury. The two became friends in 1993 when Marbury—also one of the top high school players in the country—decided to call Garnett, whom he had never met but who he knew about from highlight films.

At first the two new friends talked for hours, running up big long distance bills. "When I got the bills, I told him, 'Mr. Garnett, you don't even have a job,'" his mother told Garnett, according to *Sports Illustrated*. "Kevin's first week working at Burger King, he had to give me half his check to cover the calls. I thought I was going to have to get a blocker on the phone. One night I was eavesdropping on them, and it was all, Yeah, man, know this? and Yeah, man, know that? For hours. They must have thought it was a local call."

Marbury helped Garnett get his life together after the fighting incident. "Stephon was a real inspiration in Kevin's life," Garnett's mother recalled in *Sports Illustrated*. Stephon served as a listener, someone who was there for Kevin in a tough time. Kevin loves everyone. Kevin tried to please everyone, all his associates, all his so-called friends. But Stephon was the one telling Kevin he had to work hard, academically and athletically."

Garnett and Marbury did not meet until the summer of 1994, when Marbury traveled to Chicago. By this time the two were best friends. "Anytime you can talk to somebody on the phone without seeing their face and have the relationship we have, we didn't have to meet," Garnett explained in *Sports Illustrated*.

In their senior high-school seasons both players earned national high school player of the year honors, Garnett from *USA Today* and Marbury from Gatorade and *Parade* magazine. While Garnett was playing his rookie season in the NBA, Marbury spent one season at Georgia Tech University before declaring himself eligible for the 1996 NBA Draft.

Throughout his rookie season, Garnett tried to convince the Timberwolves to draft Marbury. Unfortunately, Minnesota held the fifth pick in the draft and most experts expected Marbury to be gone before then. The Milwaukee Bucks, picking fourth, chose Marbury, but then traded him to the Timberwolves for Minnesota's number one pick, Ray Allen from the University of Connecticut, and a future draft pick. Garnett was thrilled to be united with his friend.

WOLVES ON THE PROWL. Before the 1996–97 season Minnesota had never won more than 29 games in a season. Garnett and Marbury, however, teamed up with Tom Gugliotta to lead the Wolves to their first-ever playoff appearance. Minnesota finished the regular season with a 40-42 record, good for third place in the Midwest Division. "This year is like the Cinderella season," Garnett explained to *USA Today*. "This team has been through a lot. Eight years of negativity. Then you come along with something positive."

Garnett established himself as a star with a solid second season. He raised his scoring average to 17 points per game and his rebounding average to 8 per contest. Garnett swatted 2.12 shots per game, ninth in the NBA and first among forwards. "Even if Kevin's shot isn't on," Saunders said, "it's the other things he does—the rebounds he gets, the ones he tips to other people, the blocked shots, the intimidation inside, just knowing what to do—that make him so special."

Western Conference coaches honored Garnett by naming him to the NBA All-Star Game in Cleveland after Charles Barkley of the Houston Rockets was forced to miss the game due to an injury. Garnett scored 6 points and grabbed a team high 9 rebounds in his first contest with the best players in the NBA. "He has the running ability and agility of a 6 feet-2 inch player," Saunders told *Sports Illustrated*. "The great ones just have God-given qualities, and so when Kevin does something incredible, you don't ask why or how, you just accept it."

Minnesota got its first taste of playoff basketball, facing the Houston Rockets in the first round. The Rockets—featuring future hall-of-fame players Hakeem Olajuwon, Charles Barkley, and Clyde Drexler—swept the Timberwolves in three straight games, but Garnett gained the respect of his more experienced foes. "He can be as good as he wants to be," Barkley explained to *Esquire*. Garnett scored 17.3 points per game in the series and grabbed 9.3 rebounds a contest.

By the end of the 1996–97 season, Garnett had established himself as a player and as a man. "I think it has a lot to do with being more comfortable," he revealed in *Esquire*. "And I feel like I'm starting to get respect. I think the way I've played, the way I've conducted myself, has done that. But all I ever heard from the first day was 'This is a man's league, kid.' The only way you can get them to treat you like a man is to play like a man."

By the end of the season, some experts compared Garnett and Marbury to the great Utah Jazz duo of Karl Malone and John Stockton. "[T]hey might want to be Stockton and Malone, guys who play together in one place a long time," Saunders told *Sports Illustrated*. "Magic, [Larry] Bird, [Kevin] McHale, [Bill] Russell, [Jerry] West. You associate those guys with their franchises. I think that appeals to Kevin and Stephon."

THE FRANCHISE. The Timberwolves feel that Garnett possesses a unique blend of size, skills, and enthusiasm. He also is a tenacious defender, one of the best in the NBA at his position. At seven feet tall, he is one of the league's tallest small forwards. To survive in the NBA, Garnett must add weight to his 220-pound frame, but his body is still developing. "He's incredible," McHale said in the *Sporting News*. "In a few years, nobody's going to be able to touch this kid."

In addition to his physical skills, Garnett displays an incredible love for the game. "He's a throwback, in the sense that he's just a guy who loves playing; that's what he's all about," McHale explained in *Sports Illustrated*. "When the ball is in his hands, he just lights up. It's playtime. It's like putting crayons in a kid's hands."

The young superstar knows that the most important goal for an NBA player is to win a championship. "I want to be known as the man that led them to the dance," Garnett admitted to the *Sporting News*. "I think every player in the league wants that—to be labeled as the man that brought us to the dance and won." Minnesota made a commitment to its young superstar when they agreed to a $125 million contract extension with Garnett following the 1996–97 season.

OFF THE COURT. Garnett lives in Minnetonka, a suburb of Minneapolis. He has three dogs and owns five different automobiles. Garnett has an older sister, Sonya, and a younger sister, Ashley. He is a spokesperson for Nike.

Garnett made his film debut when he played the legendary star Wilt Chamberlain in the movie "Rebound." His sports heroes are Tony Dorsett, former running back for the Dallas Cowboys, and Magic Johnson. In his free time, Garnett likes to play pool, air hockey, and Nintendo.

Fulfilling a promise to his mother, Garnett is taking college courses in accounting at the University of Minnesota. "I've been blessed with a lot of great qualities, not just on the court but in the classroom," he explained. "Growing up, books weren't the first thing on my mind. Not to say I was dumb or that I made bad grades, it's just that sometimes I knew I could have tried a lot harder. I could have made the honor roll if I really wanted to. I know one day I'll step away from this game. God forbid, if anything happens to me, I want to have something to fall back on."

Basketball is still Garnett's first love, regardless of how much he is paid. "I don't play basketball for the money," he confessed in *Sports Illustrated*. "I don't play it for the crowd.

HARD ROAD TO FOLLOW

Many people worry that Garnett's success will encourage more high-school players to skip college and move directly to the NBA. He warns other young players that he only made it through hard work. "[It's] not that easy," Garnett confessed to *Esquire*. "I know that now. What I've found out is that it's not just accepting the money, the chance to play in the pros. It's accepting the responsibility of playing in a man's league. Now don't get me wrong, I don't consider myself [a] grown-up yet. But I have found out fast, you better be ready to act like a grown-up in this league."

When I didn't have a friend, when I was lonely, I always knew I could grab that orange pill [basketball] and go hoop. I could go and dunk on somebody. If things weren't going right, I could make a basket and feel better."

 WHERE TO WRITE:
C/O MINNESOTA TIMBERWOLVES,
600 FIRST AVE., N.,
MINNEAPOLIS, MN 55403-1414.

Sources

Atlanta Journal-Constitution, February 23, 1996; November 24, 1996.
Esquire, March 1997.
Jet, May 29, 1995; October 23, 1995.
Los Angeles Times, March 20, 1996; February 9, 1997; April 10, 1997.
Newsweek, December 4, 1995.
Sport, November 1996.
Sporting News, May 22, 1995; March 4, 1996; April 8, 1996.
Sports Illustrated, May 22, 1995; June 26, 1995; March 11, 1996; November 1, 1996; January 20, 1997; April 21, 1997.
Sports Illustrated for Kids, April 1996.
USA Today, April 16, 1997.
Additional information provided by the Minnesota Timberwolves and the Gannett News Service.

Maurice Greene

1974–

American sprinter Maurice Greene's mouth runs almost as quickly as his legs. Since he was a young child he predicted he would someday be the fastest man in the world. Greene did little to back up his promise until the summer of 1997. It was then that he broke through, winning the men's 100-meter championship at the U.S. Track and Field Championships. Greene followed that performance by defeating world-record holder and defending Olympic champion Donovan Bailey in a classic showdown at the 1997 World Track and Field Championships in Goteburg, Sweden. After years of bragging, he actually was "The World's Fastest Man."

"I am the fastest man in the world right now."
—Maurice Greene.

Growing Up

ALWAYS FAST. Maurice Greene was born on July 23, 1974. He was the youngest of four children of Ernest and Jackie Greene. Greene began training in track with coach Al Hobson at the age of eight. "He's like my son," Hobson explained to *Sports Illustrated*.

All the children in Greene's family participated in track and field. "Maurice, being the baby, always said he was going to do it better [than his siblings]," Jackie Greene said. "We encouraged all the kids in whatever they decided to do, to give it their all. We didn't let them quit. Whatever they chose to do, they had to finish it."

Greene always had confidence. When he was ten he said he would someday be the world's fastest man. At the time Greene was not even the fastest runner on his Kansas City Chargers track team. "He was always confident and energetic," Ernest Greene recalled in *USA Today*. "I told him he had to be careful his talking didn't overshadow his performance."

PICKS TRACK. Greene won Kansas state titles in the 100-, 200-, and 400-meter races for three straight years (1991–93) at F. L. Schlagle High School in Kansas City, Kansas. He also played football and had an opportunity to play that sport at Hutchinson Junior College. Greene also had many opportunities to run track at the college level.

Ernest Greene and Hobson convinced Greene to pass up college and train privately in track. "I'm a guy who stresses education," Hobson explained in *USA Today*. "But colleges can't always provide personal attention (on the track). We could work every day on mechanics and technique. We weren't pushed to run relays or score points for the team." Ewing Kaufmann—the late owner of the Kansas City Royals baseball team—provided scholarships for Greene to attend community college for two years while he trained on his own.

DEFEATS LEWIS. In April 1995 Greene defeated the great American Olympic champion Carl Lewis at the Texas Relays with a wind-aided time of 9.88 seconds. (Wind-aided means the wind was blowing toward the finish line at a speed fast enough to help the sprinters run better times. Times in a wind-aided race do not count when determining world records.) "I don't care if you're pushed by a truck, that's fast," Hobson declared in *USA Today*. "I knew then he'd set a world record." After his win over Lewis, Greene signed his autograph with 9.88 following his name.

DISAPPOINTING RESULTS. Greene finished second in the men's 100-meter dash at the 1995 U.S. Track and Field Championships with a time of 10.23 seconds. Three runners—Greene, Mike Marsh, and Dennis Mitchell—all finished with the same time, and a photograph was necessary to tell them apart. "Wow, this is the biggest day of my life," Greene declared in the *Atlanta Journal-Constitution*. "This is it."

His performance earned Greene a spot on the U.S. team that would travel to the 1995 World Track and Field Championships in Goteburg, Sweden. In a second round heat, Greene froze in the blocks when the gun sounded. The mistake meant that he was eliminated from the competition.

Greene continued to work hard to qualify for the 1996 Summer Olympics, to be held in Atlanta, Georgia. His chance at Olympic glory came to an end when he suffered a hamstring injury at the worst possible time. The injury slowed him down and he lost in the second round of the 100-meter competition at the 1996 U.S. Olympic Trials.

CHANGES COACHES. The disappointing results of the past year forced Greene to make a difficult decision. He left Hobson and in September 1996 moved to Los Angeles, California. There Greene began to train with coach John Smith, an American Olympian in 1972 and a close friend of Hobson. "I needed to learn," Greene admitted in *Sports Illustrated*.

Smith was known for developing sprinters. Two of his pupils were 1996 Olympic bronze medalist Ato Bolden of Trinidad and American 200-meter specialist Jon Drummond, and he also trained Marie-Jose Perec, a double gold-medalist

Greene runs for the finish line during the World Athletics Championships.

at the 1996 Summer Olympics. "I just thought it was time to change and take another step," Greene revealed in *USA Today*. "What better coach than John Smith? Nobody has the credentials he has. Nobody's produced more athletes. I thought if I want to be the best, I should go where the best train."

The practices Smith ran at the University of California-Los Angeles (UCLA) were tough. Smith worked on Greene's mental toughness, and both Boldon and Drummond constantly trash-talked about their newest teammate's ability. "Every day I learn something new," Greene admitted in *American Track & Field*. "Training with Boldon and Drummond is always intensive. But that helps my motivation. We always push each other. The workload is definitely higher now. Most days I am completely exhausted."

Smith worked with Greene on his start—already a strength—and made his takeoff even better. The two also helped the sprinter pace himself, saving his strength for the end of the race. "The biggest thing he's done is help me delay my acceleration," Greene told *USA Today*. "One of the problems I had was I couldn't hold on the last 20 to 10 meters." Greene also began serious weight training that added muscle to his upper body.

Superstar

TALKS A GOOD RACE. When Greene began to work with Smith he was only the twenty-fourth-ranked 100-meter sprinter in the world. Despite his low ranking, he was full of confidence. Greene promised to restore U.S. dominance in the 100-meter and to break the world record of 9.84 seconds. He had never broken the 10 second barrier in his career. By this time Greene had earned the nickname the "Kansas Cannonball."

The 1997 U.S. Track and Field Championships were held at Indiana University-Purdue University in Indianapolis, Indiana. His improvement showed as he won the men's 100-meter championship with a meet record-tying time of 9.90 seconds. Greene's result was .18 seconds faster than his previous time of 10.08 and the second-fastest 100-meter in the world up until that point in 1997. (Boldon had run a 9.89 second time.) Only six men and three Americans had ever run faster. "It's a great feeling," Greene said after his victory. "Last year was disappointing, but I knew if I trained the right way, my time would come."

TAKES ON WORLD. The 1997 World Track and Field Championships were held at the Spyridon Louis Olympic Stadium in Athens, Greece. "I'd like to set the world record here," Greene bragged in *USA Today*. "I'd like to bring U.S. sprinting back to where it's supposed to be. It hasn't gone."

The favorite in the men's 100-meter sprint was 1996 Olympic champion and world record holder Donovan Bailey of Canada. The field also included 1996 Olympic silver medalist Frankie Fredricks of Namibia and Greene's teammate Boldon.

MIND GAMES

Bailey—known for intimidating his rivals with his speed and his trash-talking—tried to get an edge on Greene throughout the early rounds of the world championships. In a semifinal heat the world-record holder pulled up next to the American champion near the finish line and stared him down, showing Greene that he was taking it easy. "Yeah, I could feel him doing that," Greene revealed in the *Los Angeles Times*. "But in the early rounds, all that matters is making it to the finals. People do things. You just have to deal with it." Bailey tried to trash-talk, but Greene did not listen. "Donovan never got into my head," he told *Sports Illustrated*.

Against this competition the winner of the race could truly claim the title of "The World's Fastest Man."

HEAD TO HEAD. The men's 100-meter competition requires the finalists to compete in four rounds of races in two days. The grueling schedule was hard on the runners, and both Greene and Bolden suffered from leg cramps. Though they were competing in the same race, the two teammates helped each other. The two runners rubbed each other's legs before races.

Before the finals, Bolden's cramps were so bad he knew he would not win the race.

"I guess I stretched Maurice better than he stretched me," he said after the race, according to *USA Today*. "I looked at Maurice before the race and gave him my blessing. He knew I wasn't going to win because of the pain on my face."

Greene drew lane three for the final. Bailey was right next to him in lane four, setting up a classic showdown. As he took his mark, Greene felt a muscle spasm in his groin. He got up out of his stance and stretched his leg, making sure he was ready. "I wanted the best start possible," Greene told *USA Today*.

When the gun fired to start the race Greene took the early lead. At 50 meters he still led, but Bailey had used an explosive closing burst to win the 1995 world championship and the 1996 Olympic title. This time, however, Greene held off the world record holder. "We hit 75 meters, and I knew he wasn't going to get me," the American sprinter explained in *Sports Illustrated* after the race. As Greene crossed the finish line first, he turned around and stuck his tongue out at Bailey.

WORLD'S FASTEST MAN. Greene's winning time was 9.86 seconds. It was the third fastest time in history and tied the record for the world championships. "I am the fastest man in the world right now," Greene declared to *USA Today*. Bailey finished second with a time of 9.91 seconds and American Tim Montgomery finished third.

Bolden—hampered by his injury—finished fifth. Although he was disappointed, he was happy for his training partner. "I am really happy for Maurice," Boldon said. "I took him under my wing when he came to work with John [Smith] and look what he has done now."

After his victory Greene fell into his father's arms and hugged him. "I worked so hard, I worked so hard," a crying Greene said after his victory, according to *Sports Illustrated*. His victory—along with that of American **Marion Jones** (see entry) in the women's 100-meter competition—marked the first time one country had won both titles at the world championships since they began in 1983. "The young ones are coming through to do the job," Greene said after the race. "I've said that it's time someone took responsibility for American sprinting and I'm just glad to have won. It's the highlight of my career."

Smith was proud of his star pupil. "He said he's going to win the nationals," Smith said. "Then he turned around and said he's going to win the world championships, and he did. I wanted, and Maurice also wanted to bring sprinting back. Now the Americans have established themselves once again as good sprinters. They never were bad sprinters. We were just going through a cycle."

LEFT STANDING. The American 4 x 100 meter relay team was one of the favorites to win the world championship title. (In the

BACK HOME

The United States has a long tradition of excellence in the 100-meter dash. From the great Jesse Owens in 1936 through the record-setting Olympic champion Carl Lewis, American men had dominated the competition. This domination, however, came to a halt in the 1990s. Since 1991—when Lewis last won the 100-meters at the world championships and Americans swept the medals—no U.S. sprinter had won an Olympic or world championship event. In fact, American men had been shut out of the medals at the 1995 world championships and the 1996 Summer Olympics.

Greene's victory marked a comeback after many experts said the U.S. program was dead. He admitted one of his goals was to reestablish American supremacy in the 100-meters. "I'm an American and this is what I came here [to the world championships] for," Greene told the *Los Angeles Times*. "I always said I wanted to bring it back home, to be the man, the world's fastest."

4 x 100, each team has four members that each run 100 meters.) The Canadian team was the defending World and Olympic 4 x 100 relay champion. Greene looked forward to a rematch with Bailey on the anchor [last] leg of the relay. "And we're going to have fun," Greene told the *Los Angeles Times* referring to the relay. "It's going to be a beautiful thing to watch."

Disaster struck the American team in the first qualifying heat. After Brian Lewis led off for the U.S., a miscommunication between himself and the second American runner, Tim Montgomery, forced the Americans to be disqualified from the race. Greene was left waiting and never got a chance to run. "I really wanted to meet Mr. Greene on the anchor," Bailey told the *Los Angeles Times*. "I really, really wanted to meet him. But that's not going to happen." Canada went on to win the gold medal.

OFF THE TRACK. Greene continues to train with Smith in Los Angeles. Despite his victory at the world championships, he knows he needs to work hard to improve. "He's still got a lot to learn," Smith told *USA Today*. Greene finished second in the voting for the 1997 Jesse Owens Award—given to the best male track and field athlete in the United States. (Allen Johnson—who won gold medals in the 110-meter hurdles and the 1,600 meter relay at the world championships—captured the award.)

City officials in Greene's home town of Kansas City, Kansas, held a reception for him after his world championship victory. They gave him a key to the city. "I always felt faster," Greene told the assembled crowd. "But not as fast as I'm going to feel. I know every time I go out on the track I have your support."

His victory at the world championships gave Greene even more confidence. "The [world] record will come, it's only a matter of time I'm sure," he said. "It is my goal for the future now that I've won the world title."

Sources

American Track & Field, July 7, 1997.
Atlanta Journal-Constitution, June 17, 1995; June 14, 1997; August 4, 1997.

Ebony, October 1997.

Los Angeles Times, June 13, 1997; June 14, 1997; August 4, 1997; August 10, 1997.

Sports Illustrated. June 23, 1997; August 11, 1997; August 18, 1997.

USA Today, August 1, 1997; August 4, 1997.

Dominik Hasek

1965–

Dominik "The Dominator" Hasek of the Buffalo Sabres is unique. He stops pucks like no other goalie in the National Hockey League (NHL). Hasek's style is unorthodox, but he has led the NHL in save percentage every year he has been a starting goalie. Three times he has won the Vezina Trophy—given to the league's best goaltender—and during the 1996–97 season he captured the ultimate prize. Hasek earned the Hart Trophy as the NHL's most valuable player in recognition of the way he lifted the overachieving Sabres to the Northeast Division title.

Growing Up

DOUBLE JOINTED. Dominik Hasek (HA-shehk) was born January 29, 1965, in Pardubice, Czechoslovakia. The country was run by a Communist government when he was born. (Communism is a governmental system characterized by the common ownership of production methods.) Today Pardubice is located in the Czech Republic.

Hasek admits that he did not make a good first impression on his hockey coaches. "They held a tryout for 6-year-old boys and my father took me there," he recalled in the *Sporting News.* "I didn't even have real skates. I had those blades that you screwed onto the soles of your shoes, but I was tall, and the 9-year-olds didn't have a goalie, so they put me in with them."

Hasek was built to be a goalie. He was double jointed and so flexible that doctors thought there might be something wrong with his knees. At the age of ten Hasek could already do the butterfly move with goalie pads on. "I could do the butterfly 180 degrees," he explained in *Sports Illustrated.* "Now I can't make it 180 degrees, but my butterfly is still very good."

TOP GOALIE. Hasek had a hard time with the strict training rules of the Communist-run hockey program. His coaches wanted the young netminder to play like all the other goalies, but he had his own style. "I watched the older goalies to see what they were doing," Hasek explained to the *Sporting News.* "I'd try it all in my practices. But those goalies would stay deep in the net and hope the puck would hit them. I wanted to do more. I had seen film of some of the National Hockey League goalies, and I wanted to make the puck bounce farther away just like they did. I wanted to be an NHL goalie. My coaches just shook their heads at the way I stopped the puck."

Hasek played for the Czechoslovakian national team for several years and soon was one of his country's top players. He won Czechoslovakian Goaltender of the Year honors five years in a row (1986–90) and Player of the Year recognition three times (1987, 1989, 1990). Hasek's talent impressed scouts from NHL teams, but the Communist government prevented its players from going overseas to play. In 1983 the

SCOREBOARD

WON 1996–97 HART TROPHY AS THE NHL'S MOST VALUABLE PLAYER.

WON THE VEZINA TROPHY—GIVEN TO THE BEST GOALIE IN THE NHL— THREE TIMES (1993–94, 1994–95, AND 1996–97).

LED THE NHL IN SAVE PERCENTAGE FOR FOUR STRAIGHT SEASONS (1994–1997).

HASEK WILL STOP THE PUCK ANY WAY HE CAN.

Chicago Blackhawks used a tenth-round pick in the NHL Draft to select Hasek in the hope that someday he might be free to leave Czechoslovakia.

NHL BOUND. In the late 1980s and early 1990s many hockey players from Communist countries began to join the NHL. The opportunity to escape came as a result of the breakdown of the dictatorships in these countries. Hasek finally was able to sign with the Blackhawks in 1990 and came to the United States to play.

Hasek expected to start in goal right away, but instead he found himself stuck behind Chicago's All-Star netminder Ed Belfour. He played in only 25 games during his first two seasons with the Blackhawks and spent most of his time with the Indianapolis Ice of the International Hockey League (IHL). In 1990–91 Hasek made the IHL All-Star first team.

SHUFFLED OFF TO BUFFALO. The reason Hasek was stuck in the minors was his size. Many hockey experts felt his slight frame would be unable to withstand the brutal NHL schedule. "I was used to playing 50 to 60 games a season in Europe for my team and the [Czechoslovakian] national team," Hasek explained to *Newsday.* "I'm only 165 pounds. People thought I couldn't play a lot of games, but I always knew I could."

Hasek became so frustrated at his lack of playing time in the summer of 1992 that he lied to Chicago's coach, Mike Keenan. "I called Mike Keenan and told him I wasn't good enough to play in the NHL," he admitted in the *Sporting News.* "I lied to him. I told him: 'I'm bad. I'm old. Let me go back to Europe to play.' But he wouldn't let me go."

The Blackhawks finally traded Hasek to the Buffalo Sabres on August 7, 1992, for goalie Stephane Beauregard and a fourth-round draft pick. Hasek and Darren Puppa shared the goaltending duties for Buffalo early in the 1992–93 season, but then the Sabres traded high scoring left winger Dave Andreychuk, Puppa, and a first-round draft pick to the Toronto Maple Leafs for future Hall of Fame goalie Grant Fuhr.

The trade for Fuhr discouraged Hasek. "I was about to give up," he confessed in the *Sporting News*. "[Fuhr] had been on five Stanley Cup champions. I had been on none. I didn't think I'd ever be a No. 1 goalie in the NHL."

BIG CHANCE. Hasek got his chance to to be the number-one goalie in Buffalo when Fuhr went down with a knee injury early in the 1993–94 season. He posted five shutouts in the month of December alone and Fuhr never got his job back. "It wasn't fun sitting on the bench but it was fun watching Dominik stone every opponent he faced," Fuhr told the *Sporting News*.

By the end of the season Hasek was the best goalie in the NHL. He finished the season with a league-leading goals

Hasek makes the save for the Sabres.

against average of 1.95 and was in goal for 30 Buffalo wins, 7 of them shutouts (a Buffalo record). Hasek became the first goalie to finish the season with a goals-against-average below 2.00 since Bernie Parent compiled a 1.89 average for the Philadelphia Flyers during the 1973–74 season and was the first European-trained goalie to lead the NHL in this important statistic. He also led the NHL in save percentage.

The NHL awarded Hasek the 1993–94 Vezina Trophy, given annually to the best goaltender in the NHL. He also finished as the runner-up for the Hart Trophy—given to the most valuable player in the NHL—to Sergei Fedorov of the Detroit Red Wings. "I thought I had the ability to be a No. 1 goalie in the NHL, but I didn't think I'd have such an outstanding season as I've had."

Hasek proved his first season was no fluke by winning the Vezina Trophy again during the 1994–95 season with a goals-against-average of 2.11 (tied for first in the NHL) and 5 shutouts (tied for first in the NHL). He led the league in save percentage for the second straight year.

Superstar

THE DOMINATOR. Hasek led the NHL in save percentage for the third straight year in the 1995–96 season with a .920 mark. His play earned him the nickname of "The Dominator." "Hasek's just incredible," New Jersey Devil defenseman Scott Stevens said. "He anticipates so well. He sees things happening before they happen. I was impressed with the way he played. He's always yelling out there, telling his defensemen to let him see the puck. He's right, if you can see the puck, chances are he'll stop it."

CINDERELLA SEASON. The Sabres did not expect to contend during the 1996–97 season. They were a young, rebuilding team whose best skater, center Pat LaFontaine, suffered a possibly career-ending head injury. Buffalo finished 15 points out of the playoffs during the 1995–96 season, and with so many young players, Hasek often was the last line of defense for his team. He consistently faced more shots per game than other NHL goalies.

Hasek enjoyed the pressure of having his team depend on him. "Twenty shots or 40 shots a game, I don't think about it at all," he revealed to *Sports Illustrated*. "In practice I face 300, 400 shots, so I don't care. I just like to play on a winning team."

Hasek almost single-handedly carried the Sabres to the 1996–97 NHL Northeast Division title, their first division championship since 1981. During the season his team was outshot 63 times, but still Hasek posted a 37-19-10 record, 2.27 goals against average (fourth in the NHL), and league-leading 92.9 save percentage, the fourth straight year he led the league in this statistic. He also posted five shutouts. "He's been our backbone this season," teammate Brian Holzinger said.

The team's success was a pleasant surprise to Hasek. "My expectations were not very high at all," he admitted to the *Los Angeles Times*. "My goal before the season was to make the playoffs. We were 15 points [out of] the playoffs last season, and I didn't even think we could make it. I don't know what is the reason for [the team's success], but we look like a different team."

PLAYOFF PROBLEMS. The Sabres faced the Ottawa Senators in the first round of the NHL playoffs. "I don't think we're ready to win the Stanley Cup, but we're ready to go far," Hasek told the *Los Angeles Times* before the playoffs began. Buffalo's championship hopes suffered a fatal blow when Hasek injured his knee in game three. The Sabres were able to defeat the Senators in seven games, but lost in five games to the Philadelphia Flyers in the second round.

A reporter in Buffalo—Jim Kelly—wrote a controversial article that reported a rumor that Hasek was not as seriously injured as he claimed. Kelly wrote that some of his Sabre teammates thought Hasek could have continued to play against Ottawa. The article upset Hasek because he felt Kelly was accusing him of letting his team down. "I was very hurt, very hurt," he explained in *Sports Illustrated.* "When I first read the article, I couldn't sleep, I couldn't read, I couldn't even talk well."

The first time Hasek saw Kelly in the Sabres locker room the two men argued. Hasek was so angry and frustrated that he pushed Kelly. The NHL stepped in and suspended the star goalie for three playoff games. Hasek apologized to Kelly and hoped the incident would not haunt him for the rest of his career. "I hope it will go away," he confessed to *Sports Illustrated.* "But maybe it takes days, weeks or months. I don't know."

MVP. Most experts felt that Hasek should win the 1996–97 Hart Trophy, given to the NHL's most valuable player. A goalie had not won the award since Jacques Plante of the Montreal Canadiens in 1962 and many felt the award should only go to a skater, not a goalie. Former Hart Trophy winner—center Mark Messier of the New York Rangers—disagreed. "The Hart Trophy is given to the best player [for] what he means to his team," Messier explained to *USA Today.* "Look at Buffalo and what was expected before the year started. I don't think anybody would have picked [the Sabres] to finish where they did."

The writers who voted for the Hart Trophy agreed with Messier, awarding the prestigious award to Hasek. He was the first Buffalo player to win the Hart Trophy. He also won the Vezina Trophy for the third time in four years, and his fellow NHL players voted him the Lester B. Person Award as the league's best player. Mike Liut of the St. Louis Blues was the only other goalie to win the Person Award, in 1981. "I always voted for players that I didn't want to face, the really best players," Hasek said. "To be recognized by my peers is the best, I was more surprised than when I won my first Vezina Trophy."

OFF THE ICE. Hasek and his wife, Alena, have a son named Michael and a daughter, Dominika. He has one sister and one

STOPPING THE PUCK

Hasek plays goal like no other netminder in the NHL. He makes saves from all positions and often seems like he has no chance to stop the puck. "People have a perception about him that he's out of position and he bends over backward and makes a dramatic save," Sabres' coach Ted Nolan explained. "He's a well-controlled goalie. If you watch in practice, he's in full control. Just when you think you have him down and out, he comes up with this unbelievable save. The only way to beat him is to throw it at the net. You've just got to tip your hat to him."

His ability to cover all the angles frustrates the best shooters in the league. "When he's in the net, his pads seem to cover post-to-post better than any goalie I've seen," Brett Hull of the St. Louis Blues told the *Sporting News.* "I had heard he likes to stay back in the goal like a lot of the European goalies we've faced. But he's just as aggressive at coming out to stop a shot. He just doesn't give you anything to shoot at."

Hasek is one of the fiercest competitors in the league. He never lets up and sometimes his teammates become frustrated because he tries as hard to stop the puck in practice as he does during games. "He's not your typical superstar," Nolan explained in the *Los Angeles Times.* "He's out there all the time, working to be better. He refuses to let anybody score on him. When they do, he looks at how they scored and how he can keep them from scoring again."

Hall of Fame goalie Ken Dryden believes Hasek is the best at what he does. "Your job [as goaltender] is to stop pucks," Dryden explained. "It doesn't matter how you do it, you do it. And it doesn't matter what part of you does it. . . . There are lots of people who play goal very stylistically and do everything technically right and who don't stop pucks. Dominik Hasek knows the job."

brother, the latter who plays professional soccer in the Czech Republic. Hasek speaks Czechoslovakian, English, and Russian.

Hasek is involved in charitable activities. He helped develop the Dominik Hasek/Variety Club Youth Hockey Program for inner-city children in the Buffalo area. He also purchases tickets for Sabres games that he donates for children to attend.

Hasek knows what his job is and he does it better than anyone else. "They say I am unorthodox, I flop around the ice like some kind of fish," he explained to the *Sporting News*. "I say, who cares as long as I stop the puck?"

WHERE TO WRITE:

C/O BUFFALO SABRES, MARINE MIDLAND ARENA,
ONE SEYMOUR H. KNOX PLAZA,
BUFFALO, NY 14303.

Sources

Los Angeles Times, April 17, 1997.
Newsday, January 1, 1994; April 13, 1994; April 29, 1994; April 30, 1994; June 6, 1994.
Sporting News, November 6, 1995; May 26, 1997.
Sports Illustrated, May 2, 1994; February 10, 1997; May 5, 1997.
Additional information provided by the Buffalo Sabres.

Martina Hingis

1980–

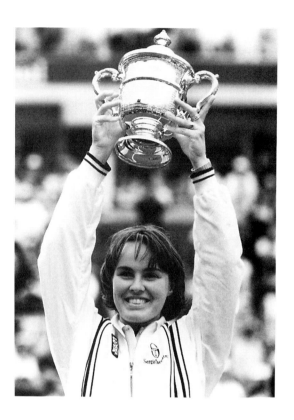

Some athletes are born winners; other have to work hard to succeed. Tennis star Martina Hingis is both. Named after legendary champion Martina Navratilova, she has great natural ability that she has worked for 14 years to develop. In 1997 Hingis became the youngest player ever to earn the number-one world ranking, taking over the top spot from Steffi Graf. She also became the youngest player in more than 100 years to win one of tennis's Grand Slam singles titles when she won the Australian Open. Hingis then added the Wimbledon and U.S. Open titles to her trophy case, dominating the women's tour like few players before her. At only 17 years old, she should have many more championships in her future.

Growing Up

WHAT'S IN A NAME? Martina Hingis was born September 30, 1980, in Kosice, Czechoslovakia (now Slovakia). She was born to be a tennis player. Hingis's parents, both highly ranked

"I play what I feel. I respond to the ball."
—Martina Hingis.

Czech tennis players (her mother was ranked tenth in Czechoslovakia), named her after their idol, the legendary Martina Navratilova, also from Czechoslovakia.

WORST THING. An only child, Hingis was only four years old when her parents divorced. She says the divorce was the worst thing that ever happened to her. "We moved five hours away, and I didn't see my father much anymore," Hingis explained in *Sports Illustrated.* "We [she and her father] still have a great relationship, and I know he wants the best for me. He's much more easygoing than my mom. I'm a lot like him, but I reached so much farther than he did." Hingis now sees her father about three times per year.

Hingis's mother Melanie Molitor hated the Communist system of Czechoslovakia. (Communism is the governmental system characterized by the common ownership of production means.) Her father (Hingis's grandfather) spent eight years in a prison for opposing the government. "The Communists wanted to break him, and they certainly did," Molitor told *Sports Illustrated.* "They didn't totally destroy him, but they had a terrible impact on him and our family."

SWISS MISS. When Hingis was seven years old, she and her mother moved to Trubbach, Switzerland. There they lived with Molitor's new husband, Andreas Zogg, a computer salesman. Trubbach is located in the Rhine Valley area of Switzerland, in the shadow of the Alps.

Hingis had a hard time adjusting to her new country, especially since she did not speak the German language used in Trubbach. "That was the second hardest time in my life," Hingis admitted to *Sports Illustrated.* "I had to go to school, but I couldn't understand anything they were saying." However, within three months Hingis had learned the new language.

HITS THE COURTS. The first sport Hingis took up seriously was skiing at the age of three, but her mother knew her daughter would be a great tennis player early on. "Since I was in her stomach, she was thinking I was going to be a great tennis player," Hingis revealed to *Sports Illustrated*. "She never thought I maybe wouldn't have the talent. In the beginning she wanted it more than I did." Molitor considered tennis a way for her daughter to escape Czechoslovakia, the way her hero Navratilova had.

Hingis first began playing tennis when she tried to hit balls back to her mother at the age of two. "Surely that was not tennis, but we tried," Molitor recalled in *People Weekly*. Molitor has always been her daughter's coach and by the age of five Hingis was spending four to five hours a day at the tennis courts where her mother taught. "But I wasn't playing tennis the whole afternoon," Hingis explained to *Sports Illustrated*. "We'd play soccer or other games too."

MOVING UP. Hingis began playing in tournaments at the age of five and at six won her first title. "When Martina was eight, she was already without competition," Peter Holik, her longtime training partner, told *People Weekly*. "She played against 16-year-olds, and she wiped them out." At the age of ten, Hingis beat her mother for the first time.

In 1993, at the age of 12, Hingis became the youngest-ever winner of a junior tournament at a Grand Slam event when she won the junior women's singles title at the French Open. She beat the record of American Jennifer Capriati, who won when she was 13. (The Grand Slam tournaments in tennis are the Australian, French, and U.S. Opens, and Wimbledon.) The next year Hingis repeated as the French Open junior women's singles champion and also won the doubles crown. She followed that up one month later by winning the junior women's singles title at Wimbledon. She was the best junior player in the world.

TURNS PROFESSIONAL. Hingis now had a tough decision to make: whether or not to become a professional tennis player.

Showing her powerful swing, Hingis slams the ball back to her opponent during the 1997 U.S. Open.

The Women's Tennis Association (WTA), the governing body of women's tennis, planned to change its rules. The WTA decided that women could not play the tour full-time until they were 18 years old. If Hingis did not turn professional immediately, she would not be able to become a full-time member of the WTA Tour for four more years.

Hingis turned professional just four days after her four-teenth birthday. She still wore braces and had to leave her public school and attend a private school that allowed her to have generous time off to play tennis. "We've worked 10 years for this," Molitor explained to *Sports Illustrated*. "It's a natural development."

Hingis won her first match as a professional, defeating forty-fifth-ranked Patty Fendick, 6-4, 6-3. "I'm not surprised," she confessed to *Sports Illustrated* after her first pro win. "I've beaten better players." Hingis lost her next match to fifth-ranked Mary Pierce, 6-4, 6-0.

GROWING PAINS. Hingis struggled in her first year on the tour. Because she was so young, her mother did not want her to serve with all her strength, fearing she would sustain an injury. Hingis also did not want to train very hard. "It was not that I did not like tennis anymore, I just did not want to do anything," she admitted to *People Weekly*.

Superstar

"CHOOSE NOW." At the 1996 Lipton International Tournament, Hingis lost to a much lower ranked opponent. Her mother told the young player that it was time to work harder. "It's either tennis or school," Molitor explained to her daughter, according to *Sports Illustrated*. "Choose now."

Hingis listened to her mother, and soon she began to see results. She won her first Grand Slam title—the Wimbledon women's doubles championship—in July 1996. "I was always sure it would happen [winning a Grand Slam title]—just not so fast," Hingis confessed in *Newsweek*. She was the youngest-ever doubles champion at Wimbledon at 15 years, 282 days.

Hingis followed up her success at Wimbledon by advancing to the semifinals in singles, women's doubles, and mixed doubles at the 1996 U.S. Open. In singles, she defeated seventh-seeded Jana Novatna in the quarterfinals before losing to top-seeded and eventual champion Steffi Graf in the semifinals, 7-5, 6-3. Hingis had five set points in the first set before losing.

THUNDER DOWN UNDER. The Australian Open is the first Grand Slam tournament of the year. Hingis arrived in Australia for the 1997 Open as the fourth-seeded player and was confident she could win. She told her mother she was ready. "Then show me," Molitor replied, according to *Sports Illustrated*.

Hingis went out and did just that. She rolled through the singles competition without losing a set. In the final, Hingis defeated Mary Pierce, 6-2, 6-2, in only 59 minutes. After match point, her mother leaped out of the stands and hugged her daughter. Hingis told her mother, according to *Sports Illustrated:* "I showed you." Her mother replied: "Yes, and I can't say I'm unhappy about it."

Hingis became the youngest female winner at a Grand Slam tournament—at 16 years, 3 months, 26 days of age—since 1887, when 15-year-old Charlotte (Lottie) Dod won Wimbledon. "It's just another record for me," she told *Sports Illustrated*.

Hingis and her doubles partner Natasha Zvereva also won the doubles title. "Next time I have to play mixed doubles, but I have to give someone else a chance to win an event," she joked to *Sports Illustrated*. She was the first woman to win both events since Navratilova accomplished the feat in 1985. Hingis also became the youngest-ever women's doubles champion at the Australian Open.

NUMBER ONE. Hingis continued to roll at the 1997 Lipton Championships. She faced her former idol, Monica Seles, in the finals. Hingis first saw Seles play when she was nine years old. "She was just great at that time," she recalled in *Sports Illustrated*. "She just looked different. She had this hair, blonde; then she cut it. I liked her personality a lot, yes."

Hingis did not show Seles respect on the court, however, whipping the great champion 6-2, 6-1. With the victory Hingis became the youngest number-one ranked player since the computer ranking system was begun in 1975. The pressure of being number one did not affect Hingis. "Why should I be worried about the future?" she asked in *Sports Illustrated*. "Right now, almost everything is perfect. I have never enjoyed tennis as much as I do now."

KEEPS ON ROLLING. The only thing that could slow Hingis down was horseback riding. She fell off her horse, injuring her knee. Although the injury required surgery, Hingis was ready for the second Grand Slam tournament of the year, the French Open.

Hingis showed no sign of her injury, cruising through the singles tournament. In the semifinals she faced Seles again. Seles had never lost a semifinal match at a Grand Slam tournament, but once again she was no match for Hingis. The young champion's record for 1997 now stood at 37-0.

In the finals Hingis faced ninth-ranked Iva Majoli of Poland. Majoli had never before reached the finals of a Grand Slam tournament, but in a major upset she defeated Hingis, 6-4, 6-2. "I won 37 matches this year," Hingis told Majoli after the match, according to *People Weekly.* "You're the only one to beat me. Great job!"

GREAT ON GRASS. Coming off her loss at the French Open, many tennis experts did not think Hingis could win at Wimbledon, the only Grand Slam tournament played on a grass surface. Hingis admitted that she did not like to play on grass. "I hate grass because you have to think differently," she confessed to *Sports Illustrated.*

Despite her dislike of playing on grass, Hingis again had little trouble reaching the semifinals. In the semifinals she defeated fellow 16-year-old Anna Kournikova of Russia 6-3, 6-2. In the finals, Hingis faced grass-court specialist Jana Novatna, who also came from Czechoslovakia.

Hingis was not nervous about playing for the most prestigious championship in tennis. "I don't feel that much pressure," she explained to *Sports Illustrated.* "It's because I've been doing this for so long it seems normal."

Novatna started fast in the finals, taking the first set, 6-2. In the second set Hingis started to play her game, mixing her shots beautifully, frustrating Novatna. The young champion came back to win the last two sets, 6-3, 6-3, and the championship. "I was there, the Wimbledon champion, standing on

COACH MOM

Because her mother is her coach, some critics have said that Hingis must have been pushed into playing tennis. But Hingis calls her mother her "mother, best friend, coach." "We always had only us two," she revealed to *People Weekly*. "She [her mother] is everything in one person." Molitor is strict about making her daughter practice, but gives her the freedom to participate in many other activities.

"People say that I ruined Martina's childhood and that I only want the money and to satisfy myself," Molitor told *Sports Illustrated*. "That's not true. I pursued this so Martina could have a chance in life. It hurts me to hear what people say, but I just continue to follow my own path."

Hingis is aware that having your mother as your coach can cause problems. Tennis players Jennifer Capriati and Mary Pierce have had serious problems because their fathers were also their managers. "We're not going to make the same mistakes," Hingis explained in *Sports Illustrated*. "In every family there are sometimes problems. Especially because she's my coach and my mother, sometimes I'm against what she wants me to do. But right now we have a great relationship. I had days when I didn't want to play tennis, but I'm glad I stayed with it because now I have a great life."

Centre Court," Hingis said after the match. "No one can take that from me. I will remember that all my life."

Hingis became the youngest Wimbledon women's champion in the twentieth century at sixteen years, nine months and five days. "I'm maybe too young to win this title," she admitted in *Sports Illustrated*.

OPEN CHAMPION. Hingis lost only her second match of the year when she fell to Lindsey Davenport in a tournament at Manhatten Beach, California, leading up to the U.S. Open. She dispelled any doubts about how well she was playing, however, when she rolled through her early matches at the last Grand Slam tournament of the season. Hingis reached the finals without losing a set.

In the finals Hingis faced 17-year-old Venus Williams, ranked only sixty-sixth in the world and playing in her first U.S. Open. Williams was the first African American woman to reach the final since Althea Gibson in 1958. Hingis came out fast, winning the first set, 6-0, in only 22 minutes. Williams played better in the second set, but still fell, 6-4. The new U.S. Open champion lost only a total of 28 games in all her matches, totally dominating one of the most difficult tournaments in the world.

"I'm very happy about my whole tennis game," Hingis told *Newsday* after the match. "I just had a great year. You know, what can I improve? Sometimes I ask myself. It's a little scary. I haven't won the French Open, so that's the tournament I want to win the most. I have many more years in front of me to maybe win it one time."

NEW YEAR. Hingis suffered through a mini-slump at the end of 1997, losing three matches after the U.S. Open. She finished the year with a 75-5 record and 12 titles. Her dominating performance in 1997 was good enough for the Associated Press to name her the Female Athlete of the Year.

The number-one player in the world proved she was still the best by successfully defending her Australian Open women's singles title, defeating Conchita Martinez in the finals, 6-3, 6-3. The victory was her fourth in the last five Grand Slam tournaments. Hingis became the youngest player—male or female—to defend a Grand Slam title in 110 years. (Charlotte "Lottie" Dodd won her second straight Wimbledon title in 1888 at the age of 16.)

Hingis realizes it will be difficult to stay on top. "To defend the title is much harder," she admitted after her victory. "There's so much pressure. This was the hardest Grand Slam I've won. Everybody told me, it's going to be harder to defend everything. I'm kind of proud of myself, what I did today. This tournament meant so much to me."

WHY SO GOOD? Hingis—at 5 feet 6 inches tall and 115 pounds—is not exceptionally big by tennis standards. She also is not very fast nor does she hit the ball as hard as some other players on the tour. What Hingis does better than any other player, however, is think on the court. By mixing power and finesse, she keeps her opponents off balance. Hingis also has the ability to know exactly the right shot to hit. "I play what I feel," Hingis revealed to *Sports Illustrated*. "I respond to the ball."

OFF THE COURT. Hingis lives in Trubbach, Switzerland. She likes to shop, ride mountain bikes, play soccer, ski, do aerobics, in-line skate, and ride horses. Hingis owns two horses, Montana and Sorrenta, and a German Shepherd, Zorro. She endorses sportswear for Sergio Tacchini. Hingis can speak English, Czech, and German. A superstitious person, she does not step on the lines when leaving the tennis court.

Hingis does not like to practice and rarely plays more than two hours a day. "Tennis is not my life," she explained to

Newsweek. "I would get bored very soon if I would think just about tennis." Hingis has an easy-going personality and loves to laugh and smile.

Hingis loves her life on the road. "Traveling is an even better education than sitting eight hours a day in class," she explained to *Sports Illustrated.* "I'm learning all the cultures, all the different nationalities and mentalities." Life on the tour does make it difficult to date. "Traveling so much, it's hard to find somebody at the tournament; you would have to go every week with someone else," Hingis told the same magazine.

Now that Hingis is at the top she wants to stay there. "I would like to prove that I am not a flash in the pan," she admitted to *People Weekly.* "The better you are, the less you want to lose."

WHERE TO WRITE:

C/O WOMEN'S TENNIS ASSOCIATION,
215 PARK AVE., SUITE 1715,
NEW YORK, NY 10003.

Sources

Los Angeles Times, September 8, 1997; January 31, 1998.
Maclean's, April 14, 1997.
Newsday, September 8, 1997; February 1, 1998.
Newsweek, May 5, 1997; June 2, 1997.
People Weekly, June 23, 1997.
Sports Illustrated, July 12, 1993; October 17, 1994; February 3, 1997; April 7, 1997; April 21, 1997; July 14, 1997.
Sport Illustrated for Kids, August 1994.
Time, September 16, 1996.
USA Today, September 8, 1997.
Additional information provided by the Women's Tennis Association.

Chamique Holdsclaw

1977–

Chamique Holdsclaw—the six-foot-two-inch forward for the University of Tennessee Lady Vols basketball team—is a winner. She has won six straight championships—four at Christ the King High School and two consecutive national championships at the University of Tennessee. Holdsclaw has earned All-American honors in her first two collegiate seasons, and many basketball experts believe she could develop into the greatest female player in history.

"I want people to say, 'That Holdsclaw kid, she really could play.'"
—Chamique Holdsclaw.

Growing Up

RAISED BY GRANDMOTHER. Chamique (sha-MEE-kwah) Holdsclaw was born August 9, 1977. She grew up in Queens, New York. When Holdsclaw was 11 years old her parents, Bonita and Willie, separated. She and her brother, Davon, went to live with their grandmother, June Holdsclaw, because their mother could not afford to take care of them. Davon eventually returned to live with his mother, but Holdsclaw had grown too close to her grandmother to leave.

BALLERINA ON THE COURT. Holdsclaw took ballet and tap dancing classes as an elementary school student. She danced with the Bernice Johnson Dance Group. As a 10-year-old Holdsclaw performed at the Lincoln Center. Her grandmother dreamed of her becoming a prima ballerina.

Holdsclaw, however, was drawn to the basketball court. During her childhood she played with neighborhood boys and more than held her own. Holdsclaw's ballet training came in handy on the court, helping her develop graceful moves going to the basket. "Everyone said it looks like I'm doing ballet sometimes," Holdsclaw revealed to the *Charlotte Observer.* "It's just a gift."

Playing on the neighborhood courts of New York with the boys—many of whom where bigger and stronger—helped Holdsclaw develop her toughness. "Chamique's got to have a level of cockiness, and she does, in order to be as good as she is," her teammate at Tennessee, Laurie Milligan, told *Newsday.* "You can tell she plays street ball in New York. You can tell she's worked hard and can also tell when she started to play she got herself swatted [her shots blocked] all the time. Every time they found a way to block her shot, she found a way to score and [that] carried over to the women's game. That's why she has such a high-arcing shot."

FOUR ON THE FLOOR. Her basketball abilities earned Holdsclaw a spot on the Christ the King High School girls basketball team—one of the top high-school programs in the United States. Before Holdsclaw arrived, the team had won two straight state Class A titles. During her four seasons at Christ the King, the school won the state championship each year, giving the program an amazing six-year title run.

In her senior season (1995) Holdsclaw averaged 24.8 points, 15.9 rebounds, 5.8 blocks, 4 steals, and 3 assists per game as the Royals lost only one game. In her four years at Christ the King, the team lost only four times and compiled a 106-4 record. "It has been a great thrill to watch her mature as a player and as a young lady," Coach Vincent Cannizzaro explained to *Newsday*. "She led by example, and was very supportive of her teammates. These are the qualities we can't replace."

Holdsclaw graduated from Christ the King as the all-time school leader in scoring (2,118 points) and rebounds (1,523). Following her senior year Holdsclaw earned both the Miss New York Basketball award—for the third straight season—and the Naismith Award as the best female high-school basketball player in the United States. "I've had a great career here," Holdsclaw told *Newsday*. "I've enjoyed every minute of it. I'm happy inside."

VOLUNTEERS TO TENNESSEE. Colleges from across the nation tried to recruit Holdsclaw, but she chose the University of Tennessee. The Lady Vols (short for Volunteers) had an outstanding program under coach Pat Summitt—winnning national championships in 1987, 1989, and 1991—but it was her grandmother who convinced Holdsclaw to travel south. "I came to New York a long time ago, about 40 years ago," June Holdsclaw explained to the *New York Daily News*. "But I love the South. And you have to remember who's coaching down there. Pat Summitt is a great coach. A great coach, with a great coaching staff."

Having Holdsclaw join her program thrilled Summitt, who claimed that her newest recruit could potentially be the best player ever at a school that had produced 14 All-Americans and 12 Olympic performers. "They expect a lot and have a lot of confidence in me," Holdsclaw told *USA Today*.

FRESHMAN PHENOM. Holdsclaw started for the Lady Vols as a freshman and led the team in scoring (16.2 points per game) and rebounding (9.1). During one stretch Holdsclaw averaged 20.3 points and 11 rebounds against the best competition in the

Holdsclaw drives the ball down the court.

country. ESPN named her the College Basketball Player of the Week for her efforts, the first time a woman had been so honored. Kodak named Holdsclaw to the 10-player All-American team, the only freshman to make the squad that year.

Despite her outstanding play, Holdsclaw still had a lot to learn. Sometimes the young freshman did not take charge of a game because she was afraid of what her more experienced teammates would think. "I tried to blend in with the team," Holdsclaw admitted to *USA Today*. "I sat back and watched. I didn't know what to do. I expected the upperclassmen to lead us."

After Tennessee lost to Connecticut, 59-53, for their first loss at home since 1991—an NCAA home winning streak record of 69 straight games—Summitt talked to the entire team. Holdsclaw had led the team with 15 points, but did not score in the final 9 minutes. Several times the freshman star had opportunities to score but held back.

Summitt told Holdsclaw that she should not worry about what her teammates thought, that she had to make big plays. "After that I didn't really care what anybody else thought," Holdsclaw explained to *USA Today*. "I knew it was what the coach wanted me to do." Senior players Michelle Marciniak and Latina Davis met with their freshman teammate and told her not to worry about the attention she was receiving.

DOWN BUT NOT OUT. Holdsclaw's freshman season almost came to a premature end in the Southeastern Conference (SEC) Women's Basketball Tournament championship game against the University of Alabama. She ran into an opponent and partially tore a ligament in her right knee. Doctors could not tell if she would be able to play in the upcoming National Collegiate Athletic Association (NCAA) Women's Basketball Tournament.

The possibility of missing the NCAA Tournament disappointed Holdsclaw. She became depressed and worried. "I just shut everybody out," Holdsclaw admitted to *Sports Illustrated*. "I felt pretty down, going to practice and not being able to participate, so I wouldn't talk to anyone."

ROOKIE PRANKS

It has become a tradition for sports teams to play pranks on rookies. When Holdsclaw was a freshman at Tennessee, her teammates told her she had to carry a broomstick around on a road trip to give the team good luck. "It's the freshman pole, and you have to carry it for the whole trip," guard Laurie Milligan told Holdsclaw, according to *Sports Illustrated*.

In reality, the freshman pole was just a broomstick that the older players found in the van that took the team to the airport. Holdsclaw thought her teammates were serious. "I thought it was a tradition, and I didn't want to break it," Holdsclaw said. A coach eventually told the freshman about the joke, but the team liked the idea so well that from now on rookie players will have to carry the broomstick.

At this point her teammates—who knew that Holdsclaw felt down—rallied around her. The fact that their star might be out for the NCAA Tournament made the rest of the Lady Vols realize that they had to pull together and play as a team. "When she went down, all the others realized they had to do more," Summitt explained in *Sports Illustrated*. "It made us a better team."

Miraculously, Holdsclaw returned for Tennessee's first NCAA Tournament game, only 12 days after her injury. "I showed her [Summitt] that I'm a person who's going to gut it out and do whatever my team needs to win," Holdsclaw told the *New York Daily News*.

FINAL FOUR. The Lady Vols rolled into the Final Four, held in 1996 in Charlotte, North Carolina. In the national semifinal game, Tennessee faced the University of Connecticut Huskies, the defending national champion. The Huskies had defeated Tennessee in the championship game the year before and had ended the Lady Vols' record home winning streak earlier in the season.

Holdsclaw denied that she had revenge on her mind. "It's not about playing UConn, it's about playing to advance to the national championship game," she revealed to the *New York Daily News*. "When you get on the level of thinking of it as revenge, that's when you get caught up in the mix."

Tennessee defeated Connecticut in overtime. Holdsclaw had a subpar game against the Huskies, scoring only nine points and pulling down six boards. However, the victory earned the Lady Vols a place in the national championship game against the University of Georgia.

NATIONAL CHAMPIONS. Before the national championship game Holdsclaw printed "Defense Wins Championships" on the side of one shoe and "'87, '89, '91, ?" on the other. The numbers represented the years that Tennessee had won the national championship and the question mark represented the possibility of adding another title to the list.

Tennessee dominated Georgia, winning the national championship 83-65. Holdsclaw was the best player on the court, scoring 16 points and grabbing 14 rebounds. "I just came out and tried to play aggressive defense," she explained to *USA Today*. "We have such a balanced team. I don't feel pressure to come out and score or rebound. We have a lot of people who can do that. I don't feel it's up to me."

> ### WHAT'S IN A NUMBER?
>
> Holdsclaw wears number 23, but says it is not in honor of one of her idols, the great Michael Jordan of the Chicago Bulls. "It's for the 23rd Psalm [in the Bible]," she explained to the *Charlotte Observer*. "My grandmother told me that one day and I thought, 'That's cool.' It surprises a lot of people."

Superstar

UNDERRATED. The Lady Vols lost their starting backcourt—guards Michelle Marciniak and Latina Davis—to graduation after the 1995–96 season. Most basketball experts felt they had very little chance to repeat as national champions. "That's OK," Holdsclaw told *USA Today*. "We'll just play hard. Maybe someone will blossom."

Holdsclaw became the undisputed leader of the Lady Vols during the 1996–97 season. She carried most of the team's offense—averaging 20.2 points—and she also grabbed 9.4 rebounds per game. For the second straight season Holdsclaw earned All-American honors. She joined Cheryl Miller, Ann Myers, and Lynnette Woodard as the only players to be named to the Kodak All-America team as both freshmen and sophomores.

Despite the outstanding play of their superstar, the Lady Vols struggled. They finished the year with ten losses—a poor record by Tennessee standards—and were the first Lady Volunteer team to drop out of the top ten in the polls since 1986. "We were setting so many bad records, we were wondering if anything positive would come out of the season," Holdsclaw confessed to *Sports Illustrated*.

REPEAT OR DEFEAT? Tennessee won their first two games of the 1997 NCAA Women's Basketball Tournament, defeating Grambling University and the University of Oregon. The Lady Vols then traveled to Iowa City, Iowa, where they continued their run of success, defeating the University of Colorado and then upsetting Connecticut—the No. 1 ranked team in the country—by a score of 91-81 to win the Midwest Regional.

Tennessee now had earned a spot in the Final Four for the third straight year. In the national semifinals— held in Cincinnati, Ohio—the Lady Vols defeated Notre Dame University, 80-66, behind 31 points by Holdsclaw. For the third straight season Tennessee would play for the national championship, this time against Old Dominion University.

MVP. Old Dominion had won 32 straight games entering the national championship final—including an 83-72 victory over Tennessee earlier in the season. Holdsclaw looked forward to the matchup with the Lady Monarchs. "I've played in a lot of big games this season," she told the *Charlotte Observer.* "I'll just go out and do what I can. We take pride in our program. We're excited to play in a game this big. Whenever you play a team the second time, and they've beaten you, there's always extra incentive."

Old Dominion put their best defender, Mary Andrade, on Holdsclaw. The Lady Monarchs hoped to stop the high-scoring forward by playing physical defense, but Holdsclaw was ready. "A lot of teams try that," she explained to the *Charlotte Observer.* "I keep moving. If they bump me, I play harder. I get fired up."

Tennessee got off to a fast start in the championship game, jumping out to an early 15-point lead. Old Dominion would not give up, however, and came back to take a 44-43 lead with only nine minutes remaining in the game. With the championship on the line, Holdsclaw took over. "I wasn't going to disappear," she told *USA Today*. Holdsclaw scored

10 points in the last seven minutes, dished out two assists, and blocked a shot.

When the final buzzer sounded, the Lady Vols had won the national championship, 68-59. Holdsclaw finished the game with 24 points, 7 rebounds, 3 assists, and 2 steals. Her dominating performance earned her recognition as the Most Valuable Player of the Final Four. "There's a lot of great players out there, but I think right now she's the best in the college game," Summitt told *USA Today*. "She's a very gifted athlete with great basketball skills. Something she has that's special is a tremendous desire to win."

The championship was Tennessee's second straight title and fifth since 1987. The only other women's basketball team to repeat as national champion was the University of Southern California in 1983 and 1984. That team was led by the great All-American, Cheryl Miller. "Only one other team has done what we've done—win championships back-to-back," Holdsclaw said in *Sports Illustrated*. "We have our place in history now."

THE BEST? Holdsclaw has a great all-around offensive game. She can score from the outside, take the ball to the basket, and play in the paint. Because so many teams double-team her, Holdsclaw has become a much better passer. She still needs to work on her defense, but has always shown a willingness to improve her weaknesses.

Her coach believes Holdsclaw can develop into one of the best female basketball players in history. "Certainly, Chamique has made a name for herself," Summitt told the *Philadelphia Daily News*. "While she is an All-America performer already, she has not seen the top of her game yet. In my opinion, if she continues to excel, improve, work and be serious about her game, I think she will become one of the best that ever played this game. I've compared her to a lot of people, but she doesn't like to be compared to anyone. She wants to be her own person. I truly understand that. She has her own style and her own game."

Holdsclaw does not want people to even think she is the best player in women's college basketball. "When the ball's in my hands, I'm one of the top two players in the country," she admitted to *Newsday* during her sophomore season. "I consider myself not the best but the next-best thing. I just know there's always going to be somebody better than me. I never want to go out there and say I'm the best because when I say I'm the best, that's when everybody's going to come at me and I'm not going to be able to do anything about it. Right now, I know I'm a good player, I'm a young player with a lot to learn. I want to be the best. I have to put a lot of work into it."

OFF THE COURT. Holdsclaw keeps in touch with her mother and father, but lists her grandmother as her parent in her University of Tennessee biography. June Holdsclaw—who works in health information at a hospital—is her granddaughter's biggest fan. "She just loves the sport, and she works so hard," June Holdsclaw told the *New York Daily News*. "She's the perfect granddaughter."

Holdsclaw is a political science major at Tennessee. She likes to keep her teammates loose by playing practical jokes. Holdsclaw wears braces and is afraid of heights.

Women's basketball is very popular at Tennessee. Holdsclaw is grateful that the fans support the team, but sometimes the attention she receives can be overwhelming. "The worst thing is you're put under a microscope because of who you are," she admitted to *Newsday*. "Everywhere you go it's like you carry 'Lady Vols' on your chest. You just have to kind of present yourself as perfect people, that's the thing. Everyone wants to comment on everything you do and everything you say and it's hard."

Never satisfied with winning, Holdsclaw wants to keep her championship streak—now at six straight years—going. The freshman class at Tennessee for the 1997–98 season was considered the best in the country. "The sky's the limit," Holdsclaw told *USA Today*. "We could be the first program to win four [consecutive] titles."

Holdsclaw, now a junior, does not think players should leave school early to turn professional in one of the two new women's leagues—the American Basketball League (ABL) or Women's National Basketball Association (WNBA). "I don't think females should be allowed to decide to go pro," she explained to *Sports Illustrated*. "The leagues need mature young ladies who have their degrees."

Holdsclaw has set a very achievable goal for her basketball career. "I want to be able to say I helped the women's game become more competitive and exciting," she revealed to *Sports Illustrated*. "I want to bring a flair to the game. I want people to say, 'That Holdsclaw kid, she really could play.'"

 WHERE TO WRITE:
C/O UNIVERSITY OF TENNESSEE,
PO BOX 47,
KNOXVILLE, TN 37901.

Sources

Charlotte Observer, March 29, 1997.
Los Angeles Times, March 31, 1996.
New York Daily News, March 28, 1996; March 31, 1997.
Newsday, February 26, 1995; April 16, 1995; December 30, 1996.
Philadelphia Daily News, March 31, 1997.
Sports Illustrated, December 2, 1996; April 7, 1997.
USA Today, October 27, 1994; March 29, 1996; April 1, 1996; March 31, 1997.

Allen Iverson

1975–

> *"I want to be the best. Years from now, when people are talking about Magic [Johnson] and Michael [Jordan], I want my name to be mentioned too. I have a lot of work to do, but that's what I want."*
> *—Allen Iverson.*

On the basketball court, point guard Allen Iverson of the Philadelphia 76ers is "The Answer," a player whose speed and skill make him one of the most dangerous all-around threats in the National Basketball Association (NBA). In his first season (1996–97) he earned the NBA Rookie of the Year award and dazzled opposing players with his lightning-quick cross-over dribble. Off the basketball court, however, Iverson has consistently made mistakes that could have cost him his career and even his life. The big question is whether "The Answer" will be remembered more for what he has accomplished as a basketball player than for the fact that he never lived up to his immense talent because he could not gain control of the controversy that swirls around him.

Growing Up

TOUGH START. Allen Iverson was born June 7, 1975. His mother Ann was only 16 and living with her grandmother at the time of her son's birth. Iverson and his mother moved from one low-income neighborhood to another around Hampton and Newport News, Virginia. His nickname as a child was "Bubbachuck."

Ann Iverson worked hard to raise her son and his two younger sisters. Iverson says his mother is his role model "because of what she went through trying to take care of myself and my sisters in the situation she was in." He never knew his father and many of his male role models were arrested for selling drugs to raise money for the family.

Life in the projects was hard. "Coming home, no lights, no food," Iverson recalled in *USA Today*. "Sometimes no water. Then when there was water, no hot water. Living in a house where the sewer was busted under the house and having to watch my sister walk around in her socks all day because the floor was wet from the sewage. The smell was making my sister sick."

HEADED FOR TROUBLE. When Iverson left the house, drugs and violence were all around him, as he related to journalist David Teel. "We talked about the environment he grew up in," Teel reported in the *Sporting News*. "He told me when he was 14 or 15 years old, his best friend was stabbed to death. He didn't see it but his best friend was murdered. He told me about a party he had been to at a hotel in Hampton where guns were drawn and a guy was murdered—and he was there for that—and how scared he was. He told me that he indeed liked to stay out late, that he liked to run around with friends, that was just a part of him that was going to be very difficult to change."

Iverson earned poor grades in school and often was involved in confrontations with students and teachers. Many times he did not come to school and teachers—who knew how bad his home situation was—took it upon themselves to pick him up and bring him to class. When Iverson was 16 he had problems with his mother and lived for almost a year with his elementary school football coach, Gary Moore. Because of his erratic behavior many rumors began that Iverson was taking drugs. He denies these rumors and insists he never took any illegal substances.

TWO-SPORT THREAT. Iverson always loved sports. Ann Iverson had been a varsity basketball player in high school at Bethel High School during the 1970s and she was her son's first coach. "His cousins taught him to dribble the ball, but his mom taught him ballhandling and the whole feel of the game," Iverson's childhood friend Dwayne Campbell told the *Sporting News*. "She was the one who taught him to go inside and drive for the hole."

Iverson pitched in baseball, but his favorite sport was football. As a 6-foot, 170 pound junior at Bethel High School he won all-state honors at quarterback (he also played safety) by passing for 1,423 yards and 14 touchdowns and rushing for 781 yards and 15 scores. He also ran 6 kickoffs back for touchdowns. The football team won the state championship.

The young athlete also starred in basketball, but only at his mother's urging. "I didn't even want to play basketball at first," Iverson admitted in *Sports Illustrated*. "I thought it was soft. My mother's the one who made me go to tryouts. I thank her forever. I came back and said, 'I like basketball, too.'"

Iverson also led his high school basketball team to the state championship as a junior, a rare double feat. He averaged 31.6 points and 9.2 assists. During his junior season the Associated Press named Iverson both the state's basketball and football high-school player of the year. *Parade* magazine named him the national high-school basketball player of the year and one of the top-10 football players in the United States. His play earned him the nickname "The Answer," which he has tattooed on his left arm.

College recruiters began coming to watch Iverson play both basketball and football. The football field was where the young athlete wanted to continue his career. "I always figured I was going to go to one of those big football schools," Iver-

Iverson takes the ball to the hole.

son told *Sports Illustrated*. "Florida State. Notre Dame. Football was my first love. Still is. I was going to go to one of those schools and play both. I just loved running the option, faking, throwing the ball, everything about football."

DISASTER STRIKES. On February 14, 1993, Iverson went with friends to the Circle Lanes bowling alley in Hampton. No one is sure about how it started, but a fight broke out between a group of African American youths and several white teenagers. The combatants began throwing chairs and several people were injured. Finally the police arrived and broke up the fight.

Several witnesses identified Iverson—whom they knew from his athletic career—as one of the instigators of the fight. He and three other African-American teenagers were arrested and charged with "malicious wounding by mob," a felony, or serious crime. The police did not arrest any of the white individuals involved in the fight.

Iverson admitted that he was involved in the beginning of the fight. He claimed that one of the white youth used racial slurs. Once the fight broke out, however, Iverson insisted that he left the bowling alley. "Sometimes I wonder how everything got so messed up," he related to *Sports Illustrated.* "All I wanted to do was play basketball, and now I'm in the middle of all this mess."

CONVICTED. Because of Iverson's athletic fame the media became interested in the case. Usually teenagers involved in similar situations were given probation and sentenced to completing community service. In this case, however, the state of Virginia decided to charge Iverson—who was 17 at the time—as an adult.

Iverson waived his right to a jury trial and let Judge Nelson T. Overton decide his fate. In a shocking verdict, Overton convicted all four teenagers and sentenced each to 15 years in prison. Overton then denied bail for the four youngsters and sent them directly to prison. Usually judges in Virginia will allow persons convicted of this type of crime to go home after paying bail while they appeal their convictions.

BACKLASH. The convictions caused a national outcry because of the harshness of the sentences and the fact that no white participants in the fight were charged. Many civil rights organizations—including the National Association for the Advancement of Colored People (NAACP)—came to Hampton to protest the judge's decision. "It's strange enough that the police waded through a huge mob of fighting people and came out with only blacks, and the one black that everybody knew," NAACP crisis coordinator Golden Frinks explained in *Sports Illustrated.* "But people thought they'd get a slap on the wrist and that would be the end of it."

Iverson was sent to serve his sentence at the Newport News City Farm, a minimum-security work camp. "I just tried to learn from everything that I witnessed while I was incarcerated," Iverson explained to the *Los Angeles Times.* "I found a lot out about myself, let me know how strong I was. I just read in the papers while I was locked up that it was over for me, there was no way I was going to be able to do this or do that. I just sat back and said, 'If I get another chance one day, I'll prove all those people wrong.' I was never scared."

RELEASED. Virginia Governor Douglas Wilder stepped in after four months and gave Iverson a conditional furlough that allowed him to be free while he appealed his conviction. In June 1995 the Virginia Court of Appeals overturned the three felony convictions against Iverson. "I was talking to his mom, but I could hear (Allen) in the background cheering," his attorney Lisa O'Donnell told the *Sporting News.* "It was the typical reaction of a 20-year-old to good news."

Because of the bowling alley incident Iverson completely missed his senior year of high school. He completed his diploma at a school for at-risk youth. Iverson knew his future was at stake. "I had to use the whole jail situation as something positive," he confessed to the *Los Angeles Times.* "I knew when I got out that my back was against the wall and that just made me work that much harder, knowing that everybody thought it was over for me. I always knew that I had to still take care of my family, even though I was coming out of jail.

HOYA HOPEFUL. Because of his problems college football recruiters stopped visiting Iverson. Several basketball coaches remained interested, but Ann Iverson knew that her son needed special attention. She asked John Thompson—the legendary basketball coach of the Georgetown University Hoyas—to help her son. Thompson—known for his strict discipline—agreed to accept the troubled young player onto his team. "I went to Georgetown because it was the best thing for me to do at the time," Iverson explained to *Sports Illustrated*. "Just play basketball."

Thompson was known for being very protective of his players, and he tried to help Iverson deal with all his off-court problems. "Regardless of what's happened in the past, Allen is a bright young man who deserves a chance to pursue a college education," Thompson told *Sports Illustrated*. "He will have to follow the same rules and accomplish the same things in the classroom as anyone else in this program." As is his regular practice, Thompson did not let Iverson or any other freshmen do any media interviews.

FRESHMAN FLASH. Iverson started slowly in his freshman season at Georgetown. Not being able to play for a year left his game rusty and unpolished. Iverson also had to learn how to run an offense at the college level. Thompson told *Saturday Night* that his point guard had to learn he was "responsible not only for himself but for managing the game, and other people." Many times Iverson thought shoot first—he led the Hoyas with 520 attempts—and pass second.

The first-year player also had to deal with fans in rival arenas who taunted and booed him, calling him a criminal and worse. "I think Allen came into the season without playing his senior year (in high school) and under a lot of emotional stress," Thompson explained in the *Sporting News*. "Regardless of how he seemed to handle it well, all of us know that it was realistic that he had to deal with it."

By the end of the year Iverson was one of the most dangerous players in the Big East Conference. He led Georgetown with 20.4 points (fourth in the Big East) and 4.5 assists per game. Iverson also finished fourth in the nation with 89 steals, a new school record. This performance earned him both the Big East freshman of the year and defensive player of the year awards.

SOPHOMORE SENSATION. Iverson came into his second college season as a more mature player. "Last year I was out of control at times," he admitted to the *Atlanta Journal-Constitution*. "This year, I've learned so much. But sometimes, people will say I'll be out of control. That's the kind of player I am."

During the off-season Iverson worked hard on his game, especially his outside shot. The season before teams dared him to shoot, backing off the lightning-quick guard so he would not go by them to the basket. Once Iverson began to make three-point baskets he was impossible to guard. "He's a bullet," DePaul coach Joey Meyer declared to the *Sporting News*. "I think he's more under control than last year. I'm really impressed with his quickness under control. Guys that move that fast often don't have control of their bodies."

Iverson had a great year in his sophomore season at Georgetown. He averaged 24.7 points (best on the team and a new Georgetown season record. Reggie Williams set the record of 23.6 during the 1986–87 season), 4.7 assists (165 total, best on the team), and 3.35 steals (116 total, best on the team). Iverson earned first-team All-American honors, and the Big East Conference named him Defensive Player of the Year for the second year in a row. "I don't feel anybody can play with me one-on-one in the country without hand-checking me," Iverson told *Sports Illustrated*.

NBA BOUND. Iverson decided to make himself available for the 1996 NBA Draft following his sophomore season at Georgetown. "After carefully weighing my options with Coach Thompson and my family, I've decided to enter the NBA," Iverson announced at a news conference. "I definitely plan to further my education, but my family needs to be addressed right now. [My mother] raised me for 20 years and did the best she could. Now I just want an opportunity to do something for her, and my little sisters, and my daughter." Iverson wanted to help his four-year-old sister Iesha, who almost died as a baby and still suffered from seizures.

Iverson thanked Thompson for giving him a chance to play college basketball. "He taught me everything I had to know to get to where I am today," he admitted in *USA Today*. "Words can't express what he did for me and for my life. He never turned his back on me when everybody else was turning their backs on me." Iverson's 23 point per game scoring average was a Georgetown record, and only eight players ever scored more points (1,539) for the school.

PHILLIE FLASH. Iverson knew that the transition from Georgetown to the NBA would be hard. "I think it's going to be difficult in the beginning," he confessed to the *Washington Post*. "But here at Georgetown, we're prepared for things like that. [Coach Thompson] gets us prepared. He lets us know about things off the basketball court, not just on the basketball court. If I have any problems, he'll be the first person I call."

The Philadelphia 76ers—who won only 18 games during the 1995–96 season—held the first pick in the 1996 NBA Draft. They announced before the draft that they had decided to use their pick to choose Iverson. He was the first point guard drafted number-one since Magic Johnson in 1979 and the smallest number one pick ever. "I wanted to be the top pick," Iverson admitted to *Sport*. "I don't really feel [any] pressure. I've been dealing with things way worse than this. This is something I like to do." Iverson signed a three-year, $9.3 million contract.

In his first NBA game Iverson scored 30 points against the Milwaukee Bucks. His cross-over dribble surprised defenders, and his speed allowed him to go right by the fastest guards in the league. Members of the Golden State Warriors admitted to taping their ankles extra tight so they would not be injured trying to keep up with Iverson. Several times the players guarding him fouled out of the game.

"I think speed is everything," Iverson declared in *Sport*. "As long as you're faster than somebody else or just as fast, you can pretty much do what you want. If you can go by guys in this league, you can make things happen, break a defense down. Somebody has to help, and whoever helps, then that's the guy you hit. And if they don't help, you got a basket."

NO RESPECT. Controversy continued to follow Iverson into the NBA. The league banned his black ankle braces and ordered referees to call carrying the ball more often. Players guarding Iverson claimed that he carried the ball on his cross-over dribble. "I figured a lot of things wouldn't go my way in the beginning because of my past and everything I went through," Iverson related to *USA Today.* "I knew people wouldn't give me a fair shake. But that's life. I look at it as another obstacle in my life, something else I have to overcome."

Iverson cockiness and trash-talking also got him into trouble. In a game against the world champion Chicago Bulls, the great Michael Jordan took the brash rookie aside. "At one point I mentioned to [Iverson], he was going to have to respect us," Jordan told the *Los Angeles Times.* "If you don't respect anyone else in this league you have to respect us. He said he doesn't have to respect anybody."

This comment led professional players—both current and retired—to criticize Iverson. When the NBA assembled the top 50 players in the history of the league at the 1997 All-Star Game in Cleveland, Ohio, Iverson's comment was a topic of discussion. "If he doesn't show any respect for the guys in this room, and for today's top players, then maybe he should read up on them," Hall of Fame center Elvin Hayes suggested in *Sports Illustrated.* "His head is in the wrong place."

MVP. Iverson had 19 points, 9 assists, 3 blocks, and 3 steals in the NBA All-Star Rookie Game. He made 7 of 11 shots and led his East team to a 96-91 win. The assembled writers named Iverson the game's most valuable player. When his name was announced, the crowd at Gund Arena in Cleveland, Ohio, erupted in boos. They wanted **Kobe Bryant** (see entry) of the Los Angeles Lakers—who scored 31 points in a losing cause—to win the award.

After the rookie game Iverson tried to explain that his comments about respecting other players had been misunderstood. What he had meant was that on the basketball court he did not fear a great player like Michael Jordan and that he felt he could hold his own with the best athletes in the world. "When Allen said he didn't have to respect anyone, what I think he really meant was he doesn't have to fear anyone," Philadelphia owner Pat Croce explained to *Sports Illustrated.*

The criticism hurt Iverson. "I wish I wasn't the one singled out," he revealed in *Sports Illustrated.* "The older guys get this idea about me from what they read in the papers. None of them have ever sat down and talked to me, and I think that's unfair. I have more love for this game than almost anyone, and that's the only thing that hurts, that they think I don't have respect for the game."

ROOKIE ROCKET. Iverson set an NBA rookie record late in the season when he scored 40 or more points in five straight games. In a game against the Cleveland Cavaliers he scored 50 points, becoming the second youngest player to reach this milestone. (Rick Barry was younger when he scored 57 points for the San Francisco Warriors on December 14, 1965.) Despite Iverson's efforts, the 76ers lost each game.

Playing on a struggling team frustrated Iverson. He needed to score, but as a point-guard he also needed to get his teammates involved in Philadelphia's offense. Iverson felt he was up to the challenge. "Point guards can do so many things," he explained to *Sport.* "They can get others involved, they can get themselves involved. You add a lot to a team if you're a point guard and you can score too. Of course you can pass the ball, hit people, get people open, but if they're worrying about your scoring ability as well, that makes you that much stronger."

In his first season, Iverson averaged 23.5 points (sixth in the NBA), 2.07 steals (seventh in the NBA), 40.1 minutes (eighth in the NBA), 7.5 assists (eleventh in the NBA), and 4.1 rebounds per game. His 1,787 points set a new Philadelphia rookie record. On the down side, Iverson also led the league in turnovers (4.4 per game) and shot only 41.6 percent from the field. Philadelphia finished 22-60.

ROOKIE OF THE YEAR. Some basketball experts felt that because of the controversy surrounding Iverson he should not win the 1996–97 NBA Rookie of the Year Award. His play, however, convinced others. "I think the Rookie of the Year has to be Iverson," Toronto Raptors assistant coach Brendan Suhr explained to *Sports Illustrated*. "He's a fabulous talent. He does great things on the court. I don't think you can hold the other stuff against him. He's a rookie, remember? And he's with a bad team. It's tough to ask a rookie to carry a team, but he tries to do it every night."

Most voters for the award agreed with Suhr. Iverson became the first 76er player to win the NBA Rookie of the Year award. He beat out Stephon Marbury of the Minnesota Timberwolves and Shareef Abdur-Rahim of the Vancouver Grizzles. "I would have always felt I was rookie of the year, even if I didn't get the award," Iverson admitted in *USA Today*. "But I wanted it bad. As a rookie, I think I made the most impact."

Despite his rough-and-tumble first year, Iverson enjoyed being in the NBA. "It's just fun," he related to the *Los Angeles Times*. "Even with all the negatives that come with it—my shorts are too low, my ankle braces being black, my crossover— even with all that, this is an experience I'll never forget."

THANKS, MOM

Iverson dedicated the NBA Rookie of the Year Award to his mother, Ann. "Without her none of this would have happened for me," he said. "If it wasn't for her, I wouldn't be anywhere near the NBA right now. Since I was young, she made me believe I could do anything I wanted to do." Iverson then handed his mother the trophy.

After he signed his first professional contract Iverson bought his mother a new house and Jaguar automobile. Ann Iverson attended almost all of the 76ers home games. "I like the person my mom brought up," Iverson told *USA Today*. "If my mom accepts me and can look at me in my eye and say I'm the same person, I'm not phony, then I'm satisfied. I can deal with what people write about me or say about me on TV."

THE FUTURE. Before his second season, new Philadelphia coach Larry Brown named Iverson the team's captain. Brown challenged his young star to be a leader and compared Iverson to Isiah Thomas, the great point guard of the Detroit Pistons championship teams. "I told Allen the players in our league set the standards, and Isiah was one of those who accepted that responsibility," he recounted in *USA Today*. "There are a lot of similarities between the two. Isiah was an unbelievable competitor. It was not an easy transition for him. He was a high scorer on a losing team early, and eventually he said the heck with it, I'm going to be a pro and demand things of

ROLE MODEL?

Iverson has made mistakes in his life. Following the 1996–97 season his Mercedes Benz automobile was pulled over in Virginia for speeding. Police found a gun and marijuana under his seat. Iverson received three years probation for a misdemeanor gun charge and NBA commissioner David Stern suspended him for the opening game of the 1997–98 season. "He [Stern] came at me like he's supposed to," Iverson conceded in *USA Today*. "Real strict. I accepted that. Somebody who has kids and looks up to me can't be in the media for what I've been in this summer. I accept any punishment that comes to me, because I deserve it. I made a mistake. It's something I have to learn from."

Despite his on and off-court problems, Iverson wants young fans to be able to look up to him. "I didn't really care how the older people, the grown-ups felt about me," Iverson said. "But I didn't want the little kids to look at me and think of me that way. I didn't want them to read things about me in the paper that aren't true. I'm not the bad guy I've been made out to be. Maybe it was because of my background, what I've come from, what I've been through. But I thought after that was over, I was supposed to be able to start with a clean slate. If somebody is coming from where I did and he's trying to do something good with his life, I'd take my hat off to him. But that hasn't happened with me."

myself and my teammates. He became a great leader. There is no reason Allen can't do that. He wants that responsibility. He has some of the same abilities, toughness and competitiveness that Isiah had. Whether he uses it like Isiah or not, I don't know."

The confidence of his new coach was important to Iverson. "It [becoming captain] means a lot to me, because I feel I am a leader on the court," he explained to *USA Today*. "Growing up, when we were in tough situations on the court, people always looked to me to do something special."

OFF THE COURT. Iverson has a daughter named Tiaura. He is a talented artist who likes to draw during his free time. "He drew me a picture of Michael Jordan dunking over [former NBA player] Dominique [Wilkens]," Dwayne Campbell told the *Sporting News*. "See, I liked Dominique and he liked Michael, so he just did this. I heard he could draw, but I never saw it before. He just sat there and sketched it so fast—and it was, like, perfect. I couldn't believe it." Iverson majored in art at Georgetown.

Reebok signed Iverson to a $40 million contract to endorse shoes. Because his nickname is "The Answer," the shoes are called "The Question." Iverson wants people to remember him for his play, not his off-court troubles. "This is my profession," he explained to *Sports Illustrated*. "I want to be the best. Years from now, when people are talking about Magic and Michael, I want my name to be mentioned too. I have a lot of work to do, but that's what I want."

 WHERE TO WRITE:

C/O PHILADELPHIA 76ERS,
CORESTATE'S CENTER, BROAD ST. & PATTISON AVE.,
PHILADELPHIA, PA 19147-0240.

Sources

Atlanta Journal-Constitution, March 23, 1996; February 9, 1997.
Jet, July 15, 1996; May 19, 1997.
Los Angeles Times, December 15, 1996; December 29, 1996.
Newsday, May 2, 1997.
Saturday Night, May 1995.
Sporting News, September 19, 1994; January 30, 1995; July 3, 1995; March 11, 1996; July 29, 1996; February 24, 1997.
Sports, March 1997.
Sports Illustrated, July 26, 1993; October 25, 1993; June 13, 1994; December 4, 1995; December 9, 1996; January 20, 1997; February 17, 1997; April 7, 1997.
USA Today, April 8, 1997; May 2, 1997; October 30, 1997.
Washington Post, May 2, 1996.
Additional information provided by the Philadelphia 76ers and the Gannett News Service.

Marion Jones

1975

"I want to run very, very fast, and I want to jump very, very far."
—Marion Jones.

Marion Jones seems to have wings on her feet. Her great speed carried her across the finish line first in the 100-meter sprint at the 1997 World Track and Field Championships, earning her the title of "The World's Fastest Woman." The speed that made her a world champion also helped Jones lead the fast break for the University of North Carolina women's basketball team that won the National Collegiate Athletic Association (NCAA) championship in 1994. A world-class athlete in two sports, Jones is just beginning to hit her stride.

Growing Up

SUPPORTIVE MOM. Marion Jones was born October 12, 1975 in Los Angeles, California. Her parents divorced when she was just a baby, and her mother's second husband died when Jones was in sixth grade. After that Jones's mother—also named Marion—worked two jobs to support her children.

Jones's mother moved to the United States from Belize—a country in South America—when she was 21. Jones says her mother taught her how to be a good person and hard worker and always stressed the importance of education. "She has been my supporter and the biggest influence in my life," Jones explained in *Sports Illustrated for Kids.*

LOVES TO PLAY. As a child Jones liked playing outside for as long as she could. "The only time I'd come in was to grab a piece of fruit and go to the bathroom," she recalled in *Sports Illustrated for Kids.* "I don't sit down very easily."

Jones became interested in sports by hanging out with her brother, Albert. "He was always involved in athletics with his friends," she told *Sports Illustrated for Kids.* "I got exposed to a lot of different sports and learned to love them all." Jones played T-ball, baseball, and softball, participated in gymnastics, and took ballet and tap-dancing lessons.

At the age of five Jones began running track, and she first played organized basketball when she was 11. She impressed track coach Jack Dawson with the way she blazed down the court while playing basketball. "She was dribbling and running faster than the other girls could run," Dawson explained to *Sports Illustrated for Kids.* "I felt confident that she could be an Olympian." Dawson invited Jones to join his track club. Soon she began to dominate the club's competitions and won a national high-school title as an eighth-grader.

BEST OF ALL TIME. In 1989 the Jones family moved from Sherman Oaks to Camarillo, California. Jones attended Rio Mesa High School and attracted national attention in two sports. She became the first freshman in history to win California state high-school titles in both the 100- and 200-meter dashes. The next year (1990) she repeated as champion in

> **SCOREBOARD**
>
> WON GOLD MEDAL IN THE 100-METER SPRINT AT 1997 WORLD TRACK AND FIELD CHAMPIONSHIPS.
>
> HELPED LEAD THE UNIVERSITY OF NORTH CAROLINA TAR HEELS TO THE 1994 NCAA WOMEN'S BASKETBALL CHAMPIONSHIP.
>
> ONE OF THE GREATEST HIGH-SCHOOL TRACK ATHLETES IN U.S. HISTORY.
>
> JONES WANTS TO CAPTURE GOLD AT THE 2000 OLYMPIC GAMES IN SYDNEY, AUSTRALIA.

both events. In basketball Jones averaged just under 25 points per game for the girls' varsity team in her sophomore season.

Before her junior year Jones transferred to Thousand Oaks High School. She continued to dominate high-school track, winning five state titles and setting a U.S. high-school record in the 200 meters (22.58 seconds). One of Jones's titles came in the long jump, an event she had only recently taken up. She jumped 22½ feet, the second longest in history by a high-school girl. Jones had the special pleasure of working with Mike Powell, the world record-holder in the long jump.

Jones also won several national junior track championships. As a sophomore she won the National Junior Championships in the 100 and 200 meters and had a national-best time of 52.91 in the 400 meters. Gatorade named Jones the Circle of Champions National Girls Track and Field Athlete of the Year, the first non-senior, male or female, to win that award. She also won the award as a junior and senior, becoming the only athlete to win the award more than once.

In 1992—at the age of 16—Jones set the national high-school record of 11.14 in the 100 meters, at the time the sixth fastest ever run by a female. Her time of 22.58 in the 200—still a national high-school record—ranked at the time as the ninth fastest ever by a woman and is still the fastest time for a woman under the age of 18. "Nothing before and nothing probably for a long time to come can match Marion," track official Doug Speck told *Sports Illustrated*. "I'm not sure people realize how lucky we've been to watch her."

By the end of her senior year Jones had established herself as one of the greatest high-school track athletes in U.S. history. She had a chance to travel to the 1992 Summer Olympics in Barcelona, Spain as a high-school junior. Jones finished fourth at the U.S. Olympic Trials in the 200 meters—missing the team by .07 seconds—and fifth in the 100 meters. She earned a spot as a member of the 100-meter relay team, an accomplishment she called the highlight of her track career. Jones turned down the invitation, however, saying that

she was too young and that she felt she would have other chances to run in the Olympics.

TAR HEEL BOUND. In addition to her success in track, Jones also was California's best female high-school basketball player as a senior. In her final season she averaged 22.8 points and 14.2 rebounds, numbers good enough to earn California Interscholastic Federation Divison I Player of the Year honors. In her two seasons at Thousand Oaks, Jones led her school to two state-championship games, and they won the title in 1992.

Many colleges recruited Jones, trying to convince her to attend their schools. Some wanted her to run track, while others wanted her to play basketball. Jones wanted to do both. She finally chose the University of North Carolina because the coaches there promised that she could participate in both basketball and track.

NATIONAL CHAMPIONS. Jones was an instant success with the Tar Heels basketball team, earning a starting job at point guard in her fourth game. "I saw myself as a leader on that team," she explained in *USA Today*. "Any time you're put at the point guard position you have to be some type of leader." Jones had to work extra hard on her passing and ball handling to make the transition from playing forward in high school to point guard in college.

Jones averaged 14.2 points, 4.3 rebounds, 2.9 assists, and 3.2 steals per game in her freshman season. Her speed—which earned her the nickname "Flash"—made it impossible to catch her on a breakaway. "You cannot prepare for a player that fast," Purdue Boilermaker coach Lin Dunn explained to the *Los Angeles Sentinel*.

North Carolina had a great 1993–94 season. They won the Atlantic Coast Conference (ACC) tournament championship and were ranked among the best women's teams in the country. The NCAA Women's Basketball Tournament named North Carolina as a top seed, and the Tar Heels progressed all the way to the national championship game.

The 1994 NCAA Women's Final Four was held in Richmond, Virginia. Jones got into foul trouble early in the championship game against Louisiana Tech and spent much of the contest on the bench. The Tar Heels trailed 59-57—with time running out—when Charlotte Smith hit a championship-winning three-pointer for North Carolina. The national championship title was the first ever for North Carolina and the first ever for an ACC school. The Tar Heels finished the season with a 33-2 record.

ON TRACK. During the 1994–95 season, Jones became the first sophomore in North Carolina women's basketball history to score 1,000 career points. The ACC named her to the conference's first team and Jones also earned honorable mention All-American honors. North Carolina finished the season 30-5, but fell to Stanford University in the regional semifinals of the NCAA tournament.

Playing basketball limited the amount of time Jones could devote to track. She could not run full-time in 1994 or 1995 because of the length of the basketball season. Jones set an ACC record with a long jump of 22 feet, 1 3/4 inches that captured second place at the 1994 NCAA Women's Track and Field Championships. She also earned All-American honors the same year in the 100 meters, 200 meters, and the 4 x 100 meter relay. The next year Jones earned All-American honors in the long jump and the 4 x 100 meter relay.

While most athletes would be happy with these results, Jones was not satisfied. Her sprint coach at North Carolina, Curtis Frye, knew she had the size, speed, and attitude to be a great sprinter. "She's one of those athletes who is just different," Frye said in *Sports Illustrated*. "I've seen her run the 40 [yard dash] with football players, and then the football players stopped running with her. I've seen her dunk a basketball. She's going to do things in track and field that only a few athletes have ever done."

OLYMPIC DISAPPOINTMENT. The upcoming 1996 Summer Olympics in Atlanta, Georgia, made Jones think about her love for running track. "I tried to tune out track and field; that was the easiest way to get through it for me," she revealed to *Sports Illustrated*. "But the love never died. Every time there was a national championship or some other big meet, I'd remember what it was like, and I'd miss being at that level. I was envious. I knew I could be there."

Jones decided to sit out the 1995–96 basketball season in order to train for the Olympics. "Getting a chance to compete in the Olympic Games, especially those Games being contested in the United States, is a chance of a lifetime," she explained to the *Los Angeles Times*. "I want to give my best shot to making the U.S. track and field team, and I don't want to ever regret not giving it my best."

Jones's Olympic dream came to a crashing end in August 1995. She broke her foot during a practice for the World University Games basketball team. Jones then again broke the same foot—bending the screw that had been inserted to help the break heal—when working out on a trampoline in December of the same year. She could not recover in time to try out for the American Olympic team.

BACK TO NORTH CAROLINA. During the season that Jones missed, the North Carolina women's basketball team struggled to a 13-14 record and missed the NCAA tournament. Jones returned to basketball for the 1996–97 season and helped return North Carolina to the elite of women's college basketball. She averaged 18.8 points, 4.7 rebounds, 4.3 assists, and an ACC-leading 3.2 steals.

The biggest contribution Jones made to the Tar Heels was her leadership. "It's unbelievable how big a factor Marion is," her teammate, Jessica Gaspar, told *USA Today*. "The person she is, the way she speaks, she wants to take that leadership. We missed it a lot. A lot tried to step up and be leaders last year. It was hard." Jones finished as one of the five finalists for the Naismith Award—given annually to the top women's collegiate basketball player—and the Associated Press named her to their All-America third team.

North Carolina earned a number-one seed in the 1997 NCAA Women's Basketball Tournament, but were upset by George Washington University, 55-46, in the East Regional semifinals. "We had some good looks at the basket, but it goes back to putting the basketball in," Jones, who finished with only 10 points, explained to the *Los Angeles Times*. The Tar Heels finished the season at 29-3.

TRACK FULL TIME. In 1997 Jones graduated from North Carolina with a degree in communications. Having earned her degree, she decided to give up her final year of basketball eligibility. In three years at North Carolina Jones averaged 16.8 points, scored 1,716 total points, pulled down 469 rebounds, had 334 steals, and dished out 403 assists.

During Jones's career the Tar Heels finished with a 92-10 record, and each season she played the team won the ACC Tournament. Jones started for North Carolina for three seasons and never missed a game. "Marion plays with such confidence, such leadership," North Carolina coach Sylvia Hatchell told the *Atlanta Journal and Constitution.* "She just spreads that to the rest of the team. She has such a presence with her leadership and confidence and the fact that she can make the big play. Not just defensively, but offensively as well."

With her college basketball career over, Jones decided to train seriously for track. "Track is my life now," she told *USA Today.* "Of course, if you asked me a couple of months ago, I would have said basketball." Jones began working with coach Trevor Graham, a sprinter from Jamaica who won a silver medal in the 4 x 100 relay at the 1988 Summer Olympics in Seoul, South Korea. Graham improved her mechanics—incredibly important in an 11-second race where one small mistake can be the difference between victory and defeat—and encouraged her to stick to a diet without junk food.

After a few workouts Jones broke the 11-second barrier in the 100-meter dash for the first time in her career. His new pupil impressed Graham. "She's self-motivated, the hardest-working girl I've ever coached," he explained to *USA Today.* "She picks up things so fast. I can move on with Marion very fast. I think that's what she likes. I've got so much stuff to show her that it's not boring."

Jones enjoyed being able to concentrate only on track. "For the first time, I got the chance to focus on one thing in my life," she revealed to the *Los Angeles Times.* "For the past four years, I've had school, I've had basketball, and I've had track and field. For the first time, over the past 16 weeks, I've had only one thing to concentrate on and try to be successful in. In high school, I did both sports and, when I got to college, I thought I could do both sports and be successful. But at this level, I now know that a lot more training is involved. I didn't want to give up basketball, but last year watching the Olympics on television really motivated me to get back to my first true love."

Superstar

NATIONAL CHAMP. The 1997 U.S. Track and Field Championships were held at the campus of Indiana University-Purdue University in Indianapolis, Indiana. Jones entered the national championships—her first since 1992—as a longshot to win any events. In the 100-meter dash she had to face two-time defending Olympic champion Gail Devers, and the long jump had been dominated for several years by Jackie Joyner-Kersee, perhaps the greatest female athlete ever.

The competition did not discourage Jones. She set a personal best time of 10.92 in the semifinal heat of the 100-meter dash. Only seven American women had ever run faster, and Jones's time was the best by a woman in 1997.

Suddenly Jones became the favorite to win the national championship when Devers had to withdraw from the competition with a calf injury. Despite running into a headwind, Jones won the final in a time of 10.97. She was so far ahead of the other runners that she slowed down with 10 meters to go and cruised across the finish line.

Jones did not stop with one victory. She also defeated Joyner-Kersee—the seven-time defending U.S. national long jump champion—with a leap of 22 feet 9 inches. The jump was one inch longer than the best Joyner-Kersee could produce. The winning jump by Jones was the longest, at the time, by a woman in 1997.

WORLD CHAMPIONSHIPS. The 1997 World Track and Field Championships were held in Athens, Greece. Entering the world championships Jones had four of the six fastest times of the year in the 100 meters, including the second-fastest time of 10.90. (Devers had the fastest time of 10.89.) She also had the fourth longest long jump of the year.

Jones also had a chance to do something no woman had ever done: win the 100-meter dash, long jump, and the 4 x 100 meter relay at the world championships. In order to be successful she knew she had to stay focused. "There's always chaos at big meets," Jones explained to *Sports Illustrated.* "Whoever handles the chaos wins."

FASTEST WOMAN. The main competition for Jones in the 100 meters was 37-year-old veteran sprinter Merlene Ottey of Jamaica. She had won four silver medals at the world championships and had earned 33 medals in international competition. Because of her injury at the U.S. Track and Field Championships, Devers did not qualify to compete in the world championships.

The women's 100-meter finals got off to a rough start. The runners took their marks, the gun sounded, and the athletes exploded down the track. Then there was a second shot, signifying a false start. Ottey did not hear the second shot right away and ran 60 meters down the track.

It took nearly three minutes for the runners to prepare to start the race again. Jones tried not to let the delay bother her, bouncing in her lane. "I don't think it had any significance in my race," she revealed to the *Los Angeles Times.*

The second start of the race was clean, and Jones took an early lead. Twenty meters from the finish her stride began to break down and her arms swung wildly at the side of her body. "I felt myself decelerating [slowing down]," Jones explained in *USA Today.* "That wasn't the best part of my race, but I gained so much at the beginning it helped at the end." Jones and Zhanna Pintusevich of the Ukraine crossed the finish line at practically the same time. Pintusevich began to celebrate for photographers, thinking she had won the race.

Jones knew differently, however, and coolly walked around the track. When the official results were posted, she was the world champion. "I thought I had it on the lean, but with the celebrating she did, I had my doubts," Jones revealed in the *Los Angeles Times*. "But then I looked over to the stands and saw some of my American teammates with their thumbs up. That was when I found out I had captured the gold."

The winning time of 10.83 posted by Jones was the best in the world in 1997. "I always dreamed I could do it; I always knew I would," she told *USA Today*. "I didn't know when. But at this time last year, I didn't think I'd be here talking about my first victory at the World Championships." Pintusevich finished second with a time of 10.85 seconds.

SECOND GOLD. Jones still had two more events to compete in after her victory in the 100 meters. She finished tenth in the long jump with a leap of 21 feet 9 inches. "I couldn't get my steps right," Jones confessed in *USA Today* after fouling on her first two jumps. Liudmila Galkina of Russia won the gold medal with a jump of 23 feet 13/4 inches.

Jones's last chance to win a second gold medal came as a member of the U.S. 4 x 100 meter relay team. (During the 4 x 100 competition, each team has four runners, each running 100 meters.) The U.S. squad—made up of Jones, Devers, Inger Miller, and Chryste Gaines—blew away the competition. The Americans won the gold medal with a time of 41.47 seconds, the second fastest time ever. (The world record of 41.37 was set by East Germany in 1985.) "This team will break the world record," Jones boasted in *Sports Illustrated*. "It's too good not to."

Despite her two world championship gold medals, Jones knew she could still improve. "I'm disappointed I'm not leaving with three gold medals," she confessed to the *Los Angeles Times*. "I'll take the two, [but] I've got so far to go in the long jump. I don't feel I've even scraped the surface in terms of what I can do."

THE FUTURE. After her world championship performance in track, Jones admitted she has considered returning to her other love: basketball. She has thought about playing in one of the two new women's professional leagues in the U.S.—the Women's National Basketball Association (WNBA) or the American Basketball League (ABL). "I'm going to sit back and see how the leagues do," Jones explained to the *Los Angeles Times.* "Maybe way, way down the road, I'll perhaps venture back to my other love. But right now I'm definitely focused on running."

Jones plans to continue to participate in track through the 2000 Summer Olympics in Sydney, Australia. She wants to win four gold medals at the 1999 World Track and Field Championships in Seville, Spain—the 100 meters, 200 meters, the long jump, and the 4 x 100 meter relay. The legendary Jesse Owens and Carl Lewis both accomplished this feat at the Olympics (Owens in 1936 and Lewis in 1984), but no woman has ever won these four events in one year at either the world championships or the Olympics.

OFF THE TRACK. Jones's boyfriend—C. J. Hunter—is a shotputter. "None of this matters if you're not happy in life with yourself and the people around you," she revealed to *USA Today.* "That's what C. J. provides." Hunter won a bronze medal in the shot put at the 1997 World Track and Field Championships.

Jones has very simple goals for her future in track and field, as she told *Sports Illustrated:* "I want to run very, very fast, and I want to jump very, very far."

WHERE TO WRITE:
C/O U.S.A. TRACK & FIELD,
ONE HOOSIER DOME, SUITE 140,
INDIANAPOLIS, IN 46225.

Sources

Atlanta Journal and Constitution, March 2, 1997; March 3, 1997; June 16, 1997; August 4, 1997; August 10, 1997.

MARION IS THE NAME

Jones's performance at the world championships led experts to begin comparing her to the greatest track and field athlete in American history, Carl Lewis. The comparison flatters Jones, but she wants to make a name for herself. "It's a great comparison," she admitted to the *Los Angeles Times.* "But my name is Marion Jones, not Carl Lewis."

International Herald Tribune, August 4, 1997.

Los Angeles Sentinel, May 26, 1994; May 24, 1995.

Los Angeles Times, September 13, 1995; January 10, 1996; March 23, 1997; August 2, 1997; August 4, 1997; August 10, 1997.

Newsday, February 4, 1997.

Sports Illustrated, August 2, 1993; June 23, 1997; August 11, 1997; August 18, 1997.

Sports Illustrated for Kids, November 1994.

USA Today, March 11, 1997; April 25, 1997; July 31, 1997; August 4, 1997; August 11, 1997.

Additional information provided by the University of North Carolina.

Hilary Lindh

1969–

Skier Hilary Lindh has been moving fast her entire life. She first put on a pair of skis when she was two and has been going downhill ever since. In 1992 Lindh won a silver medal in the downhill race at the Winter Olympics in Albertville, France. In 1996 she earned a bronze medal in the downhill at the World Alpine Ski Championships and then—in a surprise finish—won the gold medal in the same event in 1997. Giving up another chance to ski for Olympic gold, Lindh retired in 1997 as one of the most decorated American female skiers.

"[You] have to have the dream you're going to be the best in the world."
—Hilary Lindh.

Growing Up

JUNEAU'S GOLDEN GIRL. Hilary Lindh was born May 10, 1969, in Juneau, Alaska. She grew up as the only child of Craig and Barbara Lindh in the state's capital city. Juneau is located between a mountain range and an ocean channel. The only way to reach the city is by boat, helicopter, or plane.

Lindh's grandparents moved to Alaska in 1956, three years before the territory became a state.

Lindh had one goal as a child. "I knew I wanted to be famous," she recalled in *Sports Illustrated for Kids*. "But I didn't know if it was going to be in a sport or if I would write books or be a research scientist."

HITS THE SLOPES. Lindh put on her first pair of skis at the age of two and began racing at seven. There were not any mountains around her home with chairlifts. Lindh had to hike a thousand feet up a trail to get to one little tow rope that pulled her on her skis up to the top of the mountain. Lindh also cross-country skied, played soccer, baseball, and basketball, and ran cross-country as a child.

Growing up in Alaska, Lindh was unfamiliar with the world of skiing. "I used to dream about going to the Olympics and winning a gold medal," she revealed in the *Christian Science Monitor.* "I had no idea what that meant, but I thought that would be pretty cool. There was a long learning process I guess in even finding out what it entailed because I had no idea there was anything like World Cup racing. We were pretty secluded up in Alaska, we didn't have access to that like most kids."

LEAVES HOME. When she was 14 Lindh decided to leave home in order to find better competition than that available in Alaska. She moved to the Rowmark Ski Academy in Park City, Utah, which is near the headquarters of the U.S. Ski Association. Lindh attended high school there and lived with a family in the area. Her own family supported her decision because they wanted her to be the best skier she could be.

The decision to leave home paid off. Lindh began skiing in both junior and senior level races, and in 1986—at the age of 16—she won the downhill race at the World Junior Championships. (The downhill is the sport's fastest race. It requires the skier to travel down the mountain at great speeds and involves fewer turns than other ski races.) Lindh's rapid rise was slowed when she damaged cartilage in her right knee in 1987 and missed two months of skiing.

NATIONAL TEAM. In 1988 Lindh began competing on the World Cup circuit. The World Cup circuit includes ski races held throughout the world; only the best skiers compete. In her first downhill—at Zinal, Switzerland—Lindh finished tenth.

Lindh qualified for the U.S. Olympic team that would compete at the 1988 Winter Olympics in Calgary, Alberta, Canada. Her best result at the games was a twenty-third place finish in the Alpine Combined event. (The Alpine Combined requires each competitor to ski a downhill and slalom race.) Her first Olympic experience was valuable for Lindh, because she learned that she would have to improve to do well in Olympic competition. "It was just a matter of being determined," she explained to *Sports Illustrated for Kids.*

SILVER STAR. Lindh is a shy person and being a part of the national team was hard on her. She did not feel like she fit in with such a large group of people. "It was hard to get attention," Lindh revealed to *Sports Illustrated.* "Not that I wanted special treatment, but I wanted recognition from the coach. I wanted some connection, for the coaches to know I was alive."

The United States women's team struggled in the downhill. From the years 1988 to 1991 no American woman finished the World Cup season ranked higher than twentieth. Lindh continued to compete and earned a position on the United States team for the 1992 Winter Olympics in Albertville, France.

Lindh worked hard to ignore the distractions that went along with the Olympics. She tried to concentrate on her skiing, because the course did not favor her style of skiing. Lindh's strength is her ability to glide, an important skill best suited for smooth, straight courses. The Olympic course, however, was full of bumps and twists and turns.

When her time to ski came, Lindh made the most of it. She tore down the course and when she crossed the finish line her time was good enough for the silver medal, .06 seconds out of first place. Lindh was the first American woman to finish second in the downhill in more than 20 years. "I'd wanted to win an Olympic medal since I was 10 years old," Lindh told *Women's Sports and Fitness.*

CAREER TAKES OFF. Winning an Olympic silver medal gave Lindh increased confidence. "The medal gave me credibility," she explained to *USA Today.* "I always believed in myself before, but I hadn't had a breakthrough. Now I believe I can be on the podium [finishing in the top three in a race], and I can sense other people believe that about me, too."

Lindh finished in the top 15 in five races in late 1992 and early 1993, but then tore the lateral collateral ligament in her knee in a fall in Haus, Austria. The injury occurred in the same knee Lindh had hurt in 1987. "I fell right in the thick of things," she told *USA Today.* "If I had continued the season, I felt like I would have been on the podium."

Lindh returned from her injury to begin the 1993–94 season. She finished first in the downhill at Sierra Nevada, Spain—the last downhill race before the 1994 Winter Olympics—to capture her first World Cup victory. Lindh skied the long course in a winning time of 2 minutes, 4.21 seconds, .01 seconds ahead of second-place Melane Suchet of France.

The victory was the first in the downhill for an American woman in eight years on the World Cup circuit. Lindh wanted to use the victory as a springboard to the Olympics. "I'm heading into the Olympics skiing the best that I can," she explained to *USA Today.* "The fact that I've won a World Cup race only adds to my confidence. It gives me a good feeling. I know that in any given race, I can win."

Lindh did not want expectations to be too high for her performance at the 1994 Winter Olympics in Lillehammer, Norway. "I think it's going to be pretty stressful," she told *USA Today*. "From the moment I won the silver medal, people said, 'All right, get a gold next time.' But it doesn't work that way. There aren't a lot of people who have won medals at consecutive Olympics."

TEAMMATES AND RIVALS. During the 1992–93 season a new American ski talent burst on the World Cup scene. Picabo Street became the best female skier on the team while Lindh was out with an injury. For the next three years the two teammates became fierce rivals, on the slopes and off.

Lindh's second Olympic performance was not as successful as her first. She finished seventh in the downhill at the 1994 Winter Olympics. "The Olympics are so tense, it's incredible," she confessed to *Sports Illustrated*. "I remember being in the starting gate. I could hear my heart beating. I could feel it in my throat. And I didn't like feeling that way." Street finished second in the race and her outgoing personality made her an immediate star in the United States.

BEST SEASON. The two teammates continued to battle on the World Cup circuit. During the 1993–94 season Lindh finished fifth in the final World Cup standings while Street came in eighth. Lindh began the 1994–95 World Cup season fast, winning the first downhill race at Vail, Colorado, with a time of 1:45. "When Hilary came in with that time, it was like she had dropped a bomb," Street's coach, Chris Hanna, told *Sports Illustrated*.

Lindh followed up her season-opening victory with a second-place finish in her next race, at Lake Louise, Alberta, Canada. She finished .76 of a second behind Street. The one-

DANGEROUS SPORT

The downhill is one of the most dangerous events in sports. The skiers achieve high speeds and often race on icy courses. A serious accident is always a possibility and skiers have died during races.

Lindh won her first World Cup race just four days after Austrian star Ulrike Maier died after breaking her neck in a downhill race in Germany. When an accident happens, other skiers think about their competitors and their families. "We were all thinking about Ulrike and about her daughter," Lindh explained to *USA Today*. "But you have to separate your thoughts about that and the race. If you're thinking about that, you risk an injury. Ulrike's accident was freaky. We all know it can happen. Fortunately, it doesn't happen very often."

MOTHER EARTH AND PLANET HOLLYWOOD

The relationship between Lindh and her teammate Picabo Street has been stormy over the years. The two skiers are very different. Journalist Charlie Meyers of the *Denver Post* gave the two skiers nicknames: Mother Earth (Lindh) and Planet Hollywood (Street).

Lindh is quiet and shy, while Street is outgoing and has attracted a great deal of media attention. Lindh does not like to be called shy. "I hate being characterized as the strong, silent type," she admitted to *Sports Illustrated*. "When I was younger, people said I was shy, but that was because I didn't make small talk. I'm not silent in personal situations. But I've always disliked people who are overbearing, people who have to make an impression by being loud. I'm not loud or boisterous, and I think that's a good thing. I want to be worthy of respect because I excel at what I do. Classy. That's how I want to be defined. A class act."

Other experts have commented that Street is a natural talent while Lindh has had to work hard to succeed.

two finish marked the first time American women had accomplished this feat since Holly Flanders and Cindy Nelson turned the trick in 1982 at Arosa, Switzerland.

Lindh's hot streak continued the next day. She won the downhill race on the same course, giving Americans three straight World Cup downhill victories. The victory was Lindh's third career win, tying her with Holly Flanders, Cindy Nelson, and Bill Johnson for most World Cup downhill wins by an American skier.

By the end of the 1994–95 season, Lindh and Street stood atop the World Cup downhill standings. Street took the title after winning five straight races and six overall. Lindh

Lindh likes to be known for her hard work. "I don't think anyone reaches the international competition level without natural talent," she explained to *Women's Sports and Fitness.* "Besides, what's wrong with hard work? I do work hard, and so does everyone on the team. I want my skiing to speak for itself."

The differences between the two athletes are not important as long as they both succeed in winning. "If anyone can talk herself into a result, it's Picabo, and if anyone can work her way into a result, it's Hilary," Diann Roffe-Steinrotter, television commentator and former Olympic skiing gold medalist, told *Sports Illustrated.* "When push comes to shove, Hilary always lays down a good run. She's serious, and she produces for her country. She's not the most exciting personality, but then this is about winning."

Even though the two athletes are not friends, Lindh says they learned to get along. "I would say we are not close friends," she admitted to the *Juneau Empire,* "but we are on friendly terms and we wish the best for each other, and that's all there is to it. I have a lot of respect for her."

was right behind her teammate, finishing second in the standings after winning two races. The teammate's combined eight victories was one more than the total for American women since the World Cup series began in 1967.

Lindh felt that the competition between herself and Street was good for both of the American skiers. "We're pushing each other," she explained to *Women's Sports and Fitness.* "We have a really competitive group. Everybody wants to be the best, so the intense competition is great for the whole team, not just the two of us."

STRUGGLES ON THE SLOPES. Street repeated as World Cup downhill champion during the 1995–1996 season and won the downhill at the 1996 World Alpine Ski Championships in Spain. Lindh won a bronze medal in the same race, her best result of the year.

Lindh was disappointed with her 1995–96 season. "I guess you could say it's been character building," she explained to *Skiing*. The 1996–97 season also started badly for Lindh. Bulging disks in her back caused her great pain, and her coach, Ernst Hager, quit. In her first two races, she finished thirty-second and twenty-third.

The season was tough, too, for the American team. Street injured her knee in December 1996 and missed the rest of the year. Leading up to the world championships no United States skier—male or female—had won a medal in a World Cup event. "It was frustrating watching us not ski well, and it's sometimes tough to understand why that happens," Lindh told *USA Today*.

Her injuries and poor performances made Lindh consider retiring. "I thought last year, after winning a [bronze] medal at the worlds, that I could quit and feel good about it, but it didn't work out that way," she admitted to *Sports Illustrated*. "Considering how this season started, sometimes all that kept me going was that this [world championship] could be it."

Superstar

TENTHS OF A SECOND. Lindh's performances improved as the 1996–97 season went on. She finished ninth and fourth in the final two downhill events before the world championships. Lindh arrived at the World Alpine Ski Championships—held in 1997 in Sestriere, Italy—full of confidence.

In her final practice run before the world championship downhill final, Lindh turned in a great run. She finished second to Katja Seizinger of Germany and sent a message to the rest of the field. "She terrorized the Europeans with that run," Paul Major, U.S. skiing official, explained to *Sports Illustrated*. "You could see it in their eyes. Just when they think we're not a factor—and having seen what we've done this season, we weren't a factor—we show up."

WORLD CHAMPION. The sun came out just before Lindh's turn to ski in the final event. She was ready to go when her time came. "Before the race, I was getting more and more up for it," Lindh revealed to the *Juneau Empire*. "I was so ready to go, I was in the lodge just shaking I was so excited."

Lindh blistered down the course, and her gliding ability enabled her to maintain her speed all the way to the bottom. When she looked up at her time—1 minute, 41.18 seconds—she realized she had beaten Seizinger—then in first place—by .57 seconds. Now Lindh had to wait to see if her time would hold up.

Heidi Zurbriggen of Switzerland had a chance to snatch victory from the American. As Zurbriggen crossed the finish line, however, she was .06 seconds behind Lindh—the same amount of time by which Lindh had lost the gold medal at the 1992 Winter Olympics.

When the final skier finished, Lindh was still in first place, making her the world champion. Her margin of victory was hard for the winner to imagine. "You can hardly conceive [think of] anything that takes that long—six one-hundreths [of a second]," Lindh explained in *Sports Illustrated*. "You think about how such a little time can make such a big difference in your life."

Lindh looked at her victory as the highlight of her career. "I was amazed at the difference between a gold and the other colors," she revealed to *USA Today*. "It was a huge difference. It was incredible. People ask me if I ever thought in my wildest dreams I could do it. Of course, I did. That's why I kept skiing. To ski as long as I have, you have to have the dream you're going to be the best in the world. I think it's funny that people continue to be surprised when I do well at a major race. This isn't the first time this has happened. But some people just don't get it. I may not be the [typical] champion ski racer in terms of having won a lot of World Cup races. But what I've done deserves respect."

With her victory, Lindh captured the only medal of the world championships for the American team. "In the United States, the only thing that matters is the big events—winning the worlds or the Olympics is the only way you get recognition," she explained to the *Juneau Empire*. "That automatically makes us have that as our bigger goal."

OFF THE SLOPES. Lindh lives in Park City, Utah. She likes to read and go camping and hiking. Lindh plans to finish her college degree in biology at the University of Utah now that her skiing career is over. "Aside from education being important to my parents and grandparents, I personally care a lot about it," she told the *Chrisitan Science Monitor*. "I don't like to feel unproductive and I like to exercise my brain a little. Also, I'm obviously fairly goal-oriented, so there's always something I want to learn more about or improve. Basically, I get bored if I don't have some kind of challenge."

In a surprise move, Lindh announced the end of her 13-year career in March 1997, only a year before the Winter Olympics in Nagono, Japan. "[The decision] has to come from inside me," she explained to the *Christian Science Monitor*. "I can't decide to ski for somebody else. It has to come from the heart. I think you just get to the point where finally your priorities change. It's not that I don't love ski racing anymore, but there are so many other things I want to do. The most exciting thing is not knowing exactly what those things are."

WHERE TO WRITE:
C/O U.S. SKI ASSOCIATION,
P.O. BOX 100,
PARK CITY, UT 84060.

Sources

Christian Science Monitor, March 18, 1997.
Juneau Empire, February 15, 1997; February 20, 1997; March 13, 1997; March 21, 1997.
Los Angeles Times, February 19, 1997; March 14, 1997; March 21, 1997.
Salt Lake Tribune, February 16, 1997.
Skiing, October 1996.
USA Today, January 14, 1994; February 3, 1994; February 25, 1997.
Women's Sports and Fitness, January-February 1996.
Additional information provided by the U.S. Ski Team.

Curtis Martin

1973–

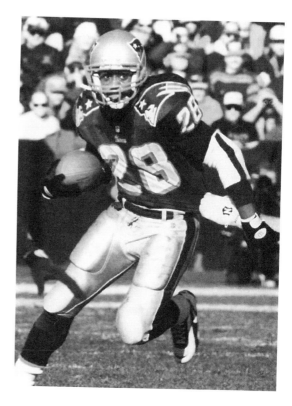

Running back Curtis Martin of the New England Patriots has been running his entire life. Growing up, he had to run from the crime and drugs that ravaged his neighborhood. At the University of Pittsburgh Martin had to convince the critics who doubted his ability. In his first National Football League (NFL) season, the rookie running back led the American Football Conference (AFC) in rushing, despite the fact that his coach called him a "one-game wonder." After three seasons, Martin has nothing left to prove and runs only from opposing defensive players.

> "No matter how many times I run the ball, I don't want to get tired."
> —Curtis Martin.

Growing Up

SURVIVING. Curtis Martin was born May 1, 1973. His parents' names are Rochella and Curtis Sr. Martin grew up in the tough Homewood and Wilkinsburg sections of Pittsburgh. His grandmother—Eleanor Johnson—was murdered in the family home when Martin was in fourth grade.

The entire family lived in fear for two years until Martin was able to identify the killer at the police station. "They showed me pictures of all these different guys and asked me if any of them looked familiar," he recalled in *Sports Illustrated.* "I didn't really recognize any of them, but just to give them something, I pointed at this one guy and said, 'I think I've seen him.' They investigated, and it turned out this guy was the killer. Looking back, that's how I know God was looking out for me."

LIVING ON THE EDGE. Martin hung out at clubs as a teenager. Several of his friends were killed and many times he was in the wrong place at the wrong time. "I'm basically a good person, but just from being in the wrong place at the wrong time, I came real close to dying," Martin explained to *Sports Illustrated.* "So many of my friends have gotten killed, and my best friend, Jamont Harris, [was shot] our senior year [of high school] and died. We played football together in high school—he was the quarterback—and some guy mistook him for another guy."

Gangs ruled Martin's neighborhood, and he tried to resist joining them. "Back then, being around guys who were dopers and gangbangers, I ran scared, for sure," he admitted to the *Atlanta Journal-Constitution.* "If you knew where I came from and what I've been through, you'd be amazed that I survived."

NEW FAITH. Martin claims that the only thing that turned his life around was when he became a devout Christian. "I've seen a lot of things, shootings, people getting killed, one of my family members got killed," he explained to the *New Pittsburgh Courier.* "I know I've been in situations where it could've been me. I have never been the type of person who would go to church. I always had my little relationship with God. I thought that was good enough. But it just so happened I went [to church] one day and the preacher just touched me by what he was saying. It seemed like everything he was saying was related to my life."

RUNNING FROM TROUBLE. Martin loved football as a child and sneaked into Three Rivers Stadium to see his favorite team—the Pittsburgh Steelers of the NFL. Despite his allegiance to the Steelers, Martin's favorite player starred for one of their arch-rivals, the Dallas Cowboys. He admired Tony Dorsett, the Hall-of-Fame running back who won the Heisman Trophy at the University of Pittsburgh before going on to play with the Cowboys. Martin also was a fan of Walter Payton of the Chicago Bears, the NFL's all-time leading rusher.

Despite his love for the game, Martin played only one season of football at Allderdice High School. He became an instant sensation. Martin ran for 1,705 yards on 229 carries (7.4 yard average) and scored 20 touchdowns. Four times he rushed for over 200 yards in a game. Martin made the All-State first team and both the *Pittsburgh Post-Gazette* and the *Pittsburgh Press* named him the City League Player of the Year.

PANTHER PICK. When it came time to choose a college, Martin decided to stay home and attend the University of Pittsburgh. Pittsburgh coach Johnny Majors also coached Dorsett during the great running back's glory years. "[Martin] has some of Tony's natural elusiveness," Majors told the *Atlanta Journal-Constitution.*

Martin filled in for injured starting tailback Jermaine Williams as a freshman during the 1991 season. He gained 556 yards on 114 carries, an average of 4.9 yards per carry, and caught 20 passes for 179 yards. In a game against the University of Minnesota, Martin gained 170 yards on the ground. He had an even better year in his sophomore season, gaining 727 rushing yards.

The rookie ball carrier displayed the ability to quickly hit the hole in the offensive line and showed great determination, often refusing to be tackled. "Curtis is a perfect role model for a running back," Skip Peete, his running back coach at Pittsburgh, said. "If you want to observe the way a

Martin runs the football down the field during the Patriots playoff game against the Jacksonville Jaguars.

player is supposed to practice, Curtis is the one you want to watch. Every time he steps onto the field, he only knows one speed—and that is full speed."

SUCCESS AND DISAPPOINTMENT. During the off-season before his junior season Martin participated in a rigorous conditioning program. The extra work paid off as he earned the starting tailback job and had a breakout season in 1993. Martin rushed for a career-best 1,075 yards and averaged 5.1 yards per carry. In a game against Syracuse, he ran for 206 yards. Martin also caught 33 passes for 249 yards. He accounted for 47 percent of the Panthers' offense.

Many publications selected Martin as a member of their preseason All-American teams before his final year at Pittsburgh, and he was a candidate for the Doak Walker Award, given annually to the best collegiate running back. He insisted he was not interested in individual awards. "The main thing I hope for is for the team to do well," Martin claimed in the *New Pittsburgh Courier*. "I am more of a team player. I'm not the type of person who will look out for myself only. I have always been the type of person who would look out for others before I look out for myself."

Martin ran for a career-best 251 yards in the opening game of his senior season (1994) against the University of Texas. Disaster struck in the Panthers' second game, however, when he severely sprained his ankle against Ohio University. The injury forced Martin to miss the rest of the season.

PITTSBURGH TO PATRIOTS. Martin now had a decision to make. He could have returned to Pittsburgh for one more year, but he made up his mind to enter the 1995 NFL Draft. The New England Patriots used a third-round pick (seventy-fourth overall) to choose Martin. He was the tenth running back selected in the draft behind such stars as Heisman Trophy winner Rashaan Salaam from the University of Colorado and Ki-Jana Carter from Penn State.

Martin impressed his new coach—Bill Parcells—in the preseason. He gained 190 yards on 52 carries. The rookie also displayed breakaway speed and proved that he was difficult to tackle. Parcells had led the New York Giants to two Super Bowl titles by emphasizing a strong running game and powerful defense. "My goal when I came in was just to make the team," Martin revealed to *USA Today.* "I felt that if I didn't hold anything back and stayed healthy, everything would take care of itself."

FAST START. Parcells made Martin his starting running back for the team's opening game of the 1995 season, against the Cleveland Browns. The Browns tried to intimidate the rookie, but their tactics did not work. "We hit him with everything we had—stuff about his family," Cleveland defensive end Rob Burnett admitted in *Sports Illustrated.* "We tried to get him mad, but he wouldn't respond, and that's no fun. After a while it's like talking to a wall." Martin responded to the Browns' defenders by saying "God Bless You" and pulling off another great run.

The Patriots trailed 14-9 with only 24 seconds left in the game. New England had the ball on the Cleveland one-yard line and quarterback Drew Bledsoe handed off to Martin. Three Cleveland defenders hit him in the air, but he stretched and placed the ball over the goal line. "I just tried to soak it all in," Martin told *Sports Illustrated* after the game. "It seems like this stuff only happens in movies."

Martin celebrated wildly, pumping his fist in the air. New England won the game 17-14 and Martin finished with 102 yards on 19 carries in his first professional game. His performance included a 30-yard burst off tackle on his first carry in a regular-season game.

ONE-GAME WONDER. Parcells played down Martin's big first game, calling him a "one-game wonder" after he rushed for just 186 yards in the next five games. The rookie tried not to let his struggles get him down. "I tried to turn that comment into a positive motivation," Martin explained. "When he called me a one-game wonder, my thoughts were, 'I'm going to try to make myself a two-game wonder, a three-game wonder, a four-game wonder.' Hopefully, I did."

Martin broke out with 127 yards in a 27-14 win over the Buffalo Bills and two games later rushed for 166 yards and two touchdowns in New England's 20-7 victory over the New York Jets. "We're getting a feel for each other," Martin said, referring to his offensive line. "I'm starting to read the blocks a lot better. I'm learning the way the fullback blocks a lot better."

ALL-PRO. Martin finished his first season with an AFC-leading 1,487 yards rushing—the fourth most ever by a rookie—and a Patriots' record 14 touchdowns. Nine times he rushed for over 100 yards in a game. The Associated Press named him the 1995 NFL Offensive Rookie of the Year and the *Sporting News* named him NFL Rookie of the Year. His fellow NFL players elected him to the Pro Bowl all-star game, the only rookie so honored. "His best attribute is his tremendous stamina," Parcells said. "He seems to enjoy the competition and the workload. He's playing with a little more confidence than he was at the beginning of the year."

ROOKIE RUSHERS

In 1995 Martin produced the fourth most rushing yardage for a rookie in NFL history. The following chart lists the all-time rookie rushers, the year of their first season, and how many rushing yards they gained:

Eric Dickerson	1983	1,808
George Rogers	1981	1,674
Ottis Anderson	1979	1,605
Curtis Martin	1995	1,487
Barry Sanders	1989	1,470

Superstar

SUPER SEASON. Martin gained fewer yards (1,152, fifth in the AFC) and had 53 fewer carries in 1996 than in his rookie season, but he developed into a better all-around player, improving his receiving and blocking skills. He led the AFC with 17 touchdowns (14 rushing, 3 receiving). Martin became only the second back in New England history to rush for more than 1,000 yards in consecutive seasons. (Jim Nance accomplished this feat in 1966 and 1967.)

More importantly, Martin was part of a winning team in 1996. New England won 11 games and captured the AFC East Division title. "[Last year] we won six games," Martin explained to *Sports Illustrated.* "I couldn't be happier."

AFC CHAMPS. In the first round of the playoffs the Patriots faced his hometown team, the Pittsburgh Steelers. On the day of the game a thick fog shrouded Foxboro Stadium. Cutting through the fog like a knife, Martin ran for 166 yards and 3 touchdowns in a 28-3 New England victory. "Everything went my way, and it was just one of those days when, even if I did something wrong, the results ended up right," Martin told the *Atlanta Journal-Constitution.* "Sometimes there's no accounting for a series of [events] that ends up in a day like this one."

Martin set team playoff records for points (18), rushing yards (166), and longest touchdown run (78 yards). "That might be my longest run ever," Martin declared in the *Detroit Free Press.* "College, Pop Warner, everything. To me, the Steelers are my second-favorite team. I kind of worry about when I go home, how infamous I'll be." Martin's scoring runs covered 2, 23, and 78 yards.

New England welcomed the visiting Jacksonville Jaguars to Foxboro Stadium for the AFC Championship Game. The Patriots were rude hosts, whipping the upstart Jaguars 20-6. Martin gained only 59 yards on 19 carries and scored a touchdown. For the second time in franchise history New England had advanced to the Super Bowl.

SUPER STRUGGLE. The Green Bay Packers stood between the Patriots and the NFL championship. The Super Bowl was held in the Louisiana Superdome, but the story before the game was the future of Parcells. Rumors swirled that Parcells would leave the Patriots and agree to coach the New York Jets during the 1997 season.

New England played a valiant game, but came up short in the Super Bowl. The Packers captured a 35-21 victory, with the big play being a Super Bowl-record 99-yard kickoff return by Desmond Howard. Martin gained 42 yards rushing in the loss, and scored on an 18-yard scamper, setting a New England career record with 5 postseason touchdowns. The loss extended the losing streak for the AFC in the championship game to 13 games.

SOLID SEASON. Parcells did leave the Patriots to coach the Jets following the Super Bowl. Pete Carroll took over as head coach, and he relied on Martin to carry the load for his offense. In an early season matchup with Parcells and the Jets, Martin set a team record with 40 carries. He gained 199 yards and scored a touchdown in the Patriots' 27-24 overtime victory.

"Curtis Martin played just a phenomenal game," Carroll told *USA Today.* "From start to finish, he was in control. He never looked to come out. He never hesitated at any call we made. He would have carried it 50 times if we needed him to."

For the 1997 season Martin rushed for 1,160 yards— becoming the first running back in franchise history to rush for 1,000 yards in three straight seasons—and scored 4 touchdowns. He also caught 41 passes for another 296 yards and one score. New England repeated as AFC East Division champions, despite the fact that their superstar running back missed the final three games of the regular season with a separated shoulder.

Just as he was recovering from his shoulder injury, Martin suffered a groin strain that forced him to miss New England's 17-3 playoff victory over the Miami Dolphins. In the next round the Patriots traveled to Martin's hometown of Pittsburgh to play the Steelers. "I'm just looking forward to somehow, someway—miraculous or whatever it must be—to play in that game," Martin related to *USA Today* in the days leading up to the game. Unfortunately, the injury kept him on the sidelines as New England lost a low-scoring contest, 7-6.

OFF THE FIELD. Martin has a daughter named Diamond. He is friends with rappers Dr. Dre and Snoop Doggy Dog, and his cousin is rapper Sam Sneed. Martin majored in public administration at Pittsburgh.

Martin is very religious, reads the Bible every day, and leads prayer meetings for his teammates. His favorite passage from the Bible is Deuteronomy Chapter 28: "The enemies who rise up against you will be defeated before you. They will come at you in one direction but flee from you in seven."

Although he carries the ball a lot, Martin always wants to run more. "I feel I shouldn't get tired," he revealed to *USA Today*. "That's my goal. No matter how many times I run the ball, I don't want to get tired."

WHERE TO WRITE:
C/O NEW ENGLAND PATRIOTS, FOXBORO STADIUM,
60 WASHINGTON ST.,
FOXBORO, MA 02035-1388.

Sources

Atlanta Journal-Constitution, January 6, 1997; January 8, 1997.
Detroit Free Press, January 6, 1997.
Los Angeles Times, November 25, 1996; November 7, 1997.
New Pittsburgh Courier, August 27, 1994; December 20, 1995.
Newsday, January 4, 1998.
Sports Illustrated, September 11, 1995; January 13, 1997.
Sports Illustrated for Kids, December 1, 1996.
USA Today, December 29, 1995; September 16, 1997; December 29, 1997.
Additional information provided by the Gannett News Service, the University of Pittsburgh, and the New England Patriots.

Tino Martinez

1967–

Tino Martinez—the slugging first baseman of the New York Yankees—believes in hard work. As a child he tore a hole in the backyard fence by hitting baseballs off a tee in an effort to perfect his swing. The hard work paid off as Martinez has established himself as one of the most feared hitters in major league baseball—first with the Seattle Mariners and then with the New York Yankees. In 1997 he arrived as a superstar, producing the best numbers of his career and finishing second in the balloting for American League Most Valuable Player. Despite his success, Martinez remembers the lessons he learned from his father, the hardest working man he ever knew.

"I've always believed that the answer to your problems is working harder."
—Tino Martinez.

Growing Up

FAMILY BUSINESS. Constantino Martinez was born December 7, 1967, in Tampa, Florida. He was the second of three sons of Rene and Sylvia Martinez. Sylvia Martinez was a school teacher and her husband was the general manager at the Villazon Cigar Company, a business owned by the Martinez family. Martinez's great, great grandparents came to the United States from Spain.

During summer and Christmas vacations Martinez and his brothers worked at unloading 100-pound crates of tobacco with their father. The warehouse was extremely hot and the work was hard. Working with his father taught Martinez a valuable lesson. "It was Dad's way of telling me what hard work is all about," he explained in *Sports Illustrated.* "He never came right out and said it, but his message was, Stay in school, work hard and do something with yourself or else you could be unloading tobacco your whole life. Working in the factory wasn't exactly something that my brothers and I looked forward to, but we learned from it. It taught me to work hard as a player."

HARD WORKER. All of the Martinez boys—Tino and his brothers Rene Jr. and Tony—played baseball. Martinez began practicing hitting by himself in his backyard when he was 13. He hit a ball off the tee, something he did so many times that he tore a hole in the fence. "Every day, year round," his older brother, Rene Jr., recalled in *Sports Illustrated.* "When the hole opened up in the fence, he covered it with a net and kept going. If he was bored and had nothing to do, he'd go back to the tee and hit."

Martinez knew he would have to work in order to succeed. "The only way I thought I'd be able to make it is if I kept practicing hitting," he explained in *Newsday.* "I had to hit. I'm not fast, and I don't have a great arm."

Rene Martinez Sr.—an all-county center on the Jefferson High School football team—forbade his son from playing football because he was afraid his son would get hurt. He sponsored, coached, and watched his son's baseball teams.

Martinez wore number 23 in honor of his two favorite players—second baseman Ryne Sandberg of the Chicago Cubs and first baseman Don Mattingly of the New York Yankees.

TAMPA TERROR. Martinez starred at Tampa Catholic and Jefferson High School. He led Tampa Catholic to the Florida State Championship in 1982 and helped Jefferson High School reach the finals in 1985. "Tino was always on time, he got good grades and the girls loved him," his coach at Jefferson High, Pop Cuestal, told *Newsday*.

Martinez continued his baseball career after his high-school graduation, playing for the University of Tampa. He earned Division II All-American honors three times and set school career records for batting average (.398), home runs (54), and RBI (222). Martinez also earned academic All-American honors. "He's a perfectionist within himself," his manager at Tampa, Kenny Dominguez, declared in *Newsday*.

In 1988 Martinez played for the U.S. team that won the gold medal at the Summer Olympics in Seoul, South Korea. He hit 2 home runs and had 4 RBI in a 5-3 gold-medal-winning game against Japan. "I don't know how anything can top this," Martinez admitted to *Sports Illustrated*. He also earned most valuable player honors at the World Amateur Baseball Championships in Parma, Italy, by hitting .413, with 4 home runs and 18 RBI. Martinez was a finalist for the Golden Spikes Award, given to the best college baseball player in the United States.

MARINERS AND MARTINEZ. The Seattle Mariners selected Martinez with the fourteenth overall pick in the 1988 amateur baseball draft. In his first professional season—in 1989 with Williamsport of the Eastern League—he batted .257 with 13 home runs and 64 RBI. The young first baseman also displayed a solid glove, leading the league first basemen in fielding percentage (.995), putouts (1,260), assists (81), total chances (1,348), and double plays (106).

The next year (1990) Martinez had a break-out year. Playing for the Calgary (Alberta, Canada) Cannons he hit .320, with 17 home runs and 92 RBI. *USA Today* named Mar-

Martinez keeps his eye on the ball as he scores his one-hundredth RBI.

tinez the Minor League Player of the Year. The Mariners called him up to the big league squad late in the season and Martinez played in his first major-league game on August 22, 1990 against the Texas Rangers. He batted .221 in 24 games in his first stint with Seattle.

HARD TIMES. Martinez suffered a great loss when his father died on January 4, 1990, from a brain tumor at the age of 48. "[I] didn't have the motivation to go and practice," Martinez explained in *Newsday*. "Although I knew he [his father] would have wanted me to play, it was still hard to get up and to work out, to try and get myself going."

Martinez especially missed talking with his father during a batting slump. "Go back to the basics," his dad would tell him, according to *Sports Illustrated*. "Are you hitting enough off the tee? Are you taking extra batting practice?"

On the field, Martinez was stuck in the Mariners' minor league system. Seattle already had two fine first basemen—Pete O'Brien and Alvin Davis—on the major league team. Martinez began the 1991 season back in Calgary, and again he dominated. He earned recognition as the Pacific Coast League Most Valuable Player after hitting .326 and scoring 94 runs.

Playing in the minors frustrated Martinez. "It's hard watching guys I've played with go up and play, and I don't get a chance," he admitted in *Sports Illustrated*. "But what good would complaining do? When I was sent down this spring, I knew I had to put up good numbers again. I didn't want to hit .200 and have people think last year [1990] was a fluke. The toughest part is no one has told me anything about their plans. I've been left in the dark."

MAJOR LEAGUER. Martinez rejoined the Mariners on August 22, 1991, and this time he was there to stay. He made the team in spring training in 1992 and put together a solid rookie year. Martinez played 136 games, hit .257, knocked 16 home runs, and drove in 66 runs.

The next two years Martinez developed into a solid—yet unspectacular—major league ballplayer. His 1993 season was cut short when he tore the a ligament in his left knee and missed the final 50 games of the season. Martinez underwent surgery and returned for the 1994 campaign at full strength. Unfortunately, the season was cut short by a player strike, caused by a disagreement between players and baseball team owners. Martinez had hit 20 home runs in 97 games when baseball shut down.

BREAK-OUT YEAR. Martinez was happy when Lou Piniella became manager of the Mariners in 1993. Piniella and his father had grown up together and had been fishing buddies in Tampa. "I've known his family since I was a young kid myself," Piniella told *USA Today.* "I grew up on the same block on St. Conrad Street with his dad, Rene. We played sandlot ball together. Then his dad became a real good football player. When I was 13, we moved to Cordelia Street, where I lived right across a playground from his mother, Sylvia. I've known 'em forever."

Through the 1994 season Martinez was a .254 hitter with only 57 home runs and 201 RBI. Both the Mariners and their first baseman were ready for a break-out season in 1995. Martinez batted in an order that included American League batting champion Edgar Martinez, slugger Jay Buhner, and superstar center fielder Ken Griffey Jr.

The Mariners won the American League West Division title in 1995—their first in 19 years of existence—and Martinez was a big reason. He set career bests in several offensive categories, including average (.293), hits (152), home runs (31), and RBI (111, fifth in the American League). Martinez broke the team record for home runs by a first baseman of 29 set by Alvin Davis in 1987. American League manager Cito Gaston of the Toronto Blue Jays named him as a reserve to his first All-Star Game, and he singled in one pinch-hit at-bat.

REFUSE TO LOSE. In the Division Series the Mariners faced the New York Yankees. Seattle lost the first two games at Yankee Stadium. They now would have to sweep all three games at home in the Kingdome (the Mariners' home field) to win the series. In game three Martinez hit a two-run homer and drove in another run in a 7-4 Mariner win. The fans in the Kingdome carried signs that read "Refuse to Lose."

Seattle also won game four, 11-8, and then won the series with an exciting 6-5, 11-inning victory in game five. Martinez batted .409 with 5 RBI and one home run in the series. The Mariners then lost the American League Championship series to the Cleveland Indians in 6 games, but the 1995 season was the best in franchise history. "I was happy to be a part of the team that finally got [the Mariners] over the hump and into the playoffs," Martinez told *Newsday*.

YANKEE BOUND. Despite their playoff success, the Mariners decided they needed to save money. Martinez was due a big raise after his All-Star season in 1995, and he expected Seattle to trade him. "When we knew we were going to trade Tino, I asked him where he would like to go," Piniella explained in *USA Today*. "He said New York. That's a positive in itself. It takes a special person to be able to play in New York."

The Yankees showed interest because their longtime first baseman—Don Mattingly—had retired from baseball. Seattle traded Martinez and pitchers Jeff Nelson and Jim Mecir to New York for pitcher Sterling Hitchcock and third baseman Russ Davis. The Yankees signed their new first baseman to a five-year, $20 million contract. "I always rooted for the Yankees as a kid," Martinez revealed in *USA Today*. "Mattingly was my favorite player."

In honor of Mattingly—who wore number 23, the same as Martinez had on the Mariners—the newest Yankee decided to change his number to 24. "I wouldn't wear 23 if it was offered to me," Martinez explained to *Newsday*. "I have respect for him. Obviously he's one of the greatest Yankees ever. I'm interested to see what's going to happen here. I have no idea what to expect. All the people back home in Tampa are Yankee fans. They knew somebody had to come in and be the first baseman so they're excited I got the chance. It's an honor to be the next guy after Mattingly. I can't replace Don Mattingly. I can only play like I'm capable of and put up numbers like I'm capable of. Don Mattingly was a great ballplayer. He brings a lot of leadership and experience to a team. I hope I can bring that to this team."

DON MATTINGLY

First baseman Don Mattingly played 14 seasons with the New York Yankees. He batted .307 during his career with 222 home runs and 1099 RBI. In 1984 Mattingly won the American League batting championship with a .343 average and in 1985 he earned American League Most Valuable Player honors with a .324 average, 35 home runs, and 145 RBI. Mattingly was one of the best fielding first basemen ever and won nine consecutive Gold Glove Awards (1985–94). The Yankees honored their longtime captain in 1997 by placing a plaque with his likeness with those of other great New York players in the center field area of Yankee Stadium.

FIRST SERIES

Martinez attended his first World Series in 1981 when the New York Yankees faced the Los Angles Dodgers. His father received tickets from his childhood friend, Lou Piniella, then an outfielder with the Yankees. Martinez, his father, and his two brothers traveled to the Bronx for the first two games of the Series. The Yankees won both games, then lost four straight in Los Angeles to lose the Series. They did not play another World Series game until 1996 with Martinez starting at first base for New York.

REPLACING A LEGEND. New York fans loved Don Mattingly and felt that he had been treated unfairly by Yankee owner George Steinbrenner. The fans at Yankee Stadium took out their frustrations on Martinez, booing him on Opening Day. "I knew they were booing me because they wanted Mattingly," he confessed to *Newsday*. "I wasn't surprised or disappointed. I totally understood."

Replacing Mattingly was difficult for Martinez. He hit only .196 in the first three weeks of the season. "I tried to impress people right away," Martinez admitted to *Sports Illustrated*. "I swung too hard. I was over-anxious. It wasn't because I was replacing Mattingly. I wanted to show my teammates what I could do and live up to the contract. Every day I drove to the park thinking, 'This is the day I'm going to get four hits.'"

Mattingly himself had a talk with Martinez and told him to relax and play his game. Martinez finally broke out of his slump with back-to-back game-winning home runs. He finished the season with a .292 average, 25 home runs, and a team-high 117 RBI. Martinez's RBI total was the most for a Yankee first baseman since Mattingly had 145 in 1985. Martinez also led American League first basemen in fielding percentage (.996).

BENCHED. The Yankees won the 1996 American League East Division title. They then defeated both the Texas Rangers and Baltimore Orioles to reach the World Series for the first time since 1981. There the Yankees would take on the National League champion Atlanta Braves.

The day-in-day-out grind of playing for the Yankees took its toll on Martinez. By the end of the regular season he was exhausted. The big first baseman slumped and lost his power swing. Martinez was not a factor in New York's winning the American League pennant. He did not have an RBI against either the Rangers or Orioles and was batting only .205 through game two of the World Series.

When the World Series moved to Atlanta for games three, four, and five Yankee manager Joe Torre had to make a decision. He had to bench either Martinez or slugger Cecil Fielder—who had been acquired earlier in the year from the Detroit Tigers and had been playing at designated hitter. During the World Series, the designated hitter is not used at the home field of the National League team.

Fielder had come up with several big hits in the playoffs, so Martinez sat on the bench. "I think Tino has been putting a lot of pressure on himself, and Cecil has been swinging the bat really well," Torre said. "I still feel very loyal to Tino, but you're at a point now where you talk to Tino and he understands."

The decision was hard for Martinez to deal with. "I was hurt," he admitted to *Sports Illustrated.* "Deeply hurt. I had busted my butt day in and day out and never asked for a day off all year. I was definitely mad. But I kept it to myself. I walked back to my locker and, after a minute, told myself, 'O.K., be ready to come off the bench. You don't want to come in and do something bad because you weren't ready to play.' I never have talked to Joe about it." Martinez finished the Series one for eleven, but New York won the championship in six games.

Superstar

SOMETHING TO PROVE. Martinez came into the 1997 season wanting to show that his poor performance in the World Series was a fluke. "He didn't have the Series he wanted to have," former Yankee star outfielder and Hall of Fame member Reggie Jackson told *Newsday.* "I know he was upset. Over the winter, he set his mind to proving to people he was better than he showed."

Martinez usually started slowly—hitting only .240 during his career in April—but that all changed in 1997. He began the season hot and stayed that way. Martinez set a major-league record with 34 RBI in April. (Barry Bonds of the San Francisco Giants set the previous record in 1996 with 32 RBI.) He also became the first player to reach 40 RBI in his team's first 30 games since Roy Campanella of the Brooklyn Dodgers in 1953. Martinez also became only the third Yankee—joining Babe Ruth and Mickey Mantle—to hit 15 home runs in the club's first 40 games, hitting 16 in that time span.

At one point in May, Martinez led the major leagues in RBI, was tied with Ken Griffey Jr. for the major-league lead in home runs, and was batting .350. "Honestly, I haven't done anything different this year," Martinez admitted to *USA Today*. "I had the best spring training of my career. I was locked in. I got my swing down, my mechanics down. I was feeling great and I knew I had a chance to start fast. It just carried over to the season. The only thing I can say is that I'm seeing the ball real well. I think I'm picking up pitches a lot quicker. As soon as it comes out of the hand of the pitcher, I can pretty much tell if it is a curve or fastball. I'm able to lay off nasty pitches down out of the strike zone."

His early home run barrage had some experts discussing whether Martinez might be able to challenge the record of 61 set by Yankee outfielder Roger Maris in 1961. "Obviously, I'm not going to hit 60 home runs," he declared to the *Sporting News*. "That's ridiculous. I'm not that kind of hitter. I consider myself a run-producer, an RBI guy, more than a home run hitter or someone who's going to win a batting title. And I'm just lucky right now that I'm swinging the bat well while there've been runners in scoring position."

MVP RUNNER-UP. Martinez could not keep up his torrid early pace for the entire season, but he did produce the best numbers of his career. He finished the year with a .296 average, 44 home runs, and 141 RBI. "The work ethic Tino has is that two hits are never enough and three RBIs are never enough," Torre told *Sports Illustrated*. "That's what makes for great years." Martinez finished second in the voting for American League Most Valuable Player behind his former teammate, Ken Griffey Jr.

The Yankees could not repeat their playoff magic of 1996. They finished the 1997 season in second place in the American League East Division behind the Baltimore Orioles, but qualified for the post-season as the wild card team. New York faced the Cleveland Indians in the Division Series. The series was close, but the Indians ended the Yankees dream of repeating with a five-game victory. "It's tough," Martinez admitted to *Newsday*. "We had quite a few opportunities."

OFF THE FIELD. Martinez lives in Tenafly, New Jersey, with his wife, Marie, and his three children, Olivia, Tino Jr., and Victoria. The Yankees now train one mile from Martinez's boyhood home in Tampa, and the field at Jefferson High School is now named after Martinez's father.

Martinez works hard on his game. He continues to hit off a tee before batting practice begins, fields extra practice ground balls, and lifts weights four times a week. "I've always believed that the answer to your problems is working harder," Martinez explained to *Sports Illustrated*. "In the end, even if the numbers aren't there, at least I'll know I worked hard. It's a lesson I learned from my father. No one worked harder than he did."

Martinez loves to play in Yankee Stadium. "It's a great place to hit," he told *USA Today*. "I see the ball well here. There's a good hitting background. There is a lot of space for line drives in left-center. I try to hit line drives. And if you hit the ball to the right, you have a chance to hit a home run."

The Yankee slugger looks forward to many more accomplishments in his career. "I'm happy with where I'm at, but I will not be content or satisfied," Martinez declared to *USA Today*. "I want to win another World Series. There are many more things I want to do."

WHERE TO WRITE:

C/O NEW YORK YANKEES, YANKEE STADIUM,
161ST ST. & RIVER AVE.,
BRONX, NY 10451.

Sources

Los Angeles Times, October 23, 1996.

Newsday, October 8, 1995; October 10, 1995; October 15, 1995; December 6, 1995; December 8, 1995; February 3, 1996; March 31, 1996; October 14, 1996; October 16, 1996; October 17, 1996; October 23, 1996; May 11, 1997; October 7, 1997.

New York Daily News, December 7, 1995.

Sporting News, June 2, 1997.

Sports Illustrated, October 10, 1988; July 22, 1991; February 5, 1996; June 9, 1997.

USA Today, May 12, 1997; May 21, 1997.

Additional information provided by the Gannett News Service and the New York Yankees.

Mark McGwire

1963–

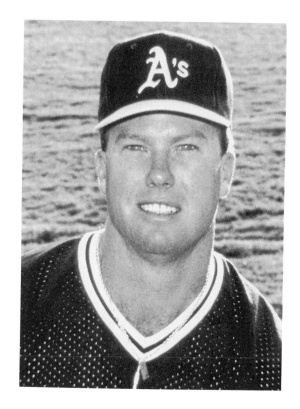

M ark McGwire, the hard-slugging first baseman of the St. Louis Cardinals, put his name into the record books in 1997 with one of the greatest home-run-hitting displays ever. He hit 58 home runs, which tied the record for the most ever hit by a right-handed hitter and represented the most in the major leagues since Roger Maris of the Yankees set the record with 61 in 1961. In addition, McGwire joined the legendary Babe Ruth as the only player to hit more than 50 home runs in each of two consecutive seasons. McGwire has been one of the most feared hitters in the game since he hit 49 home runs as a rookie in 1987.

"I think hitting a home run is the hardest thing to do in sports. You just have to see the ball, hit the ball, take it from there."
—Mark McGwire.

Growing Up

BIG FAMILY. Mark David McGwire was born October 1, 1963. He was the second of five sons of John McGwire, a dentist, and his wife Ginger. All five McGwire boys grew to at least 6 feet 5 inches and weighed more than 210 pounds.

Dan McGwire starred at quarterback for the University of Iowa and played with the Seattle Seahawks and Miami Dolphins of the National Football League.

John McGwire suffered from polio as a child. (Polio is a disease that attacks the central nervous system.) The disease forced him to spend seven months in bed. Even after he recovered, he walked with a limp and had to wear a leg brace. Despite his disease, John McGwire learned how to play golf and box and once rode a bicycle from San Francisco to Santa Barbara, California, a distance of over 300 miles. He did not neglect his studies, either, becoming a dentist.

LOVES GOLF. McGwire grew up in a comfortable and loving home in Claremont, California. "I had a middle-class upbringing," he explained to *Sports Illustrated.* "I was always just a basic athlete, nothing extraordinary. But I was a hard worker. And I liked to do a lot of that work where people couldn't see me. I'd throw balls against a cement wall or set a ball on a tee and hit it."

McGwire's first love in sports was golf. He actually quit playing baseball at one point to concentrate on golf. "Golf was the first game I learned," McGwire recalled in *Sports Illustrated.* "My dad taught me how to grip a club when I was five, and I never had another lesson. But I won some tournaments, and in my junior year in high school I quit baseball to work on my golf game. The thing I liked about golf was that you were the only one there to blame when something went wrong. I missed baseball, though, and I went back to it." In addition to golf and baseball, McGwire also played soccer.

MAKES HIS PITCH. McGwire began playing Little League baseball at the age of eight. He hit a home run in his first at-bat and then set a Claremont Little League record with 13 home runs at the age of ten. In addition to playing first base,

McGwire was the ace pitcher of his team. By the time he reached high school he could throw the ball almost 90 miles per hour.

At Damien High School, McGwire pitched and played first base. His pitching impressed the Montreal Expos, who drafted McGwire in the eighth round of the major league baseball amateur draft. McGwire also received a scholarship offer to play for the University of Southern California (USC). Rather than turn professional, he decided to accept the offer to play for the Trojans.

TROJAN STAR. McGwire compiled a 4-4 record in his freshman season at USC with a 3.04 earned-run-average (ERA). He credits his coach, Rod Dedeaux, with helping him develop his game. "In college I started taking the game seriously," McGwire told *Sports Illustrated*. "My coach, Rod Dedeaux, was a strong influence on me, particularly in the mental aspects of the game. 'Don't make the same mistake once,' he'd say." During his freshman year McGwire met Kathy Hughes, a ballgirl for the team. The two married in 1984.

After his freshman season, McGwire traveled to Alaska to play in a summer league. Southern California assistant coach Ron Vaughn decided to use the practice time in Alaska to test out McGwire's ability to play first base. Vaughn saw that his young player could be a great hitter. "I had seen him hit in high school and practice," Vaughn explained in *Sports Illustrated*. "I couldn't see wasting him on the mound."

McGwire returned to USC and proved that Vaughn was correct. He hit .319 in his sophomore season and broke the school record for home runs with 19. (The previous record was 17.) In addition to his hitting heroics, McGwire led USC with a 2.78 ERA and earned a 3-1 record. "I still say Mark has a major league arm," Dedeaux told *Sports Illustrated*.

SETS SCHOOL MARKS. In his junior year McGwire gave up pitching completely. Concentrating solely on his hitting, he shattered his own single-season home run record with 32 round-trippers, batted .387, scored 75 runs (tying the USC

McGwire shows his powerful home run swing.

single-season record), and knocked in 80 runs in only 67 games. The American Association of College Baseball Coaches named him to their first team All-America squad.

During his three seasons at USC McGwire set school and Pacific-10 Conference career records with 52 home runs. He also set USC records for runs-batted-in or RBI (150) and most total bases in a career (369) and in a season (216). U.S.A. Baseball made him a unanimous choice for the 1984 U.S. Olympic Baseball team that would play in the first-ever

Olympic competition. McGwire helped lead the United States to the gold medal.

TURNS PRO. The Oakland Athletics (A's) drafted McGwire in the first round (tenth pick overall) of the 1984 amateur baseball draft. He quickly worked his way through the minors, hitting .298 and averaging 24 homers and 109 RBI in two full seasons. McGwire did struggle in the field, because the A's wanted to convert him to third base. In one season McGwire made 41 errors playing the hot corner.

McGwire got his first taste of the big leagues in 1986, coming up to the A's late in the season. He got his first hit on August 24, 1986, against Tommy John of the New York Yankees, and the next day he hit his first career major league home run against the Detroit Tigers. During his first stint with Oakland, McGwire batted only .189 with three home runs, while making six errors in the field.

ROOKIE SLUGGER. McGwire struggled to make Oakland's big league roster in 1987. He managed to make the team as a reserve infielder, but got off to a slow start, hitting only .187 early in the year. It was April 20 before he got his first start at first base, and his season took off from there. By the time the All-Star break arrived, McGwire had hit 33 home runs, the first rookie to ever hit over 30 round-trippers by that point in the season. He also became the only rookie to hit 5 home runs over the course of two games. McGwire earned selection to the American League All-Star team.

McGwire's fast start began baseball experts talking about whether he could break the single-season home run record of 61 set by Roger Maris of the New York Yankees in 1961. The media pressure on McGwire was intense. "It really took a toll on me," he admitted to *Sports Illustrated*. "I never wanted to be in the public eye. All I want away from the ballpark is to be with my family and friends, but I can't even go into a restaurant now without being bothered. And everybody knows me as Mark McGwire the baseball player. I don't want to be just the baseball player. I want to be myself."

ROOKIE OF THE YEAR. The rookie slugger's home run production slowed down after the All-Star Game, but not by much. McGwire finished the season with a major-league-leading 49 home runs (tied with Andre Dawson of the Chicago Cubs), a new major league record for rookies. (The old record of 38 was set by Wally Berger of the Boston Braves in 1938 and tied by Frank Robinson of the Cincinnati Reds in 1956.) He hit .289, had 118 RBI (third in the American League), and led the majors with a .618 slugging percentage. McGwire became only the second player—Carlton Fisk of the Red Sox in 1972 being the other—to earn unanimous selection as American League Rookie of the Year.

McGwire had a chance to hit 50 home runs, but skipped the A's final game to go home for the birth of his first child, Matt. "I told myself that I'll have another shot at 50, but I'll never have another first child," he explained to the *Sporting News*. "I've never regretted it."

DYNASTY. The A's hung close to the Minnesota Twins in the American League West Division in 1987, but finished second to the eventual World Series champions. Over the next four years, however, Oakland dominated the West Division, winning the title each year. For three straight seasons (1988–90) the A's won the American League pennant, and in 1989 they won the World Series championship over their cross-bay rivals the San Francisco Giants.

McGwire teamed up with outfielder Jose Canseco to form the "Bash Brothers." They earned the nickname because of their ability to bash baseballs over the fences. McGwire continued to hit the ball hard with 32 home runs in 1988 (third in the American League) and 33 in 1989 (third in the American League). When he hit over 30 home runs again in 1990, McGwire became the first major league player to hit more than 30 round-trippers in his first four seasons. His improved defense won McGwire a Gold Glove Award for fielding excellence in 1990.

SLUMP. For the next four years (1991–94) McGwire struggled. There were several reasons for his slump. His family, which was very important to him, fell apart and he and his wife, Kathy, divorced. McGwire also started to feel the strain of a serious back injury.

McGwire hit rock bottom in 1991 when he batted a career-low .201 with only 22 home runs. His manager, Tony LaRussa, took him out of the lineup late in the season so that he would not hit under .200. The A's fell to fourth place, failing to win their division for the first time in five years.

His batting slump bothered McGwire. "How bad did it get?" he said in *Sports Illustrated*. "Well, for the first time, I disliked baseball. It was frustrating trying to climb out of a hole that got deeper and deeper. I started joking in the clubhouse that I was going to give up baseball to shoot pool for a living, or maybe, like some of my friends, become a policeman. I was joking, but there was an element of truth in what I was saying."

Watching the playoffs on television for the first time in four years affected McGwire. "I wasn't planning on watching the playoffs or the World Series, but I did," he explained in *Sports Illustrated*. "It hit me what I'd had. Sometimes you don't realize what you had until you see someone else in your place. Watching the playoffs and the Series got me pumped up."

HARD WORK. McGwire changed his approach to hitting following his horrible 1991 season. Hitting coach Doug Rader worked with his big slugger, trying to convince him to make adjustments at the plate. "Pitchers made adjustments to me, but I wasn't making adjustments to them," McGwire explained to *Sport*. "I didn't realize this game was mental until my terrible season in '91. Sometimes you get to a certain level and you think you don't have to work as hard. I'm not saying I didn't work: I'm saying I could have worked harder. But when you get distracted from what you love to do, failure usually follows." McGwire also started seeing a psychiatrist to help him work through both his on- and off-field problems.

In 1992 McGwire returned to form, hitting 42 home runs (second in the major leagues) and leading the major leagues by hitting a home run every 11.1 at-bats. He raised his average to .268 and led the American League in slugging percentage (.585). United Press International named him Comeback Player of the Year. Oakland returned to the playoffs, but lost to the eventual World Series champion Toronto Blue Jays in the American League Championship Series.

LONE SURVIVOR. Over the next four seasons McGwire missed 274 games due to back and foot injuries. He played only 27 games in 1993 and 47 in the strike-shortened 1994 season. Despite missing 33 games in 1995, McGwire still hit 39 home runs in only 317 at-bats, only the seventh player to hit more than 30 home runs with under 400 at-bats. He also tied a major-league record when he hit 5 home runs over the course of two games for the second time in his career. (Ralph Kiner of the Pittsburgh Pirates is the only other player to accomplish this feat, which he did in 1947.)

Oakland had a record of 264-318 in the three seasons following their last division title in 1992. LaRussa, his coaching staff, and several players, including relief ace Dennis Eckersley, left the A's following the 1995 season and went to the St. Louis Cardinals. When catcher Terry Steinbach signed a free-agent contract to play with the Minnesota Twins, McGwire was the last Oakland player left from the team's glory years.

Superstar

50 HOME RUN CLUB. McGwire enjoyed playing for new manager Art Howe and the group of young players that replaced his former teammates. "I'm having the best time of my career," he confessed in the *Sporting News*. "I love these young guys. The coaching staff is great. And that says a lot considering the teams I've been on."

The Oakland Coliseum—where McGwire had played his entire career—was one of the worst parks for home run hitting in the major leagues. The stadium was refurbished before the 1996 season to accommodate the Oakland Raiders football team. The changes made to the centerfield wall blocked the wind that had turned many a fly ball into a long out.

As a result, McGwire had the best season of his career so far in 1996. He hit 52 home runs—becoming only the fourteenth player to hit over 50 in one season—despite missing 30 games with injuries. His total was the most in the major leagues since George Foster of the Cincinnati Reds hit 52 in 1977, and the most in the American League since Roger Maris's record-breaking season in 1961. McGwire set a major league record by averaging a home run every 8.13 at-bats and became the first player to hit 50 home runs while playing fewer than 140 games.

In addition to his home run heroics, McGwire hit .312, 26 points better than his highest previous batting average, which he achieved in his rookie year. He led the majors in home runs, slugging percentage (.730), and on-base percentage (.467), only the tenth player in major league history to lead in all three of these categories. During one stretch of 162 games spanning the 1995 and 1996 seasons, McGwire hit 70 home runs.

RECORD BREAKER. Oakland reacquired fellow Bash Brother Jose Canseco prior to the 1997 season. Having Canseco back in the lineup helped McGwire, since other teams could not pitch around the big first baseman. McGwire started fast for the A's, hitting 11 home runs in April and 34 by July 16. Once again he was in position to challenge Maris's home run record.

Unfortunately, McGwire was the only bright spot for Oakland. Trade rumors swirled around the A's because McGwire was eligible to be a free-agent after the 1997 season and wanted to play for a winning team. Not knowing what would happen distracted the Oakland superstar, who hit only five home runs in July.

TO THE CARDS. The uncertainty ended on July 31—the major league trading deadline—when the A's traded McGwire to the St. Louis Cardinals for minor league pitchers T. J. Mathews, Eric Ludwick, and Brady Raggio. "Sometimes you get stuck in one place too long," McGwire told *USA Today.* "If you get a change, you get a second wind." At the time of the trade

McGwire held the Oakland franchise record for home runs in a season (52) and in a career (363).

McGwire—who had hit 34 home runs at the time of the trade—now had to adjust to a new league. (The Cardinals belong to the National League.) "You know what the biggest adjustment was?" he asked in *Sports Illustrated*. "It wasn't the pitchers. I told myself that I adjusted for pitchers in the American League, so there wasn't much change there. The biggest adjustment was the batter's boxes. Just standing in these different batter's boxes. Just feeling comfortable. It's all a question of feeling comfortable. That all goes into hitting."

The adjustment slowed down McGwire's home run pace. He had only one home run in the first ten days of August, and at one point he went 45 at-bats without a home run. Soon McGwire felt comfortable and returned to the form he showed earlier in the season. By the time September began he had 43 home runs.

McGwire felt his mid-season slump cost him a chance to break the single-season home run record. "I've always said—I've been saying it for 11 years now—that the only way anyone's going to hit 62 home runs is if he has at least 50 going into September," he explained in *Sports Illustrated*. "It would be just too difficult otherwise. You get close and you don't see many pitches to hit. Every pitcher just starts working on you every at-bat."

On September 16 McGwire signed a three-year, $28.5 million contract with St. Louis. That night he hit a 517-foot home run, the longest ever hit in Busch Stadium. On the last day of the season McGwire hit his fifty-eighth and final home run of the season.

MCGWIRE AND THE BABE. McGwire tied or set several home-run records in 1997. His 58 home runs tied the record for the most home runs ever hit by a right-handed hitter. (Jimmie Foxx of the Philadelphia Athletics hit 58 home runs in 1932 and Hank Greenberg of the Detroit Tigers matched that number in 1938.) McGwire became the only player other than Babe Ruth to hit more than 50 home runs in each of two consecutive seasons. (Ruth accomplished this feat twice, first with 54 in 1920 and 59 in 1921, then again with 60 in 1927 and 54 in 1928.) He also became the first player to hit 20 or more home runs in each league during one season and the first player to hit 20 or more home runs for two different teams in the same season.

BODY SHOP. McGwire has now taken his place as one of the greatest home-run hitters in major league history. If not for injuries, his statistics would be even more amazing. McGwire thought about giving up baseball in 1996 when he hurt his right heel. He rejected that idea when he thought about what his father had gone through. "My father had polio at age 7," McGwire told *Sport*. "He never had a chance to play sports when he was a kid. When I look at my father, it makes my injuries so [unimportant]."

OFF THE FIELD. McGwire is single and lives in Alamo, California. He maintains a close relationship with his son, Matt. "Everything I do in the game is for him," McGwire revealed in *Sport*. "We have such a great relationship. I could be away from him for a month or so and come back and it's like we just missed yesterday." When McGwire hit his fiftieth home run in 1996 he gave the ball to Matt.

McGwire likes going to comedy clubs and says that laughter is the best medicine. "The wonderful thing about

TWICE AS NICE

Only six players have hit over 50 home runs in a season more than once. The following chart list these players, the years they accomplished this feat, and how many home runs they hit each year.

Babe Ruth	1920 (54)
	1921 (59)
	1927 (60)
	1928 (54)
Jimmie Foxx	1932 (58)
	1938 (50)
Ralph Kiner	1947 (51)
	1949 (54)
Willie Mays	1955 (51)
	1965 (52)
Mickey Mantle	1956 (52)
	1961 (54)
Mark McGwire	1996 (52)
	1997 (58)

comedians is that they take some of our greatest fears and laugh them off," he explained to *Sports Illustrated*. "They make something funny out of some very serious stuff."

Despite playing baseball in front of thousands of fans, McGwire is a very shy person. "I was always the kind of kid who liked to sit in the back of the room and just blend in," he recalled in *Sports Illustrated*. McGwire still likes to golf and can hit the ball over 300 yards.

By signing with the Cardinals, McGwire passed up the chance to sign an even bigger contract with another team. He signed with St. Louis because he loved the city and the way the fans there support baseball. "I hope more players feel the way I feel," McGwire explained to the *Atlanta Journal-Constitution*. "Granted, there's a lot of money out there, and you've always thought of getting as much as you can because you don't know how long your career is going to last. But you know, if you're happy at a place, for you to take less dollars, well, I think the first and foremost thing in the game of baseball is you've got to be happy with yourself."

McGwire will donate $3 million of his salary to the Mark McGwire Foundation, a fund that assists abused children. "Let's just say children have a special place in my heart," he told the *Sporting News*. "It's a time in my life that I want to help them out." Because of his great season and his charitable work the *Sporting News* named McGwire the Sportsman of the Year for 1997.

McGwire realizes how hard his job can be. "I think hitting a home run is the hardest thing to do in sports," he admitted in *Sports Illustrated*. "Because you can't plan to hit a home run. You can't try. As soon as you try, you can't do it. You just have to see the ball, hit the ball, take it from there."

The game of baseball is still fun for McGwire. "When a round ball meets a round bat perfectly, there's just a feel . . . I don't know if anybody but a baseball player could relate to it," he told a television interviewer. "It's a game where millions of Americans would love to play and only a few get to the big leagues. We're so fortunate."

WHERE TO WRITE:
C/O ST. LOUIS CARDINALS, BUSCH STADIUM,
250 STADIUM PLAZA,
ST. LOUIS, MO 63102-1722.

Sources

Atlanta Journal-Constitution, September 21, 1997.
Los Angeles Times, September 29, 1997.
People Weekly, August 31, 1987.
Sport, April 1997.
Sporting News, August 5, 1996; September 2, 1996; September 29, 1997.
Sports Illustrated, July 13, 1987; September 14, 1987; July 4, 1988; August 4, 1988; August 27, 1990; September 30, 1991; April 27, 1992; June 1, 1992; June 19, 1995; August 26, 1996; September 29, 1997.
Sports Illustrated for Kids, May 1997.
USA Today, September 11, 1997; September 29, 1997.
Additional information provided by the University of Southern California and the St. Louis Cardinals.

Shirley Muldowney

1940–

Drag racing legend Shirley Muldowney has always lived life in the fast lane. During her career she has driven cars at speeds exceeding 250 miles per hour (MPH). Three times Muldowney captured the National Hot Rod Association (NHRA) Top Fuel world championship—the most by any driver, male or female—and won 17 NHRA races, the second-most in history. The most successful female driver in motor sports history, she returned to drag racing in 1996 and hopes to continue to be competitive in the sport she loves.

Growing Up

DADDY'S LITTLE GIRL. Shirley Muldowney was born as Shirley Roque on June 19, 1940, in Burlington, Vermont. She grew up in Schenectady, New York, with her father, Belgium, a taxicab driver and professional boxer, and mother, Mae, who worked in a laundry. Muldowney's childhood was uneventful. "I remember very little about my young years," Muldowney admitted in *Sports Illustrated*.

Belgium Roque—who fought under the name Tex Rock—taught his daughter to be tough. One day he gave Muldowney some advice after she came home complaining about bullies at school. "'You pick up a board, you pick up a pipe, you pick up a brick, and you part their hair with it,'" Mae Roque recalled her husband saying in *Sports Illustrated*. "There was no more coming home beat up. She went out and took care of herself. She was all thrilled."

FIRST LOVE. Muldowney never did well in school and at the age of 13 she began to skip classes. It was at this time that she began to date a boy named Jack Muldowney, who was two years older and interested in racing cars. "Jack was a member of a car group—I won't say gang—but a car club," Muldowney explained in the *Sporting News*. "I had eyes for Jack, and I wanted to be a part of this recreation. They would street race a bit, and that was how I got started."

Muldowney learned how to drive in her boyfriend's car and soon was racing on the streets of Schenectady, New York. She fondly remembers her first car. "My first car was a 1951 Mercury," she related to *Ms*. "All souped up, lots of carburetors—it was a street-racing machine. I raced on the back streets when the police weren't looking."

The young racer kept her activities a secret from her parents. "They didn't know I was doing it, but my dad was kind of a real outgoing guy," Muldowney admitted in the *Sporting News*. "I wouldn't describe him as a daredevil, but kind of an anything-goes sort. When he did find out about [the racing], he thought it was great."

BEGINS CAREER. Muldowney quit school in 1956—at the age of 16—and married Jack. (She returned to school eight years later to get her high school diploma.) With her husband as her mechanic, she began to earn a reputation for her racing skill. "Guys would come from Amsterdam, Glens Falls, Albany," Muldowney recalled in *Sports Illustrated*. "I'd race them, and when I'd turn around, they'd be going the other way. It was very satisfying. I'd say the first time I ever took my life in my own hands and got away with it was when I really appreciated what I was capable of."

In 1959—at the age of 19—Muldowney began racing professionally. Jack built and maintained the cars and led the pit crew. Drag racing—a one-on-one duel between two cars—became a professional sport in the early 1950s. The first National Hot Rod Association (NHRA) championship was held in 1955.

Spectators—many of whom did not believe women should be race drivers—booed Muldowney. "It was brutal, awful," she confessed to *USA Today*. "I can't imagine what the heck I was thinking about in the early days, but I wanted to [drive] so bad. And I had so much fun, I just overcame all the other stuff. When I started strappin' it on 'em, and I mean big-time stuff like top speed at the meet, No. 1 qualifier race after race, they knew I was there to stay."

The reaction of the fans was the least of Muldowney's problems. "I always knew this wouldn't be an easy profession," the 5 feet-4 inch, 108-pound driver admitted to the *New York Times*. "But the attitudes against me didn't bother me. Trying to hold on to a 1,700-pound car with a 2,000-horsepower engine is hard work, and anyone that says different is out of his mind."

TRAIL-BLAZER. Muldowney soon gained a national reputation as a talented driver. In 1965 she became the first woman to obtain a license from the NHRA to drive a gas-burning dragster in the Top Gas category. At one race Muldowney earned the nickname "Cha, Cha" when someone wrote it on her car in shoe polish.

Muldowney raced mostly in one-on-one competitions at small race tracks. Many times promoters invited her as a pub-

Muldowney waits at the starting line in her custom-built dragster.

licity stunt, but soon she proved she had real talent to defeat leading male drivers like Tommy Ivo, Gary Beck, and Larry Dixon in head-to-head duels. Muldowney won several regional titles in the early 1970s and appeared headed toward national stardom.

PARTNERSHIP ENDS. Just as her racing career was taking off Muldowney's personal life crumbled. She and Jack divorced in 1972, leaving her to raise their teenaged son, John, alone. Muldowney had difficulty devoting enough time to her racing.

In 1971 Muldowney moved to Armada, Michigan, and teamed up with a fellow racer, Conrad "Connie" Kalitta. The two traveled the country, often racing each other in "grudge match" Funny Car races. (A "funny car" is a fiberglass replica of an American street car, but with a dragster frame and engine.) Kalitta built and maintained both of their cars.

Muldowney captured the International Hot Rod Association (IHRA) Funny Car title at the 1971 Southern Nationals, in Rockingham, North Carolina. The next year she was the runner-up for the same title. Muldowney's career almost came to an end at the 1973 U.S. Nationals in Indianapolis, Indiana. Her dragster crashed, and she was left with second-degree burns on her face. The heat was so intense that Muldowney's eyelids melted shut. She spent several months in the hospital recovering from her injuries.

FRESH START. Drag racing went through major changes in the early 1970s. The cars used in the Top Gas category of racing were dangerous. The engines sat right in front of the driver, and often explosions caused serious injuries. Don "Big Daddy" Garlits—who lost part of his right foot in an explosion—designed new cars that had the engines behind the driver. Soon Top Fuel—as the new cars were called—replaced Top Gas dragsters on the NHRA circuit.

Muldowney resolved to return to racing following her recovery. She decided to become the first woman in Top Fuel racing. (Top-fuel dragsters are stiletto-shaped, 24-foot cars that rocket down quarter-mile strips in less than six seconds. They require strength and quick reflexes to control, as well as a parachute to slow down at the end of the race.) Muldowney's first full year of Top Fuel drag racing was 1974. She painted her car hot pink, her trademark color for the rest of her career.

At the 1974 U.S. Nationals, Muldowney reached a top-speed of 241.58 MPH, the second fastest time in the event. The next year she became the first female professional to reach the finals of an NHRA national event. Muldowney also became the first professional female driver to finish a race in under six seconds. The American Auto Racing Writers and Broadcasters Association named her to the 1975 Auto Racing All-America team.

In 1976 Muldowney continued to make history. She won the NHRA Spring Nationals, the first woman to win an NHRA national event in a professional category. Muldowney added a victory in the Winston World Finals and posted the best time (5.77 seconds) and speed (249.30 MPH) of the season. *Drag News* named her the "Top Fuel driver of the year."

Superstar

WORLD CHAMPION. Muldowney became the best drag racer in the world in 1977 by winning the Winston World Championship, a season-long competition. By winning three Top Fuel races in a row Muldowney became the first driver—male or female—to accomplish this feat. During one competition she broke the drag-racing speed record with a speed of 253.52 MPH. The U.S. House of Representatives presented Muldowney with an Outstanding Achievement Award.

Muldowney and Kalitta ended their personal and professional relationships in 1978. He returned to racing, and she became the captain of her team. Despite her success, Muldowney had a hard time finding a sponsor for her team after her split with Kalitta. Without a sponsor, Muldowney concentrated more on the better-paying match races and less on NHRA national events.

"I went after the [points] championship because I was sure it would bring me a big sponsor," she explained to the *New York Times*. "Well, it didn't happen. My sponsors said, do it one more time and we'll give you more money. That really changed my attitude. I broke my back [in 1977] to win, and now I feel like I'm starting all over from scratch. This year [1978] I simply can't afford to go for the championship."

BACK ON TOP. By 1980 Muldowney had earned enough money to win the Top Fuel Winston World Championship for the second time. She became the first driver in NHRA history to win the championship twice. Muldowney won four NHRA national events and had a 21-4 record in all her national events that season. In addition, she finished second in the

HEART LIKE A WHEEL

In 1983 a movie about Muldowney's life—*Heart Like a Wheel*—was released. Actress Bonnie Bedelia, who played Muldowney, earned a Golden Globe nomination for her performance. Beau Bridges co-starred as Connie Kalitta. Muldowney described the movie to *Ms.*: "I thought we would end up with a racing film. And I wouldn't have done it if I didn't think it was good for the sport. But not everyone is a racing enthusiast, so to tell a story that would touch many people, we had to tell more than a racing story. I think the movie does that very well."

American Hot Rod Association (AHRA) world championship. The next year (1981) Muldowney became the first woman to win that championship.

Muldowney repeated as the Top Fuel Winston World Champion in 1982. She captured four NHRA national events on her way to becoming the first driver to ever win this important championship three times. Muldowney got to the top by refusing to lose. "I mentally prepare myself by envisioning getting beat and how humiliating that is for me," she revealed to *Ms.* "I do not want to lose, either for myself, or for my crew—they work so hard to make me do as well as I do. I want to win to 'get even.' Call me anything you want, but winning says it all. A racer is a special breed of person."

HORRIBLE CRASH. Muldowney's career and life almost came to an end on June 29, 1984, at the Grand Nationals in Montreal, Quebec, Canada. Her front tire blew out and the debris caused her wheels to lock. The car crashed into the wall, flew 600 feet in the air, and disintegrated.

"I knew it took a left. It impacted head-on into an embankment, and I hit twice," she told the *Sporting News.* "I can't tell you where my legs went because I continued another 500 feet with just the cage over my head. It was broken off at the top of my legs. That was a rough ride."

The accident left Muldowney seriously injured. She suffered a severed right thumb, partially severed foot, fractured pelvis, three fractures between the ankle and knee of the right leg, compound fractures of both ankles, torn cartilage in her left knee, two broken fingers on her right hand, and neck injuries. "At first we couldn't find her because the car was destroyed," her crew chief, Rahn Tobler, explained to the *Detroit Free Press.* "When we finally got to her, she was in the roll cage, unconscious, with her head slumped down. Her thumb was off and she was covered with mud. I lifted her visor and she stirred and said, 'I'm hurt. I'm really hurt.'"

Doctors worked for 12 hours on the injured driver, cleaning her wounds, reattaching her thumb and foot, and setting her broken bones. "When I woke up in the intensive care unit," Muldowney recalled in *People,* "I hurt so bad I didn't care whether I'd make it or not."

Muldowney could not leave the hospital for four months. In the next year she underwent five additional operations. The driver's left ankle was fused—meaning she could not bend it—and her right leg was five-eighths of an inch shorter than her left. Doctors advised Muldowney to never race again. "I was crushed," she admitted to *People.* "I thought, 'My life is ruined.' People said, 'Oh, you're a fighter,' but when I was alone in bed at night, it was hard to deal with."

COMEBACK. Muldowney was too tough and competitive to give up the sport she loved. She worked hard at grueling therapy to get back on her feet. "Driving is a way of life for me, my bread and butter," she explained to *People.* "And I'm not interested in doing anything else right now. I wasn't ready to give up the cockpit. I was forced out of it. The accident took a lot out of me, but it didn't kill my will to win. Anybody who's counting me out is dreaming."

In October 1985 Muldowney announced she would be back in the driver's seat for the 1986 racing season. In her first qualifying run—at the Firebird International Raceway in January 1986—her parachute failed to open and she had to stop her car with her foot brakes. Despite this scare, Muldowney set a career-best time in 1986 of 5.42 seconds and drove her car over 267 MPH.

TEAMMATES. For most of her career Muldowney's main rival was the legendary "Big Daddy" Don Garlits. Garlits—the winningest driver in NHRA history with 35 national championships and 3 Winston world championships—kept track of his wins over Muldowney on the side of his trailer. "Somebody has got to stop Muldowney, and right now it looks like

ROLE MODEL

Shirley Muldowney has always been aware of her place as the most successful woman auto racer in history. She paints her car pink as a symbol to her female fans. "I would be a fool if I didn't paint the car pink," Muldowney confessed to *Sports Illustrated.* "The pink car stands out. The pink car is known. The women like it. Little girls love it; they come up to me and squeeze me around the legs. It's part of an image, that's all the color is. It's feminine. It's a girl's image."

More women have followed Muldowney into the sport, where speeds now exceed 300 MPH. Shelly Anderson won two NHRA events in 1996, and she gives credit to her role model. "Shirley was the one that helped women in all motor sports," Anderson explained to *USA Today.* "She made sponsors realize women could be successful."

I'm the only one standing between her and glory," Garlits once said, according to *Sports Illustrated.*

In 1989 Garlits—who had helped Muldowney financially after her accident in 1984—came out of retirement to serve as a special advisor for his one-time rival. "It is unbelievable," he confessed to *Sports Illustrated.* "If you had told me 10 years ago that I would be over here trying to make her go fast, I would have laughed. Laid on the ground and kicked my feet and laughed. At one time she was one of the best."

Garlits helped Muldowney win her last NHRA race, the 1989 Fall Nationals. She also appeared in the finals of several other national events that year. Though Muldowney continued to participate in match races, she would not win another NHRA race and entered semi-retirement.

RETURNS TO COMPETITION. In 1996—at the age of 57—Muldowney returned to competitive racing, this time on the IHRA circuit. She won three consecutive events, was the fastest driver on five separate occasions, and her top speed of 294.98 MPH set a new IHRA record. Muldowney finished second in the final IHRA points standings.

In October 1997 Muldowney returned to the NHRA, participating in a race at the Revell Nationals in Dallas, Texas. "I think it's great," fellow racer Joe Amato told *USA Today.* "She was always a fierce competitor. It's good for drag racing to have her back."

Muldowney was unsure whether she could gather enough funding to race full-time in the NHRA in 1998. The cost of racing a car for an entire season exceeds $1 million. "It still comes down to dollars and cents," Muldowney explained to *USA Today.* "How much do you want to spend? How fast do you want to go?"

OFF THE TRACK. Muldowney lives in Armada, Michigan. She married Rahn Tobler—her former crew chief—in the late 1980s. Muldowney likes to target shoot.

Muldowney is second all-time in NHRA history with 17 wins. In her later years she has become a fan favorite, even though she has not had competitive cars. "I enjoy a special situation," Muldowney told *USA Today.* "Ninety-nine percent of [drivers] can't do what I do because there is no demand for them. I'm able to drive the car and have fun, and people pay to see it. I'm in the show-business part of it now."

 WHERE TO WRITE:

79559 NORTH AVE.,
ARMADA, MI 48005.

Sources

Detroit Free Press, September 19, 1982; June 30, 1984; July 27, 1984; August 16, 1984; August 23, 1984; October 28, 1984; March 2, 1985; January 19, 1986.

Ms., October 1983.

New York Daily News, November 12, 1978.

New York Post, October 11, 1983.

New York Times, July 20, 1975; April 1, 1976; July 9, 1978; July 19, 1981; October 14, 1983.

People, September 16, 1985.

Sporting News, January 26, 1987.

Sports Illustrated, July 18, 1977; June 22, 1981; February 10, 1986; September 4, 1989.

USA Today, April 10, 1997; October 15, 1997.

Georghe Muresan

1971–

"I like [to] play basketball. I['ll] play until I can't play. . . ."
—Georghe Muresan.

Every person experiences what is called a growth spurt, a period of time when they grow rapidly. Some people grow taller than others, and some people, like center Georghe Muresan of the Washington Wizards, tower over everyone else. At seven feet seven inches tall, Muresan is the tallest player ever to take the court in the National Basketball Association (NBA). Showing that tall is not all, Muresan has developed his basketball skills to become one of the best men in professional basketball.

Growing Up

GROWING PAINS. Georghe (GHEE-yor-ghee-yay) Muresan was born on February 14 (Valentine's Day), 1971. He, and his three brothers and two sisters, grew up in Tritenii, a small town in the Romanian province of Transylvania. His father, Ispas, worked in a factory that made electrical wire.

250

Muresan was the family's youngest child, and quickly the tallest. No one else in his family is over six feet tall. Muresan's father is five feet, nine inches tall and his mother was five feet, seven inches. Muresan began his growth spurt when he was six and by the time he turned 10 he was taller than any of his family. By the time he turned 14, he was six feet nine inches tall. Clothes and shoes that fit were almost impossible to find. Muresan's nickname was Ghita (GEET-za), which means "Little George" in Romanian.

Muresan's extraordinary growth was caused by a tumor on his pituitary gland. The tumor caused this gland, which controls growth, to pump out too much growth hormone. Doctors call this disorder gigantism. Children with this disorder usually have the tumor removed early in life, but medical care was not available in Muresan's town.

TAKES UP BASKETBALL. Muresan did not play basketball as a child, despite his height. It took a trip to the dentist to get him on the court. "I never play[ed] basketball until I [was] 14 years old," Muresan recalled in *Sports Illustrated*. "I never know about basketball. My mother took me to Cluj to see the dentist. He was the dentist for the national basketball team. He looked at me and asked how tall I was. Then he asked how old I was. He did not believe I was 14. He called the coach of the basketball team, and they asked me to stay in Cluj and play basketball. I stayed that night. I never went home."

Muresan worked hard on his game, and by the time he turned 16 he had earned a spot on the Romanian national team. He studied the great basketball players of the NBA and developed a hook shot after seeing the legendary center Kareem Abdul-Jabbar play in an NBA All-Star Game.

LEAVES HOME. Romania was a Communist country ruled by the dictator Nicolae Ceausescu. (Communism is a govern-

---

SCOREBOARD

TALLEST PLAYER (7 FEET, 7 INCHES) TO EVER PLAY IN THE NBA.

TWICE LED NBA IN SHOOTING PERCENTAGE—.584 IN THE 1995–96 SEASON AND .604 IN THE 1996–97 SEASON.

WON NBA MOST IMPROVED PLAYER AWARD FOR 1995–96 SEASON.

MURESAN HAS DEVELOPED INTO A SOLID NBA CENTER, NOT JUST A BIG MAN IN THE MIDDLE.

mental system characterized by the common ownership of production means.) Life was hard for Muresan and his family. "No heat," he explained to *Sports Illustrated*. "There was no hot water. No electricity. Everyone was given half a bread a day to live. A kilogram of meat a week. There were vegetables in the summer, but not the winter. Never bananas, Never oranges. Fish? On Friday."

In 1991 the Communist government was overthrown. By this time Muresan was 20 years old and already stood seven feet seven inches tall. That same year he starred with the Romanian team at the Junior World Championships in Edmonton, Alberta, Canada, scoring 23.4 points and grabbing 11.4 rebounds per game. "He was the leading rebounder in the tournament, the second-leading scorer," his agent, Kenny Grant, told *Sports Illustrated*. "No one could stop him at that level. A lot of American colleges became very interested, but Georghe wanted to make some money. How could you blame him?"

Muresan turned down several offers to play college basketball in the United States and signed instead to play with the Pau Orthez team of the French League. During the 1992–93 season he averaged 18.7 points, 10.3 rebounds, and 2.8 blocked shots per game. Muresan took the $300,000 he made in France and bought his parents a new home in Romania. It was the family's first house with indoor plumbing and electricity.

Escaping the communist system of Romania meant that Muresan had to adjust to a new way of life. He had money to spend for the first time in his life and had other opportunities he never had before. One thing Muresan could do was learn to drive. "I had three accidents when I was [in France], learning to drive," Muresan told *Sports Illustrated*. "The first, the car was finished. The second, the car was in the garage, but not finished. The third, not so bad. Did not even have to go to the garage."

Muresan was still learning the game despite his solid statistics in his first season of professional basketball. He had never had world-class coaching and was so out of shape that he could not do even one push-up. Pau Orthez coach Michel

Gomez worked hard with his new center. "The first time he came here, psychologically he was just a kid, a child," Gomez explained in *Sports Illustrated*. "Physically, he did not accept his size. The first thing I did–before any basketball–I taught him how to walk. He walked like an old man, all hunched over. I taught him to stand straight, to be proud of his height. First, he had to walk before he could run. I did things with him that I never did with anyone else. I worked with him on the trampoline. Can you imagine that? The trampoline almost went down to the floor when he bounced. I worked with him on doing tumbling moves. I wanted him to have control of his body. We never set up any offense where he just stood still, which would have been the easiest thing to do. I wanted him to move. He was very, very slow."

BULLET BOUND. After his first season in France, NBA scouts began to take an interest in Muresan. They liked his shooting touch, but worried because he had never played against tough competition like that he would face in the NBA. Muresan thought he was ready. "I think I can match their skills," he said in *Sports Illustrated*. "Right now, today."

Muresan flew to the Palace in Auburn Hills, Michigan, site of the 1993 NBA Draft, full of high hopes. He sat in an area with other potential draftees, each waiting for their names to be called. As the afternoon dragged on, all the players sitting with Muresan had been selected and he was sitting alone.

Finally the Washington Bullets (now called the Washington Wizards) selected Muresan with the third pick in the second round (thirtieth overall). While most people expected him to be angry about not being chosen sooner, Muresan was the happiest player at the Palace. "I don't believe I've ever been so happy in my whole life," he admitted to *Sports Illustrated* the night of the draft. "Just the thrill of having my name called was the greatest excitement."

Muresan dismissed the critics who said he could not play in the best basketball league in the world. "When I am 14, I like to learn basketball," he explained in *Sports Illustrated*. "I do that. When I am 16, I like to play for the national team. I do that. When I am 19, I like to play in Europe. I do that when I am 20. I come here and I say that I can't play in NBA, it is too strong, but after a while I think I can play. I like to play in NBA."

The Bullets liked Muresan's potential. "He's potentially a fine player," Washington general manager John Nash told *Sports Illustrated*. "He hasn't played against the quality of competition players see in the U.S., so he obviously has some catching up to do." The Bullets signed Muresan to a non-guaranteed contract for the NBA minimum salary of $150,000.

Washington already had Manute Bol, until then the tallest player in NBA history at just under seven feet seven inches tall. Muresan surprised Bol when the two players went one-on-one. "You should have seen Manute," Nash recalled in *Sports Illustrated*. "He looked startled. I'll bet he had never seen someone taller than him. They played one-on-one, and right away you could see that Georghe could play. He threw a couple of jump hooks over Manute, hit a couple of jumpers. You had to say to yourself, if Manute isn't going to block him, then no one is going to block him."

TOUGH START. Muresan faced surgery before he could suit up for the Bullets. He had the tumor that had caused his incredible growth removed from his pituitary gland. The surgery was successful, but Muresan must take medication twice a day for the rest of his life.

Adjusting to life in the United States was difficult for Muresan. He did not speak English and needed an interpreter. The new Bullet also needed shoes and clothes. "We went, in Atlanta, to Freedman Shoes," interpreter Greg Ghyka recalled in *Sports Illustrated*. "It's a place where all the players in the NBA go for large-sized shoes. Georghe just became very quiet. You could see he never had seen anything like this. He must have had 15 boxes of shoes spread out around him before he was finished. I think he bought seven pairs."

TALLEST EVER. When Muresan took the court for the first time he became the tallest player ever in the NBA. He was slightly taller than his teammate Bol and Shawn Bradley of the Philadelphia 76ers, both of whom checked in at just under seven feet seven inches tall. Even though Washington viewed Muresan as a backup center, he had different plans. "People say, 'Oh, you are big, but you are not for the NBA,'" he explained to *Sports Illustrated for Kids*. "You play basketball in Europe only because you are so tall. I don't want people to say that."

Muresan worked hard during his rookie season. He lost 30 pounds his first year and began lifting weights to improve his strength. The big rookie also impressed the Bullets coaching staff with his shooting touch and passing ability. "I was one of the doubters at the beginning at the draft," Washington coach Jim Lynam admitted in *Sports Illustrated*. "I thought he had too many problems, with language and conditioning and foot speed, to overcome. What I didn't know, and I don't think anybody knew, was how hard he would work. He works as hard as anyone I've ever seen."

Muresan played in 54 games during his rookie season, averaging just 5.6 points per contest. He began to get more minutes as the 1994–95 season began, and soon he was the team's starting center. "He's big, solid and kinda strong," Shaquille O'Neal then with the Orlando Magic told *USA Today*. "He does what he's supposed to—set picks, block shots."

For the season Muresan averaged 10 points, 6.7 rebounds, and 1.74 blocked shots per game. He finished sixth in the NBA in field goal percentage (.560). "I saw definite improvement this year," Utah Jazz forward Karl Malone told *Sports Illustrated*. "He's showed he can score on anybody. There are a lot of people who don't take him seriously, but I think he's a [fine] player already."

MOST IMPROVED. By the beginning of the 1995–96 season, Muresan had firmly established himself as the Bullets starting center. Taking his place between forwards Juwan Howard and Chris Webber, Muresan gave Washington an imposing front line. Muresan earned the NBA's Most Improved Player Award with his best season so far. He led the league in shooting percentage, with a .584 mark, and ranked eighth in the NBA with 2.26 blocked shots per game. Muresan also improved his scoring (14.5) and rebounding (9.6) averages.

Muresan struggled with nagging injuries during the 1996–97 season. He led the NBA in shooting percentage for the second straight year (.604), but lower back pain slowed Muresan for most of the season. The big center's scoring (10.6) and rebounding (8.8) averages dropped, but the Bullets made the playoffs for the first time in his career. The eventual champion Bulls swept Washington in the first round, but the Bullets were one of the best young teams in the NBA. Any future success the team has will be as the Wizards, the new name of the team beginning in the 1997–98 season.

OFF THE COURT. Muresan lives in Crofton, Maryland, with his wife, Liliana. He has a Great Dane dog named Lucky. Muresan is 7-foot-7-inches tall, weighs 315 pounds, and wears size 20 shoes. His height forces him to sit so far back in his car to drive that it looks like he is in the back seat.

Muresan serves holiday meals to the homeless and visited a child in the hospital as a part of the "Make-a-Wish" program. He has made commercials for Snickers candy bars and ESPN. Muresan has also appeared in the movie "My Giant" with Billy Crystal. He learned how to speak French during his one season playing basketball in France.

Muresan likes to return to his native country in the off-season. "It is beautiful, Romania," he told *Sports Illustrated*. "I buy a house in Cluj. I buy another house for my father. I buy a bakery for my brothers. There are still many problems in Romania. But it is getting better. Every day is better."

Muresan plans to play basketball until he cannot play anymore. "I like [to] play basketball," he revealed in *Sports*

Illustrated. "I like [to] play basketball a lot. I like [to] play 26 more years, 28 more years, then retire. Hah! I['ll] play until I can't play."

WHERE TO WRITE:
C/O WASHINGTON WIZARDS,
USAIR ARENA,
LANDOVER, MD 20785.

Sources

Science World, February 23, 1996.
Sports Illustrated, July 12, 1993; October 2, 1995.
Sports Illustrated for Kids, February 1996.
USA Today, February 1, 1994; February 8, 1994.
Additional information provided by the Washington Wizards.

Gabrielle Reece

1970–

Beach volleyball star Gabrielle Reece likes to stay busy. In addition to a full season of play in the Women's Beach Volleyball League (WBVL), she models, works on television, and has written a book. On the sand, Reece led her league in kills (unreturnable spikes) for four straight seasons (1993–96) and won WBVL Offensive Player of the Year honors two consecutive times (1994 and 1995). A star athlete and popular model, she wants to show that it is all right to be big and beautiful.

Growing Up

ON THE MOVE. Gabrielle Reece was born January 6, 1970, in La Jolla, California. Her parents divorced when she was only two years old and her father—a native of the island of Trinidad—died in a plane crash when she was five years old. Reece moved to Mexico, where her mother, Terry, found a job training dolphins in a circus owned by friends. Reece participated by holding up a toothbrush, the cue for the dolphins to open their mouths.

When she was almost four years old, Reece went to live with her aunt and uncle in Amityville, New York, a village on Long Island. She lived there until she was seven years old, when she reunited with her mother. The family moved to St. Thomas, an island in the Caribbean Sea. Reece returned to Long Island during the summer to visit.

GETS IN TROUBLE. Reece had a tough relationship with her mother. She felt for most of her childhood that she had to take care of herself. As Reece entered her teens she began to run with the wrong crowd. "I started getting into trouble there [in St. Thomas]," she admitted to *People Weekly.* "I was drinking a lot, had no direction and wanted to drop out of school."

At this point her mother stepped in. She and her daughter moved to Florida and Reece enrolled at a strict Christian high school in St. Petersburg between her sophomore and junior years. After having very few limits on what she could do, Reece had a hard time adjusting to her new school. "I was considered big and mean," she revealed in her book, *Big Girl in the Middle.* "I got into a fight with three girls on the cheerleading squad the first two weeks. At the first spiritual retreat I went to I was told to go back where I came from."

TAKES TO THE COURT. Reece always was taller than her friends. She got her height from her parents. Reece's mother was six feet three and her father was six feet one. By the time Reece turned 15, she had already reached six feet, three inches in height. "I didn't agonize over my size; maybe I just knew all along that it was something that would one day work in my favor," she explained in her book, *Big Girl in the Middle.*

Her height helped Reece fit in at her new school. Some classmates and teachers suggested she try out for the school's basketball and volleyball teams. Reece had never participated in sports and says she did not have any female sports role models as a child. The people she looked up to were her parents and their adult friends.

Despite never before playing the game on an organized team, Reece become a star center on the basketball team. "I'd never played before and we went to the state championship finals that year," she recalled in her book, *Big Girl in the Middle*. Reece earned an invitation to a summer basketball camp and five universities invited her to play for their teams.

Reece played basketball for two seasons, but she did not want to continue in the sport after high school. She also played volleyball on the school team and joined a club team after the high-school season ended. Reece began to like playing volleyball and attracted the attention of Cecile Raymond, the coach for Florida State University. Raymond offered her a scholarship and Reece accepted.

SEMINOLE SLAMMER. Reece had enough potential in volleyball to earn a college scholarship, but she admits she still had a lot to learn about how to play the game. "The problem with college was that for the entire four years I thought I was faking it," she confessed in her book, *Big Girl in the Middle*. "I was athletic, sure, but I was also so tall. I had no sense ever that I actually knew what I was doing. I had a relatively successful college career, but I never once felt I really knew how to play volleyball."

Reece played middle-blocker, a position she described in her book: "I've spent my whole volleyball life as a middle blocker, the big one in the middle, the one who touches every ball. I hit and I block, period. That's what the middle blocker does, and I'm good at this."

The Seminole star was good enough as a junior in 1990 to earn the Most Inspiring Collegiate Athlete award from the Dodge National Athletic Awards Committee. That same year Reece also earned All-Metro Conference and All-South Region honors. She finished her career ranked fifth on the all-time National Collegiate Athletic Association (NCAA) blocks list. "She likes to hit the ball hard and put it back in somebody's face," Raymond said.

MODEL STUDENT. It was during her college days that Reece began her second career: modeling. In 1988 she appeared on her first magazine cover, for *Vogue* magazine. Reece tried not to let the attention go to her head. "I'm really not very pretty," she revealed to *People Weekly* at the time. "I'd describe the way I look as interesting. It's definitely different. I look at modeling as a business. I'm marketable now, but things could change. That's why I'm staying involved with school and athletics." *Elle* magazine named her "one of the five most beautiful women in the world" when Reece was a sophomore.

To accommodate her modeling career and her studies Reece spent half the year at Florida State—playing volleyball from September to December—then traveled to New York. The two worlds in which she lived were very different. "In New York my model roommates complain about [their skin] breaking out," Reece explained to *People Weekly.* "In Tallahassee [where Florida State is located] I have volleyball roommates, and we complain about hurt ankles. Some people here at FSU think I'm weird now because I'm getting to be a well-known model. It amazes me that they think I'm a celebrity or something. If they knew I was just a normal goofball like them, they'd probably chill out."

BEACH BASHER. When her college career at Florida State ended, Reece had to make a decision. She enjoyed playing volleyball, but at the time there were no professional leagues for her to join. In order to pursue a full-time career in modeling, Reece would have to travel to Europe and give up playing volleyball. Because she would not commit the necessary time she received fewer and fewer modeling offers.

One day a friend suggested that Reece begin playing beach volleyball. She played her first tournament for the Women's Professional Volleyball Association (WPVA) in January 1992. The WPVA played doubles volleyball—with two players on a team—instead of the six-person game she played in college. Reece soon realized that if she really wanted to succeed in beach volleyball she would have to move from Florida to California, where the sport was starting to take off.

Reece continued to play in the WPVA, but struggled to play well. She quit the league to practice, and while she was off the beach she learned that a new four-person league was about to be formed. Reece jumped at the chance to be in on the ground floor of the new Women's Beach Volleyball League (WBVL).

LEADS LEAGUE. Beach volleyball made a dramatic rise. Once a sport mainly played in California, the game grew until it was played throughout the United States and the world. The two-person beach volleyball game was contested at the 1996 Summer Olympics in Atlanta, Georgia, and the sport now has major television contracts.

Reece was in the forefront of making beach volleyball a major spectator sport. In her first season she served as team captain for the Lady Foot Locker team. Reece led the league in blocks (53) and kills (unreturnable spikes) with 227. "Volleyball is really fun," she told *Sports Illustrated for Kids*. "I love the teamwork. When it works, it's like clockwork."

Reece moved to Team Nike for the 1994 season. She again led the league in kills (454) and earned league Offensive Player of the Year honors. In Chicago, Reece set league records for kills (63) and attempts (173) in one tournament. In 1995 Reece repeated as Offensive Player of the Year, led the league in kills (482) for the third straight year, and also blocked more shots than any other player. For the fourth consecutive year Reece topped the league in kills (547) in 1996, a new WBVL record. "I enjoy getting the ball to go exactly where I want it, at the speed I want it to go," Reece explained.

TO THE EXTREME. In addition to her volleyball playing, Reece began working in 1993 on the television program

"MTV Sports" and later starred on another show, "The Extremists." During her time with MTV she did some dangerous stunts. Reece rock-climbed on a mountain in France, drove a drag race car, and parachuted out of a plane from 12,000 feet above the ground. "I'm not a thrill-seeker," she explained to *Sports Illustrated for Kids.* "I'd rather go to the movies. But I have a job with the television show MTV Sports on which I do a different sport every week. Some of the stuff I do is scary and difficult. But I'm willing to look like a knucklehead on TV while I try."

OTHER INTERESTS. At six feet three inches and 170 pounds, Reece is bigger physically than most models. "She's done as well as any model we've had," *Shape* editor-in-chief Barbara Harris explained in *Mediaweek.* "She is leading us in a direction not only of someone with a healthier body image but also of being your own person." Reece has appeared on the covers of several national magazines, including *Elle* and *Vogue,* and has had her picture published in many other publications and advertisements.

Reece also is a spokesperson for Nike, with her own "Air" line of cross-training shoes. She wants to use her popularity to help her sport. "I need to show that [women] volleyball players are feminine, competitive, and intelligent," Reece explained to *Sport.* "I think it's important for me to find a platform to be a representative for women's sports." She also is a spokesperson for Oakley sunglasses and Coppertone suntan lotion.

In 1997 Reece published a book titled *Big Girl in the Middle.* She hopes that her writing will help others to be successful. "I really didn't want to do the book at first," Reece admitted to *Newsday.* "I'm hoping the book is motivating for younger girls, to give them a wake-up call."

Juggling so many different interests is difficult for Reece to do. "I haven't gotten to where I want to be in volleyball," she explained to *Sport.* "You start to feel like a knucklehead, being recognized for various things, like looking a certain way or having a fashion career, and then going out and trying to be taken seriously playing a sport."

ROLE MODEL

Reece wants to be a role model for young girls and encourages them to participate in sports. "I guess most importantly, I'm here for fifteen-year-old girls," she explained in *Newsday.* "I just want to tell them that when they're in that part of their life when things are changing and they want to kill their parents, that it's O.K. and good for them to take up sports."

Even though she wants to be involved in many different activities, volleyball still comes first for Reece. "The fact is, if I take care of my sport and I'm successful there, everything else will take care of itself," she declared to *Sport.* "If I [stunk] at volleyball, it would be kind of hard to be a successful spokesperson."

OFF THE SAND. Reece lives in Marina del Rey, California. She majored in communications at Florida State. A very superstitious person, Reece wears the same style visor all season, and once changed her team's red uniforms because she was sure they brought bad luck. Her nicknames are Gabby or Gab. Reece likes to roar when she goes up for a spike or block.

In the off-season Reece continues to stick to a grueling training schedule. Her workout includes 12 different exercises. "I threw up the first time I did this workout—on my birthday too," she admitted to *Sport.* "You finish and you're tired, drenched. Forget physical, it's mentally grinding."

Reece encourages everyone to stay in shape. "Athletics keep your mind clear," she explained to *People Weekly.* "They make your life better."

Sources

Mediaweek, March 18, 1996.
Newsday, August 3, 1997.
People Weekly, October 16, 1989.
Sport, April 1995.
Sports Illustrated, February 21, 1997.
Sports Illustrated for Kids, July 1995; June 1996.

Teemu Selanne

1970–

T eemu Selanne—high-scoring forward for the Mighty Ducks of Anaheim—is one of the most feared players in the National Hockey League (NHL). Selanne—known as the "Finnish Flash"—set NHL rookie records during the 1992–93 season with 76 goals and 132 points and won the Calder Trophy as the league's rookie of the year. Selanne has been an All Star in every one of his NHL seasons and now teams with Paul Kariya to make the Mighty Ducks a Stanley Cup contender.

"It's important to do more than just play hockey. Athletes are so lucky."
—Teemu Selanne.

Growing Up

TEEMU THE TEACHER. Teemu Selanne (Tay-MOO SEH-lahn-nay) was born July 3, 1970 in Helsinki, Finland. He has a twin brother, Paavo, and another brother, Panu. Selanne attended business college and served for one year in the Finnish Army, a requirement for all Finnish youngsters.

SCOREBOARD

WON 1992–93 CALDER TROPHY AS
THE NHL ROOKIE OF THE YEAR.

SET NHL ROOKIE RECORDS WITH
76 GOALS AND 132 ASSISTS IN
1992–93.

FIVE-TIME NHL ALL-STAR.

THE "FINNISH FLASH" IS A STAR ON
THE ICE AND OFF.

Selanne taught morning kindergarten classes for three years after leaving the army. At night he played hockey for Jokerit, a Helsinki club team. "I have to do something other than play hockey and I've always loved children," Selanne told the Knight-Ridder/Tribune News Service. "I really miss those times. They were good times. When I was in the classroom, I always forgot the hockey. I would work from nine in the morning until one. Sometimes I would have to leave for game and the children would shout, 'Teemu, score 1,000 goals.' It was great."

Even though he lived in Finland, Selanne still knew about the great players of the National Hockey League (NHL). His favorite players were Guy Lafleur of the Montreal Canadiens, the great Wayne Gretzky, then with the Edmonton Oilers, and his fellow Finn, Jari Kurri. Selanne wore number 8 throughout his hockey career in Finland.

BIG BREAK. Selanne played five years for the Jokerit team in the Finnish League. He scored 33 or more goals in four of those seasons. When Selanne was 19 he faced adversity. He broke two bones in his left leg and feared that his career was over. "To me, the broken leg was the worst time of my career," Selanne recalled in *Sports Illustrated*. "It took more than a year to heal. I was so worried. I was afraid I'd never know if I could've made it in the NHL."

JETS CHOICE. With his leg completely healed, Selanne continued his hockey career. The Winnipeg Jets of the NHL selected him with the tenth overall choice in 1988 NHL Draft, even though they knew he still had to perform his military service in Finland. Selanne continued to improve his game, playing for his native country at the 1989 World Junior Ice Hockey Championships, the 1991 Canada Cup tournament, the 1991 World Hockey Championships, and the 1992 Olympics in Albertville, France.

ROOKIE SENSATION. When Selanne finally joined the Jets, the team was happy to welcome their new star. He signed a three-year, $2.7 million contract with Winnipeg. "He's been well worth waiting for," Barry Shenkarow, owner of the Jets, told *Sports Illustrated.*

Selanne started his rookie season (1992–93) fast and never slowed down. He had 33 goals by the All-Star break, then shattered the previous rookie record for goals —53—set by Mike Bossy of the New York Islanders during the 1977–78 season. "I'm sure that when I scored 30 goals, [opponents] said, 'Who is Selanne?'" he admitted in *Sports Illustrated.* "When I scored 50, it was, 'What's going on?' And then 60. I was just rolling. After games I'd come in our dressing room and laugh and say, 'I can't believe I scored a goal on that shot.'"

By the end of the season Selanne had an NHL rookie record 76 goals (he tied with Alexander Mogilny of the Buffalo Sabres for the NHL lead). He also broke the rookie point record of 109 set by Peter Stastny of the Quebec Nordiques during the 1980–81 season. Selanne finished with 132 points, fifth in the league. The NHL honored Selanne by awarding him the Calder Trophy as the league's rookie of the year. He also made the NHL All-Star Team at right wing. "He's going to put Winnipeg back on the hockey map," Jets coach John Paddock told *Sports Illustrated.*

TORN ACHILLES. Selanne continued to fly in his second NHL season. He scored his one-hundredth NHL goal in only 130 games, one game off the fastest pace to that milestone, set by Mike Bossy, who did it in 129 games. Selanne's year was cut short by a torn Achilles tendon he suffered on January 26 against the Mighty Ducks of Anaheim. The injury forced Selanne to miss the final 34 games of the season.

SMALL WORLD

Selanne learned about how small the world really is when he played for Finland in the 1992 Winter Olympics in Albertville, France. "I remember seeing my future NHL teammates Keith Tkachuk [of Team USA] and [Russia's] Alexei Zhamnov were in the Olympics, too, and we had all been drafted by Winnipeg," he recalled. "The day Russia won the gold medal, and those guys were celebrating, Alex saw me. He yelled to me, 'See you in Winnipeg.' The next year, Alex, Keith and I were linemates."

The 1994–95 season was cut to 49 games by a players' strike. The strike was caused by a disagreement between players and hockey team owners over issues like salaries and free agency. Selanne finished the season with 22 goals and 26 assists for 48 points. He finished the season with only two penalty minutes, the lowest for any player who appeared in 40 or more games.

TIME FOR ANAHEIM. Selanne made the NHL Western Conference All-Star team for the third time in the 1995–96 season. There he met Paul Kariya—superstar winger for the Mighty Ducks of Anaheim. The two hung out together and goofed around during pre-game introductions. "We were saying, there goes [Jaromir] Jagr," Kariya recalled in *Sports Illustrated*. "He's so unbelievable! And [Mario] Lemieux! He's so great!"

Kariya returned to Anaheim raving about Selanne's skills and how the Winnipeg star was the answer to the Mighty Ducks anemic offense. What Kariya did not know was that Winnepeg had been interested in trading Selanne because they believed his production had dropped off. Anaheim general manager Jack Ferreira called the Jets and struck a deal, trading forward Chad Kilger and defenseman Oleg Tverdovsky for Selanne and center Marc Chouinard.

The trade hurt Selanne at first, especially since his wife, Sirpa, was only weeks from delivering the couple's first child. "Every organization I play in, I always try to help, to do what they want," Selanne revealed to *Sports Illustrated*. "After the trade I thought, Management doesn't care. They use players."

QUACK ATTACK. Selanne's new teammates were excited when they heard the news about the trade. "There was so much excitement in the dressing room," Ducks general manager Jack Ferreira recalled in *USA Today*. "[Goalie] Guy Hebert kept saying, 'We got Teemu Selanne, We got Teemu Selanne.' The players knew what he was about."

"This is going to be like having two Paul Kariyas out there," Ferreira told the *Sporting News*. "I've seen games this year that Paul has won singlehandedly. I think Teemu will do the same thing for us."

Selanne had played 51 games with Winnipeg before the trade, scoring 24 goals and passing for 48 assists. He finished the 1995–96 season with 40 goals, 68 assists (tied for ninth in the NHL), and 108 points (tied for seventh in the league). Both Selanne and Kariya were nominated for the Lady Byng Trophy—given annually to the player who displays the most sportsmanship—the first time two members of the same team were nominated for this award. Kariya won the trophy, edging out Selanne.

The Ducks barely missed making the NHL playoffs for the first time, losing a tiebreaker against Selanne's old club—the Jets. "I was disappointed we didn't make the playoffs," Selanne admitted to the *Los Angeles Times*. "We really played so well; we just started too late." Following the season Selanne played in the World Hockey Championships in Vienna, Austria. He scored five goals and had three assists.

DUCKS! Anaheim sought to build on the team's strong finish the previous season and become a playoff team during the 1996–97 season. This plan hit a serious roadblock when Kariya missed the first 13 games with an abdominal injury. Without their superstar the Ducks struggled, going 1-10-2 during Kariya's absence. Included in this record was an eight-game losing streak.

When Kariya returned the team started to click. In Kariya's second game back, Selanne scored his first hat trick of the season (three goals in one game) in a 4-3 victory over the San Jose Sharks. The victory ended the team's eight-game losing streak, but Selanne was not satisfied with his team's play. "We still have won only two games this season," he told the *Los Angeles Times*.

Selanne finished the 1996–97 season with 51 goals (second in the NHL), 109 points (second in the NHL), and 58 assists (ninth in the NHL). The two linemates—Selanne and Kariya—finished 1-2 in the league in scoring, making them the most dangerous tandem in the NHL. "I've played with a lot of great players, guys like Eric Lindros, and we've had good chemistry, but not the kind of chemistry Teemu and I have,"

Kariya told *Sports Illustrated*. "It's so much fun playing the game when you know exactly what the other person's going to do." Selanne once again was nominated for the Lady Byng Trophy and lost for the second straight season to Kariya.

PLAYOFF BOUND. The Ducks finished with a winning record for the first time in their four-year history with a 36-33-13 mark. Their record was good enough for fourth place in the NHL Western Conference and earned Anaheim home-ice advantage in the first round of the playoffs. The Ducks lost only three of their final 23 games, an impressive closing surge. "For sure, it was unbelievable," Selanne confessed in the *Los Angeles Times*.

Anaheim played the Phoenix Coyotes in their first-ever playoff series. The Phoenix franchise had been Selanne's old team—the Winnipeg Jets, who had moved at the beginning of the 1996–97 season. Selanne claimed he did not want revenge against his former team. "Somehow it seems like five years ago when I was traded," he explained to the *Los Angeles Times*. "I really enjoy being here [in Anaheim] and playing here. I almost forgot I played there before. There are going to be lots of faces I know pretty well in the same game. But somehow it's different. They have new uniforms, lots of new players. They've come to a new city. Except that there are lots of people I know and friends in the organization, it's different. I could never say I hate the team. I had a great time there. I really respect them. But of course, I want to beat anybody."

Despite his success in the regular season, Selanne had played in only six playoff games in his career. Teammates noticed that he did not act as easygoing as he usually did. "He's definitely not as relaxed," center Steve Rucchin told the *Los Angeles Times*. "He's aware he has to be on his game every night if we're going to win."

DUCKING COYOTES. The Mighty Ducks started out fast against the Coyotes. Both Kariya and Selanne scored two goals in a 4-2 Anaheim victory in game one, then Selanne sealed a 4-2 win in game two with an empty net goal. The Ducks seemed to be well on their way to a series win.

The Coyotes turned the series around playing at home, winning the next two games. Phoenix held Selanne—he did not have a goal or assist in either game—with tough checking and physical play. Selanne did break out in game five at the Pond—he scored two goals—but the Coyotes won 5-2. Anaheim now faced elimination, heading back to Phoenix.

The Mighty Ducks took a 2-0 lead entering the third period of game six, but with the home crowd behind them the Coyotes came back to tie the score and force sudden-death overtime. With seven-and-a-half minutes gone in the extra period, Selanne picked up the puck in the Ducks' zone. He flipped it down the left side of the ice to a streaking Kariya, who ripped a blistering shot past Phoenix goalie Nikolai Khabibulin to give Anaheim a 3-2 victory to tie the series. "That shot by Paul was just unbelievable," Selanne declared to the *Los Angeles Times*.

Game seven was played at a sold-out Pond in Anaheim. "It's going to be exciting," Selanne told the *Los Angeles Times* before the game. "It's a great challenge. The Mighty Ducks dominated the final and deciding game of the series, 3-0, to win their first ever playoff series. Neither Selanne or Kariya scored in game seven, but they accounted for 10 of the team's 14 goals against Phoenix.

WORKING OVERTIME. The Ducks now faced the Detroit Red Wings in the Western Conference semifinals. Every game was a closely played defensive struggle. Game one went to overtime and game two was decided in triple overtime. Detroit won both games at home.

The series traveled to Anaheim for game three. The Ducks took a 2-0 lead on a goal by Selanne, and led 3-1 late in the second-period. Two late second period goals tied the game for Detroit, and when the Red Wings scored two quick goals in the third period, the game was all but over. Detroit won game three, 5-3, leaving the Ducks one game from elimination once again.

Many teams would quit after trailing three games to none, but the Mighty Ducks played hard in game four. For the

GOOD WORKS

Selanne believes strongly in doing charitable work and especially likes helping children. A visit to a children's hospital when he was 18 moved him so much he formed the Godfather Foundation. "I remember when I went [to a children's hospital] the first time, it was the biggest shock of my life to see small kids so sick," Selanne told the Knight Ridder/Tribune News Service. "I decided I'm going to help these kids if I can somehow."

The Godfather Foundation encourages celebrities to donate money to help sick children. Selanne donates most of the money he earns through endorsements. "It's important to do more than just play hockey," Selanne explained in *Sports Illustrated*. "Athletes are so lucky, and it doesn't take so much for us to do these things. Once a nurse at the hospital told me that after we visit, the kids don't need painkillers for a week. That made me feel so, so good, you know?"

Selanne helped raise thousands of dollars for children's hospitals in Finland and has worked with various children's charities throughout his career. In Winnepeg, Selanne donated $500 for every goal he scored through the "Jets' Goals for Kids Foundation," a total of $73,500 for 147 goals. The money went to various charities throughout Manitoba, Canada.

third time in the series the game went to overtime. Anaheim's season finally came to an end when Brendan Shanahan scored for Detroit with only 2 minutes and 57 seconds left in the second overtime period.

OFF THE ICE. Selanne and his wife, Sirpa, have a boy named Eemil Ilmari. The family owns two rottweiler dogs, Teddy and Domi. Selanne enjoys playing tennis and squash, and likes fishing and jogging. As a child he learned to play guitar and studied magic tricks with a performer friend.

Although he enjoys playing in the NHL, Selanne often misses Finland. He calls home every day to talk to family or friends and returns to Finland each summer. The fans in his native country love him. "He's like a rock star," Alpo Shonen, the former coach of the Finnish national team, explained to *Sports Illustrated*. "I don't know if he can get any more popular in Finland than he is right now."

Selanne owns a speedboat, four Jet-Skis, four go-karts, and five classic convertible automobiles. During the summer he competes in road races in Finland. "It's a four-wheel drive," Selanne told *Sports Illustrated,* describing his racing truck. "Turbo. Roll bar. The whole package." His racing nickname is Teddy Flash, a take-off on his hockey nickname. Selanne also works with fellow countryman and NHL veteran Jari Kurri at summer hockey camp in Finland.

Selanne is good at making his teammates laugh and keeping everyone loose. "I think the epitaph [saying] on Teemu's tombstone is going to read, 'I had a million friends and not one enemy,'" Coach Ron Wilson revealed in *Sports Illustrated*. "He's a guy you just love being around."

Selanne is pleasant with fans and loves to sign autographs. "Teemu always says that without fans there would be no game of hockey," his wife, Sirpa, explained in *Sports Illustrated*. "So he always signs."

The Mighty Ducks hope to fly to the Stanley Cup, and look to the "Finnish Flash" to take them there.

 WHERE TO WRITE:
C/O MIGHTY DUCKS OF ANAHEIM, ARROWHEAD POND,
2695 E. KATELLA AVE.,
ANAHEIM, CA 92803.

Sources

Los Angeles Times, April 10, 1997; April 13, 1997; April 14, 1997; April 25, 1997; April 28, 1997; May 7, 1997; May 9, 1997.
Sporting News, February 19, 1996.
Sports Illustrated, March 29, 1993; January 27, 1997; April 28, 1997; October 20, 1997.
USA Today, April 30, 1997; May 9, 1997.
Additional information provided by the Mighty Ducks of Anaheim.

Annika Sorenstam

1970–

Golfer Annika Sorenstam has one the most beautiful swings in golf. From the moment she joined the Ladies' Professional Golf Association (LPGA) Tour, that swing has helped her become one of the best female golfers in the world. Twice Sorenstam has captured the U.S. Women's Open (1995 and 1996), won the LPGA Player of the Year Award (1995 and 1997), and earned the Vare Trophy, given to the golfer on the LPGA Tour with the lowest scoring average (1995 and 1996). Only 27 years old, the Swedish star should be a dominant figure in women's golf for years to come.

Growing Up

ATHLETIC FAMILY. Annika (AH-nick-ah) Sorenstam was born October 9, 1970, in Stockholm, Sweden. She got her love of sports from her parents. Both her mother and father participated in athletics, including basketball, handball, track and field, and golf. "Sports has always been a big thing at home," Sorenstam explained to *Golf Magazine*. She often tagged along with her parents when they went to the local sports club.

FROM THE COURTS TO THE COURSE. Sorenstam's favorite sport as a child was tennis. She began playing in competitions at the age of five. Her heroes were Swedish stars Bjorn Borg and Matts Wilander. By the time she entered her teens, however, Sorenstam knew she had reached her peak and turned her competitive energies to golf.

Sorenstam learned about golf from her parents. She began playing at the age of 12 and liked the game right away. The young golfer liked the fact that she could practice by herself, and she also enjoyed seeing all the different types of golf courses. Sorenstam loved her new sport and practiced very hard to improve.

WHERE IS ARIZONA? The Swedish Golf Federation picked Sorenstam to play on the junior national team when she was 16. While playing an event in Japan, Sorenstam impressed the coach of the University of Arizona golf team with her ability. The coach offered her a scholarship, and she decided to move to the United States to play, despite not knowing where Arizona was located. "I didn't even know where it was on the map," Sorenstam explained to the *Los Angeles Times*. "I'm lucky I didn't wind up in Idaho with snow up to my waist. It was a little bit of a culture shock. I hadn't seen a cactus before."

Sorenstam starred at Arizona, becoming the best collegiate female golfer in the United States during her two seasons. She won the National Collegiate Athletic Association (NCAA) championship in 1991 and finished second in the same tournament in 1992. The NCAA named Sorenstam the College Player of the Year in 1991 and she earned All-American honors in both 1991 and 1992. She won seven collegiate titles while at Arizona.

SCOREBOARD

TWO-TIME WINNER OF LPGA PLAYER OF THE YEAR AWARD (1995 AND 1997).

TWO-TIME WINNER OF U.S. WOMEN'S OPEN (1995 AND 1996).

TWO-TIME WINNER OF VARE TROPHY, AWARDED TO LPGA GOLFER WITH LOWEST SCORING AVERAGE (1995 AND 1996).

SORENSTAM HAS SWUNG HER WAY TO THE TOP OF WOMEN'S GOLF.

TURNS PRO. The golf world began to take notice of Sorenstam when she won the 1992 World Amateur championship and finished second at the U.S. Women's Amateur Championship that same year. Her success led her to turn professional and join the WPG European Tour in 1993. That year Sorenstam won rookie of the year honors.

Sorenstam returned to the United States in 1993 and earned a spot on the Ladies' Professional Golf Association (LPGA) Tour. In 1994 she earned LPGA Rookie of the Year honors with three top-ten finishes. Sorenstam was now one of the best young golfers in the world.

DREAM TOURNAMENT. Sorenstam had always dreamed of winning the U.S. Women's Open, the most important tournament in women's golf. In 1988 she watched her countrywoman, Liselotte Neumann, win the tournament. "It was a delayed telecast, but I remember staying up all night to watch it," Sorenstam recalled in *Golf Magazine*. "I did think, 'Yeah, that could be me someday.'"

The Broadmoor Golf Club in Colorado Springs, Colorado, hosted the 1995 U.S. Women's Open. The course provided a difficult test, with greens that made putting almost impossible. Sorenstam entered the tournament on a hot streak, having won two recent European tour events.

In addition to her success on the links, Sorenstam became engaged to her boyfriend David Esch. She felt her golf game and personal life were both coming together at the same time. "All the pieces of my life are falling into place," Sorenstam said. "I am playing very relaxed golf. My confidence level is very high, and my overall game has just come together. Playing well in one tournament and then another, I think it carries over and you just have positive thoughts."

BATTLE OF NERVES. The 1995 Open was closely contested. At one point on Sunday—the final day of the tournament—

five players were tied for the lead — Sorenstam, Julie Larsen, Pat Bradley, Meg Mallon, and Betsy King. Bradley and King are members of the LPGA Hall of Fame and Mallon had won the Open once before. The competition for Sorenstam could not have been tougher.

Sorenstam separated herself from her competitors with birdies on holes 9, 10, and 11. All of a sudden she had a three-stroke lead in the most important tournament in the world. Just then the pressure got to Sorenstam. Her hands began to shake and her heart raced. She bogied holes 15 and 16 holes, and her lead was cut to one. "I didn't know a tournament could be so scary," Sorenstam admitted to *Golf Magazine*.

With the championship slipping away from her, Sorenstam got angry at herself. "I was making stupid mistakes on simple shots," she confessed to *Golf Magazine*. "I told myself, 'Stop it!'" Sorenstam steadied herself, parring holes 17 and 18. Her round—a two-under-par 68 under intense

Sorenstam plays from a fairway bunker during the 1997 U.S. Open.

pressure—was completed. Sorenstam finished the tournament at two under par.

OPEN CHAMPION. Sorenstam watched as Mallon prepared to attempt an 18-foot birdie putt that, if she made it, would force a playoff. When Mallon's putt rolled just below the cup, Sorenstam had the title. She became the thirteenth LPGA player to win the Open as her first tour victory and only the fifth foreign player to win the title.

"I can't believe it," Sorenstam told the *Atlanta Journal and Constitution*. "It's like a dream. It's the biggest tournament in the world you can win. I thought only supermen did it. For me, it's the world championship." Sorenstam cried when she called her parents in Sweden to tell them about her victory. Absent-mindedly, she dropped a wet tissue in the winner's cup.

DOMINATING. By the end of the 1995 season Sorenstam was the best player on the LPGA tour. She became the first foreign player to win the Vare Trophy, given to the LPGA golfer with the lowest per-round scoring average, with a mark of 71.00. Sorenstam captured the GHP Heartland Classic by 10 strokes, the largest margin of victory of the season. She also won the World Championship of Golf, chipping in a 45-yard shot on the first hole of sudden-death playoff to beat Laura Davies. Sorenstam led both the LPGA and European tours in prize winnings, the first player ever to do so.

The LPGA honored Sorenstam by giving her the Rolex Player of the Year Award. She was the second foreign player to win the award and only the second player—Nancy Lopez was the first—to win the Rookie of the Year Award one year and the Player of the Year Award and Vare Trophy the next. Sorenstam became only the fifth LPGA player to win the Player of the Year, Vare Trophy, and money title in the same year. (The others are Betsy King, Dottie Mochrie, Pat Bradley, and Beth Daniel.)

Sorenstam's greatest honor came when Sweden honored her as the nation's Athlete of the Year, the most prestigious award her country can bestow on an athlete. "It's hard to believe all this has happened in one year," Sorenstam admitted to the *Los Angeles Times*. "But there are a lot of things for me to work on. It's just the start of my career."

Superstar

REPEAT. Sorenstam had a hard time dealing with all the attention she received following her phenomenal season in 1995. She took some time off to try to regroup. "I had to think about the season overall," Sorenstam told the *Los Angeles Times*. "I mean, I did things I didn't think I could do in a career. Where do I go from here? The last thing I wanted to do was be burned out and be tired of golf. It's no fun if you don't enjoy it. There are other things in life that are important besides golf. When you are happy, it doesn't matter how many tournaments you win or how much money you make."

The time off helped Sorenstam prepare to defend her U.S. Women's Open title, held in 1996 at the Pine Needles Lodge and Golf Club in Southern Pines, North Carolina. "I'm going to try to pretend it's just a regular tournament," she explained to the *Los Angeles Times*. "Besides, I've won it once and there's nobody saying I've got to win it twice."

UNSTOPPABLE. Sorenstam got off to a fast start and quickly moved up the leader board. By the time the final round teed-off, she had a three-stroke lead. This time Sorenstam's nerves did not bother her, and she tore up the course on the tournament's final day. She shot a tournament-tying low round of 66 to win her second straight U.S. Women's Open, this time by six strokes.

"I was real nervous on the 18th tee," Sorenstam confessed to *Sports Illustrated*. "I knew I had a five- or six-shot lead, but it's never over until it's over. My shots went straight, my putts went in. There was nothing in the way. I felt like I could close my eyes and hit." Sorenstam became only the sixth woman to win back to back Open championships. (The others were Betsy King [1989–90], Hollis Stacy [1977–78],

Susie Berning [1972–73], Donna Caponi [1969–70], and Mickey Wright [1958–59].)

Later in the year Sorenstam won the CoreStates Betsy King Classic and defended her World Championship of Golf title. Fourteen times she finished in the top ten and seven times in the top five. Sorenstam won the Vare Trophy for the second straight season with a scoring average of 70.47, the second lowest ever. (Beth Daniel had a 70.38 average in 1989.)

THREEPEAT? Sorenstam started out hot again in 1997, winning four tournaments early in the year and finishing second twice. "The way I started this year was incredible," she admitted to the *Atlanta Journal and Constitution*. "I still can't believe it."

Sorenstam arrived at the 1997 U.S. Women's Open at Pumpkin Ridge Golf Club in Cornelius, Oregon, with a chance to make history. She was trying to become the first golfer to ever win three consecutive U.S. Women's Open titles and the first golfer to win three U.S. Opens since Willie Anderson turned the trick in 1903, 1904, and 1905. "I think about it a lot," Sorenstam told *USA Today*. "I tell myself, 'Don't think you have to win it again. You've already won it twice.'"

MISSES CUT. Sorenstam started slowly in the first round of the Open and never recovered. She missed the cut, the first time since July 1994 that this had happened to her. (Missing the cut means that your score is too high to qualify for the last two days of a tournament. About half the golfers in every tournament fail to make the cut.) "I was a little confused," Sorenstam admitted in *Sports Illustrated*. "I was a little upset. I didn't know what was happening. It's like, where am I and what am I doing? Take me away from here."

PLAYER OF THE YEAR II. Despite her disappointment at not defending her U.S. Women's Open title, Sorenstam was still the best golfer on the LPGA Tour. She won six tournaments in 1997—the most by an LPGA player since Beth Daniel won seven in 1990—and led the tour in prize money with a record $1,236,789. For the first time in two years Sorenstam failed to win the Vare Trophy, finishing second to **Karrie Webb** (see entry).

Her consistent play earned Sorenstam the 1997 LPGA Player of the Year Award. "It's like a dream," she confessed to *USA Today.* "When I won in [1995] it felt like it just happened. This time I set [winning Player of the Year] as a goal when I started the year."

OFF THE COURSE. Sorenstam is married to David Esch. The two met on the practice tee. Esch is a salesperson for Calloway golf equipment and Sorenstam is a spokesperson for the same company. She also endorses products for Titleist golf balls, Rolex watches, and Mercury automobiles. Sweden issued a postage stamp with Sorenstam's picture on it.

Sorenstam loves to fly and wants to learn to be a pilot. She likes to listen to music and cook during her free time. Sorenstam keeps track of all her statistics on a laptop computer. "I don't watch much television," she explained to *USA Today.* "I don't go to many movies because I fall asleep trying to watch them. I do enjoy working on my computer."

Sorenstam is a very shy person and does not like to talk about herself. When she was a teenager, she often tried to lose junior golf tournaments so that she would not have to give a victory speech. "I think Swedish people are known for being real shy," Sorenstam admitted in the *Los Angeles Times.* "You don't want to stand out."

Other golfers respect Sorenstam's ability and look to her for help. "When I'm struggling with my swing," fellow LPGA golfer Jill Briles-Hinton told *Golf Magazine.* "I watch Annika."

Sorenstam has earned her place as one of the best golfers in the world. "I know what I want to accomplish," she told

SIBLING RIVALRY

Sorenstam's sister, Charlotta, also is a golfer. She won the 1993 NCAA championship for the University of Texas and joined the LPGA tour in 1997. "She's a great golfer," Annika told the *Atlanta Journal and Constitution* about her little sister. "She has no weaknesses, that I know of."

The two sisters, despite playing together on the tour, do not speak very often. Their relationship is strained because of a severe case of sibling rivalry. "It seems important to her, to be as good or better than me," Annika explained in the *Atlanta Journal and Constitution.* "I guess that's hard, being my little sister. At the same time, I always root for her."

USA Today. "Golf is No. 1 with me now. I've worked hard on my game, and that's important because my goal is to be a better golfer."

WHERE TO WRITE:
C/O LADIES' PROFESSIONAL GOLF ASSOCIATION,
100 INTERNATIONAL GOLF DR.,
DAYTONA BEACH, FL 32124-1092.

Sources

Atlanta Journal and Constitution, July 17, 1995; April 1, 1996; April 8, 1996; May 29, 1996; April 26, 1997; July 6, 1997; July 9, 1997.
Golf Magazine, December 1995.
Los Angeles Times, December 3, 1995; May 29, 1996; June 2, 1996.
Newsday, November 21, 1995.
Sports Illustrated, July 24, 1995; June 10, 1996; January 20, 1997; May 12, 1997; July 21, 1997.
USA Today, May 13, 1997; May 27, 1997.
Additional information provided by the Ladies' Professional Golf Association.

Larry Walker

1966–

Growing up in British Columbia, Canada, Larry Walker—star outfielder for the Colorado Rockies—had a dream. In his dream he was playing in front of a sellout crowd—as a goaltender for the Montreal Canadiens hockey team. When his dream of playing professional hockey ended, Walker did not quit. He took up baseball as a hobby, and now he is one of the best players in the major leagues. In 1997 Walker had the season of his life and was rewarded with the National League Most Valuable Player award.

"The thing is, I just step in the box, see the ball and hit it."
—Larry Walker.

Growing Up

RHYME TIME. Larry Walker was born December 1, 1966. He grew up in Maple Ridge, British Columbia, a town about 20 miles from Vancouver. Walker is one of four sons of Larry Sr. and Mary Walker. Every member of his family has a rhyming name, including his brothers Barry, Gary, and Carey. "To tell you the absolute truth, I'm still not exactly sure how all that [the rhyming names] happened," Mary Walker admitted to *Maclean's*.

ALL IN THE FAMILY. The entire Walker family excelled at athletics. "We were a really athletic family," Walker told *Maclean's*. "I remember we were always throwing out boxes full of trophies because there was never any room in the house to keep them all."

Walker's father—a building supplies dealer—played minor league baseball for the Yakima Bears of the Northwest League in Washington state. He coached all four of his sons in Little League and acted as a hitting instructor at the Major League Baseball Camp. His son Larry traveled with him to camp several times.

As a child, Walker never thought about being a major league baseball player. "Baseball just wasn't big [in Canada]," he explained to *Sports Illustrated*. "The weather was against it. Nobody ever played baseball thinking about making the major leagues. It was just a game, just something to do."

GOAL TO PLAY GOAL. Walker's first love was hockey. He was a goaltender, and his hero was Billy Smith, the great netminder for the Stanley Cup champion New York Islanders. His father made him his first mask. "The mask had a big W painted on the front," Walker recalled in *Sports Illustrated*. "It worked pretty well until one day a guy hit it, dead on, with a slap shot. Right in the middle of the forehead. The mask broke in two. The W split exactly in the middle. There was a V on each piece now. I switched to a birdcage mask."

Walker played goal for the neighborhood team. One of his teammates was Cam Neely, a future star in the National Hockey League (NHL) with the Boston Bruins. In 1993 the Regina Pats of the Junior A level of hockey in Canada—a steppingstone to the NHL—invited Walker and his friend, Rick Herbert, to try out for their team.

The tryout turned out to be a disappointment for Walker. "Rick Herbert's father drove him and me to the tryout," he told *Sports Illustrated*. "Rick made the team. I didn't. I drove back with his father, 15 hours from Saskatchewan." Walker was the last goalie cut at the tryout. He returned the next season and the Pats cut him again. At 16 years old Walker realized his dream of playing in the NHL was not going to come true.

HOBBY BECOMES CAREER. Walker also starred in Little League baseball as a child playing shortstop and pitcher. He worked his way up through the youth baseball system in British Columbia and played at several junior championships. The Montreal Expos and Chicago Cubs showed interest in drafting Walker, but he was not interested in playing baseball. "I was just like every other Canadian kid," he admitted in *Maclean's*. "I didn't want to be a baseball player. I wanted to be a hockey player."

After failing to earn a place on a junior hockey team, Walker continued to play baseball for exercise. He earned a spot on the Canadian junior team and traveled to Saskatchewan to work out at a national training camp. During the camp Walker attracted the attention of big league scouts in attendance when he hit a long home run.

TURNS PROFESSIONAL. The Montreal Expos were one team that showed interest in Walker. The Expos—always looking for native Canadian players—signed Walker to a contract. "Sure, we're always looking for the Canadian kid," former Montreal Expos general manager Dan Duquette admitted to *Sports Illustrated*. "But I'm sure we weren't thinking Larry was going to be anything great."

Walker struggled at the 1985 Montreal minor league camp. It soon became obvious that he had not faced the kind of pitching that players who grew up in the United States faced. The variety of pitches Walker faced in camp confused him because he was used to hitting only fastballs. "I'd never seen a forkball, never seen a slider," he explained to *Sports Illustrated*. "I didn't know they existed. I had never really seen a good curveball. In Canada, as a kid, we'd play 10 base-

Walker slams a home run in a game against the Seattle Mariners.

ball games a year. Fifteen, tops. Some pitchers had a thing they called a spinner, but nothing like this."

MINOR STUGGLES. The Expos did not have high hopes for Walker. They sent him to play for the Utica (New York) Blue Sox of the New York-Penn League. The Blue Sox were a team made up of players that were not considered strong major league prospects. At 18, Walker was the youngest player on the team. In his first season he batted only .223 and hit only two home runs. "I didn't know what hit me," Walker confessed in *Saturday Night*. "I figured one season and I'm back in Maple Ridge."

Fortunately for Walker, the manager of the Blue Sox was Ken Brett. Brett is a former major league pitcher whose brother, George Brett, was a great third baseman for the Kansas City Royals. Brett recognized that Walker was a raw talent who still needed to learn how to play baseball. "He was just so tough," Brett told *Sports Illustrated*.

Coaches who worked with Walker knew he had potential. "He was very fast, very strong, and he just had a fire in him that made you think he was going to make it," Gene Glynn, who also managed Walker for a while in Utica, recalled in *Sports Illustrated*. "He was as fast a learner as I've ever seen. He never made the same mistake twice."

Montreal considered releasing Walker, but Expos hitting coach Ralph Rowe argued the team should send the young player to the Florida Instructional League. Walker slowly worked his way through the system–never earning more than $200 per week—learning as he went. Life in the minor leagues was tough. "I'd be back here in the instructional league," Walker recalled in *Sports Illustrated*. "The heat in the locker room would be about 180 degrees. No air-conditioning. You'd put on dirty uniforms, go back out there. They'd give you a cup of soup and an orange every day for lunch. One cup of juice. No more. We'd go down to that dirt diamond in the back, just work forever."

BIG LEAGUER. The hard work paid off for Walker. He hit 29 home runs in his second minor league season at Burlington, Iowa. Having a successful season took some pressure off of Walker, who constantly had to fight criticism that the only reason Montreal had signed him was because of where he was born. "By then my teammates knew I wasn't getting special treatment just because I was Canadian," Walker told *Saturday Night*.

On August 16, 1989, Walker played his first game with the major league Expos. "I went one for one with three walks," he recalled in *Maclean's*. In 1990 Walker proved he was in the big leagues to stay when he made the Montreal team in spring training. "It was Opening Day [in 1990]," he told *Sports Illustrated*. "I looked around the ballpark and felt good about the opening of the season. I said to myself, 'Hey, this is where I should be. I belong.' I really felt it. I belong."

Walker had a great first full season. He hit 19 home runs and stole 21 bases. Walker also displayed his great arm by throwing out shortstop Tony Fernandez at first base after a single to right field. Later in the year he also threw out pitcher Tim Wakefield the same way. Despite his success, Walker still was learning how to play baseball. "I was still learning the game at the major-league level, learning to hit to left field," he admitted to *Saturday Night*.

ALL-STAR. In 1992 Walker arrived as a major league star. He hit .301, had 23 home runs, and drove in 93 runs. National League managers named Walker to the All-Star team and he responded with a pinch-hit single. Proving that he had become a great all-around player, Walker won the Gold Glove for fielding excellence and the Silver Slugger Award as the most productive hitter in the National League at his position.

STRIKES OUT. Entering the 1994 season the Expos boasted the best outfield in the major leagues—Walker in right field, Marquis Grissom in center, and Moises Alou in left field. Montreal held the best record in the major leagues—74-40—when the player's strike brought the season to a premature end. The strike was caused by a disagreement between players and baseball team owners over issues such as salaries and free-agency.

Walker's play was a big reason for Montreal's success. He batted .322 with 19 home runs and 86 RBI. He put up these numbers despite suffering a torn rotator cuff in his shoulder. The injury prevented Walker from throwing, so he moved from right field to first base. "He's the type of player who can win a team a pennant," former Expos general manager Dan Duquette told *Sports Illustrated*. "He's getting better and better."

LEAVES MONTREAL. During their history the Montreal Expos had a tough time convincing their players not to leave as free agents. Many players did not like living in Montreal because of the cultural difference in the French-speaking city. The Expos also could not afford to pay players as much money as other teams.

Walker, unlike other players, wanted to play in Montreal. He even took French lessons to better fit in. Despite being Canadian, Expo fans did not warm up to their superstar. "It would be different for a player from Quebec [the province in which Montreal is located]," Walker explained to *Saturday Night*.

Following the 1994 season Walker sought a long-term contract. The Expos—trying to save money—refused. Montreal decided to use younger and less expensive players. Walker did not understand the Expos' decision. "The fans [gave me a hard time] early this season [in 1994] because they thought I wanted more money," he said in *Saturday Night*. "Thing is, I wanted to stay in Montreal. The organization didn't want to make a commitment."

HEADS FOR THE MOUNTAINS. The decision by the Expos not to offer him a long-term contract hurt Walker. "All the way comin[g] up in the minors the guys in the Expos' front office told me how much they needed a Canadian guy, a power hitter with the big-league club," Walker told *Saturday Night*. In addition to Walker, Montreal also traded starting pitcher Ken Hill, centerfielder Marquis Grisson, and relief ace John Wetteland.

In April 1995 Walker signed a four-year, $22.5 million contract with the Colorado Rockies. He loved playing in front of sell-out crowds at Coors Field. "I've got a great ball club to play on and 50,000 people to play in front of," Walker revealed in *Sports Illustrated*. "I played in Montreal, so this is definitely not something I'm used to. Plus, the ball does travel better here. There's no better place to play."

Walker earned his money during his first season with the Rockies, hitting .306, with 36 home runs (second in the National League behind teammate Dante Bichette's 40) and

101 runs-batted-in (RBI). He also finished second in the league in extra-base hits (72), total bases (300), and slugging percentage (.607). Colorado, in only their second season of existence, won the National League West Division title. The Rockies lost in the Division Series to the Atlanta Braves, but they seemed to be one of baseball's up-and-coming teams.

SLOWED BY INJURIES. Walker had developed into an All-Star performer despite a history of injuries. He missed the entire 1988 baseball season with a knee injury and had to have surgery following the 1994 season to repair a slightly torn rotator cuff in his right shoulder. Only once through the 1995 season had Walker played more than 140 games and he had been on the disabled list three times.

The worst injury of Walker's career came on June 9, 1996 when he ran into the centerfield fence and broke his collarbone. He missed 60 games and was not at full speed when he returned in August. Walker batted .276 for the season, and just .142 on the road. Without their star outfielder, the Rockies failed to repeat as division champions.

Superstar

CAREER YEAR. Walker was determined to have a huge season in 1997. "All I try to do is stay healthy," he explained to *Sports Illustrated.* "I owed it to the organization, I owed it to the fans. I get paid to play this game, and I didn't want to sit on the bench this year—at least not every day." Unfortunately, Walker slipped on a rock while fishing during the off-season and separated his shoulder.

Walker's shoulder healed in time for spring training. Showing that he was healthy, he tore up the National League early in the season. By the time of the All-Star Game Walker led the major leagues in hitting at .398 and in total bases, slugging percentage, on-base percentage, and extra-base hits. He also had 25 home runs and 68 runs batted in. "Sometimes this year I've even surprised myself," Walker confessed to *Sports Illustrated*. "I'll hit one down the leftfield line in one at bat and down the rightfield line the next. Sometimes it's like, 'Wow, how'd I do that?'"

ALL-STAR SHOWDOWN. Walker received criticism from fans and the media when he decided to sit out a game against fire-balling left-hander Randy Johnson of the Seattle Mariners. Even though many left-handed batters sit out against Johnson, no one else had ever admitted that fact. "I could have lied and said my knee hurt, but I told the truth," Walker explained to *Sports Illustrated*. "Randy Johnson is the best pitcher in the game, and I didn't want to face him. A lot of guys don't face him. I didn't think it was that big a deal."

Fans voted Walker to the starting team for the 1997 All-Star Game. Who was the starting pitcher for the American League? Johnson. When Walker came to the plate to face the "Big Unit," Johnson threw the first pitch over his head. Walker turned his helmet around and switched batter's boxes for the next pitch.

CHANCE FOR HISTORY. Walker kept his batting average around the .400 mark throughout July. His hot hitting had the baseball world talking, wondering if he could finish the season above the magic .400 mark. The last time a hitter had batted over .400 was 1941, when the great Boston Red Sox left fielder Ted Williams did the trick. Walker realized his chances of reaching the magic mark were slim. "I don't mind people asking me [about hitting .400], because I know it's not going to happen," he told *Sports Illustrated*. "I'm a career .285 hitter."

In addition to trying to bat .400, Walker also had a chance to win the Triple Crown. The Triple Crown involves leading either the American or National Leagues in batting average, home runs, and RBI. The last time a National League player won the Triple Crown was Joe Medwick in 1937 for the St. Louis Cardinals. The last player to win the Triple

Crown was Carl Yastrzemski of the Boston Red Sox in 1967. Walker led the league in hitting and home runs, and was second in RBI late in the season.

Walker credited staying in the lineup with his big year—he played a career-high 153 games in 1997—even though his knee and shoulder bothered him throughout the season. "It's just being in there all the time," Walker told the *Sporting News*. "That's been my downfall in past years, being injured and not being in the lineup every day. This year, for the most part, I've stayed fairly healthy and I've been able to be in the lineup almost every day."

MVP. Behind the play of Walker Colorado stayed in the National League West Division race until late in the season. Despite falling short to the San Francisco Giants, Walker's season was worthy of Most Valuable Player consideration. He finished with a .366 batting average (second in the National League), 49 home runs (first in the National League), and 130 RBI (second in the National League).

Walker led the major leagues with 409 total bases, the seventh-most in National League history and the most since Stan Musial of the St. Louis Cardinals had 429 in 1948. He had the third highest batting average for someone with 49 home runs or more. (Only Babe Ruth had higher batting averages, a feat he accomplished twice.) Walker came within 4 hits and 10 RBI of winning the Triple Crown.

Some experts said that Walker's numbers were made better by playing at Coors Field, but he actually hit more home runs on the road (29) and batted .346 away from home. "I'm really happy about that," he explained to the *Sporting News*. "This year I think I've proven I can hit outside Denver."

Showing outstanding speed for a big man, Walker also stole 30 bases, and his defense earned him his third Gold Glove Award. "He has had the kind of season players dream of," Tony Gwynn of the San Diego Padres, who beat out Walker for the National League batting crown, told *USA Today*. "There is no question he is MVP of our league."

The baseball writers who voted for the National League Most Valuable Player Award agreed with Gwynn. Walker far out-distanced Mike Piazza of the Los Angeles Dodgers and **Jeff Bagwell** (see entry) of the Houston Astros to win the award. He was the first Canadian player ever to be so honored. "I've done something good for me personally, and I've done something good for my country," he said. "I hope a lot of kids in Canada are looking. If I can be any kind of role model and incentive for them not to give up on the dream of playing in the big leagues one day."

OFF THE FIELD. Walker lives in West Palm Beach, Florida, in the off-season. He is an amateur magician and likes to play practical jokes on his teammates. Walker's favorite rock band is Metallica. He now holds the record for most home runs hit by a Canadian player, breaking the record of 194 held previously by Jeff Heath.

Fame has not changed Walker, something he is proud of. "The people back home will say to me, 'Boy, you haven't changed at all,'" he explained to *Sports Illustrated*. "To me, that's the nicest thing anyone can say to you." Walker does not like to wear dress clothes and his nickname on the Rockies is "Dirtbag." "I have lots of nice clothes, I just don't wear them," he confessed to the same magazine. Walker hosts a half-hour weekly radio talk-show.

Walker is still a hockey fan and still dreams about what might have been. "I'd much rather be playing hockey than doing this," he admitted to *USA Today*. "It's the game I love. I gave up on it at an early age. I'll never know what could have happened."

BEHIND THE SCENES

Fans sometimes forget that ballplayers are people just like them. Walker is divorced from his wife, Christa, and has a daughter, Brittany. He loves his daughter, but does not get to see her as much as he would like. Once Walker had to leave after a visit and Brittany did not want him to leave. "She didn't want me to go; then she asked if she could come with me," Walker recalled in *Sports Illustrated*. "That just killed me. I get on the bus and sit down next to [teammate] Billy Swift, and he just looks at me. Tears are streaming down my face. That's something the public doesn't see. We hurt. We're human. We have feelings. Believe me, I feel very guilty about it. I can spoil her to death when I see her, but that doesn't change the fact that when she wakes up in the morning, I'm not there."

Someday Walker hopes he can lead his team the baseball's ultimate prize: a World Series championship. "I'll take the worst year of my career next year [1998], and if I walk away with a World Series ring, people can talk about how bad I was all year and I wouldn't care," he admitted to *Baseball Weekly.* "The ultimate is going all the way."

Unlike other players, Walker does not take batting practice and does not study opposing pitchers. He has a simple approach to hitting, as he told the *Sporting News:* "The thing is, I just step in the box, see the ball and hit it."

 WHERE TO WRITE:
C/O COLORADO ROCKIES, COORS FIELD,
20TH AND BLAKE ST.,
DENVER, CO 80204.

Sources

Atlanta Journal-Constitution, July 20, 1997; September 14, 1997; November 14, 1997.
Baseball Weekly, November 12, 1997.
Los Angeles Times, September 12, 1997; September 20, 1997; September 21, 1997; November 14, 1997.
Maclean's, August 24, 1992.
Newsday, November 14, 1997.
Saturday Night, October 1994.
Sporting News, July 14, 1997; October 6, 1997.
Sports Illustrated, July 9, 1990; July 27, 1992; April 5, 1993; May 2, 1994; June 13, 1994; April 17, 1995; July 31, 1995; April 14, 1997; July 14, 1997; October 6, 1997.
USA Today, May 22, 1997; October 1, 1997; November 13, 1997; November 14, 1997.

Karrie Webb

1974–

Australian golfer Karrie Webb has taken the Ladies' Professional Golf Association (LPGA) by storm. In 1996 she won rookie of the year honors while becoming the first woman ever to win over $1 million during one season. Webb followed up her rookie success by capturing the 1997 Vare Trophy, given to the player with the lowest per-round scoring average during the year. She and **Annika Sorenstam** (see entry) from Sweden give the LPGA a one-two punch, and their rivalry should carry the woman's game into the next century.

"Karrie is going to be a star for many years."
—LPGA veteran Nancy Lopez.

Growing Up

WONDER FROM DOWN UNDER. Karrie (Kahr-ee) Webb was born December 21, 1974, in Ayr, Queensland, Australia. She is the oldest of three daughters of Robert and Evelyn Webb. Webb's father worked in construction and her mother operated a cafe. Ayr is a town best known for growing sugarcane and is 10 miles inland from the Great Barrier Reef.

Webb loved sports as a child and participated on local boys' teams. She also played guitar and tap danced. Webb took up golf along with her parents at the age of eight. Her grandmother—who loved the game—bought the young athlete her first set of clubs. "I was born to play," Webb admitted in *People Weekly*.

MOVING UP. When Webb was 11 her grandparents sent her on a trip to see her golfing idol—fellow Queensland native Greg Norman, then the number-one ranked male player in the world—play at the 1986 Queensland Open. After seeing Norman play and getting his autograph, Webb gave up other sports and concentrated on golf full-time.

Webb and her friends pretended to be great golfers. "We'd play the last round of the Masters and I'd be Greg Norman, someone would be [Nick] Faldo and someone would be Seve [Ballesteros]," she recalled in the *Los Angeles Times*. "We would have our own little tournament."

Webb worked hard to improve her golf game. "Karrie was very determined," her coach, Kelvin Haller, the greenskeeper at Ayr Gold Club, recalled in *Sports Illustrated*. "You didn't have to chase her down to practice; she'd be there before you. She was winning tournaments from the beginning, beating girls much older than she was." Haller emphasized golf basics and good rhythm in her swing.

Soon Webb was winning nearly all the junior tournaments in Australia. At the age of 16 she made the Australian national junior team and won the national junior championship. As part of the national junior team Webb traveled and played tournaments in Asia and Paris, France.

TURNS PRO. Webb finished high school in Ayr and worked at her family's lunch stand. No college coaches recruited her to play golf, and she had to make a decision. A month before her twentieth birthday Webb and her caddy and fiance Tom Haller—the nephew of her coach—decided to take on the professional golf tour. The two borrowed $5,000 from her grandparents and began to tour professionally.

In late 1995 Webb joined the WPG European Tour. Traveling through Europe was hard because she needed to adjust to different countries, languages, and currencies every week. "You can get [cheated] if you don't think quickly enough," Webb told *Golf Magazine*. She saw snow for the first time when she played a tournament in the shadows of a glacier in Austria.

Webb dominated the European Tour in 1995, winning that year's Women's British Open by six strokes. She finished in the Top-10 in seven other tournaments and won the third-most money on the tour. Webb won the tour's rookie of the year award.

Superstar

TAKES ON UNITED STATES. Her success in Europe made Webb confident enough about her game to join the LPGA Tour, the toughest women's circuit in the world. "Although I played in Europe last year, I knew this is where I'd play," Webb told the *Dallas Morning News*. "This is the ultimate tour because it is, more or less, a world tour. All the best players are here, the competition is great and I love competing."

At 21 years of age, Webb was the youngest player on the LPGA Tour. She started strong in her rookie season. In her

WEEK AT GREG'S

At the age of 17 Webb won a tournament sponsored by her idol, Greg Norman. The first prize was the chance to spend a week with Norman at his home in Hobe Sound, Florida. "It was a dream come true," Webb declared in the *Los Angeles Times*.

Webb impressed her idol. "They had to do everything I did, live the life of a professional for a week, to see if they had the dedication required," Norman recalled in *Sports Illustrated*. "If I was up at dawn, they were up at dawn. If I lifted weights, they lifted weights. If I hit 400 balls, they hit 400 balls. Karrie was right there the whole way, whereas the boy couldn't keep up. She had the right attitude. It was obvious that she had the game and the mental toughness to succeed. I would say she's one of the most promising young players, male or female, that I've seen."

Webb credits Norman with improving her short game and helping her keep her head still while putting. "He was great," she explained to *Golf Magazine*. "Not many people get to meet their idol."

first five tournaments she claimed her first LPGA win—the HealthSouth Inaugural—finished second twice, and had two other Top-10 finishes. She won $241,638, more than any other player had won in their first five tournaments. "There's not a flaw in her game," veteran tour player Meg Mallon declared in the *Los Angeles Times*. "She's awfully good."

Her fast start surprised Webb. "I wouldn't have expected in my wildest dreams to start off as well as I have," she admitted to the *Los Angeles Times*. "I don't worry about how long it's going to go. I'm just going to ride it out. One day or one tournament, I'm going to play bad. That's just the facts of life. But at the moment, I just don't think I can shoot a really bad score."

ROOKIE OF THE YEAR. By the end of the 1996 season Webb had won four tournaments—including the first-ever LPGA Tour Championship—and led the LPGA Tour in prize winnings. She won $1,002,500, a tour record. Webb also became the only rookie—male or female—to win over one million dollars. "It feels great because no one can ever say she was the first to win a million dollars except me," she told the *Los Angeles Times*. "It's always going to be in the record books. No one can change that." Webb was the first rookie to lead the LPGA in winnings since Nancy Lopez in 1977.

Webb's consistently strong year—in which she finished in the top-five twelve times in 25 tournaments—earned her the LPGA Rookie of the Year award. "I'm more proud of my consistency than the four wins," she explained in *USA Today*. "I had five seconds and seemed to be in contention almost every week. It was all unexpected, I certainly didn't think I'd do that well, but when I got in contention, I managed to keep my game under control." Webb finished second to Laura Davies—who won two fewer tournament and almost $100,000 less in prize money—for the LPGA Player of the Year award.

Golf experts have compared Webb to Tiger Woods—the young star of the men's PGA Tour—but she wants her accomplishments to stand on their own. "I don't think you can ever stop people from making comparisons, and some of those comparisons make me very honored that I can even be in the same sentence as Nancy Lopez," Webb told the *Columbian*. "But I want to make my own name."

RIVALRY. The 1997 LPGA season became a duel between two of the best young golfers in the world—Webb and Annika Sorenstam of Sweden. Sorenstam had won the 1995 LPGA Player of the Year award and had earned the Vare Trophy— given to the player with the lowest scoring average—in 1995 and 1996. "I think the rivalry is more in the eyes of the media," Webb revealed in *USA Today*. "Sure, it's a rivalry in the sense that we both want to be number 1, we both want the money title and the Vare Trophy. But we get along with each other. We both want to be the best players that we can be."

BRITISH REPEAT. The biggest win of 1997 for Webb was when she won her second consecutive Women's British Open. In the third round she fired a course-record 9-under-par 63 to take an 8-stroke lead and 18-under-par-score into the final round. "I'm ecstatic, speechless—this is my best score ever," Webb declared in the *Los Angeles Times*. "I've never played that well before."

Webb's final score of 269 (19 under par) shattered the previous record of 274 set by Jane Geddes in 1989. Her 8-stroke margin of victory matched the record set by Karen Lunn in 1993. "I am over the moon," Webb told *Newsday*. "I played great golf all week and everything just fell into place. The British Open is such a special tournament to me because it's the first one I ever won."

VARE TROPHY. Webb and Sorenstam were battling for the most important LPGA titles entering the last tournament of the year—the LPGA Tour Championship in Las Vegas, Nevada. Sorenstam led in prize money and in the race for Player of the Year honors, while Webb held the edge for the Vare Trophy. Sorenstam had won six tournaments and Webb three.

Webb was the defending champion, but did not feel any extra pressure to win the tournament. "It's a big tournament," she explained to *USA Today*. "If I play well, there will be a good outcome. I can't think about all the things I could do if I win the tournament. All I can do is try to play myself into contention."

Sorenstam won the season's final tournament in a three-way playoff. The victory helped her earn the money title with a tour record $1,236,789 to Webb's $987,606. The win also gave Sorenstam the LPGA Player of the Year award. Webb finished first in the race for the Vare Trophy, winning with an average score of 70.00 to Sorenstam's 70.04. She also finished first on the LPGA Tour in rounds under par (66) and Top-10 finishes (21 times in 25 tournaments). "That's amazing to me," Webb said. "I've just been really consistent. If one part of my game is off, another part seems to pull me through."

WHY SO GOOD? What sets Webb apart from other golfers is her ability to concentrate and her intense desire to win. "Ever since I turned pro, all I've wanted to do is compete," she declared to *Sports Illustrated.* "I just love it. I love the pressure and being in contention. I love it much more now as a pro than I did as an amateur. And the amazing thing is that I'm on the LPGA tour and I've had that pressure every week."

OFF THE COURSE. Webb lives in Orlando, Florida. She likes to skydive, play basketball, listen to dance music, read, and go fishing. Webb's success has led to her nickname: "Cash and Karrie."

Webb broke up with her fiancé Tom Haller in 1996. With her busy schedule she does not have time for dating. "I'm not into that sort of thing," Webb explained to *People Weekly.* "I'm concentrating on golf."

Norman and Webb now have a mutual admiration society. Norman faxed Webb congratulations after she won the 1995 British Women's Open. She appeared on a "This Is Your Life" television segment for Norman.

Webb enjoys her job. "I don't know what my secret for success is," she admitted to *Golf Magazine.* "I just love being out here. I've dreamed about this since I was a kid."

WHERE TO WRITE:
C/O LADIES' PROFESSIONAL GOLF ASSOCIATION,
100 INTERNATIONAL GOLF DR.,
DAYTONA BEACH, FL 32124-1092.

Sources

Atlanta Journal and Constitution, April 24, 1997; July 13, 1997.

Columbian, July 10, 1997; September 15, 1997.

Dallas Morning News, May 20, 1996.

Golf Magazine, August 1996; February 1997.

Los Angeles Times, March 28, 1996; November 24, 1996; November 25, 1996; August 16, 1997; August 17, 1997; October 30, 1997; November 23, 1997.

Newsday, October 3, 1996; August 18, 1997.

People Weekly, April 28, 1997.

Sports Illustrated. March 25, 1996; May 13, 1996; January 20, 1997; May 12, 1997.

USA Today, March 3, 1997; March 27, 1997; April 30, 1997; May 14, 1997; November 20, 1997.

Additional information provided by the Ladies' Professional Golf Association (LPGA).

Pernell Whitaker

1964–

Boxer Pernell "Sweet Pea" Whitaker fights by one motto: You cannot hit what you cannot catch. During his career he won the 1984 Olympic gold medal and six professional titles in four weight classes. Whitaker, however, is best known for the fights he did not win: a controversial draw against Julio Cesar Chavez and a tough loss to Oscar De La Hoya. Long considered the top pound-for-pound fighter in boxing, Whitaker has taken his place as one of the best ever in his sport.

"If I don't want God to hit me, he's not going to hit me."
—Pernell Whitaker.

Growing Up

PROJECTS PRODUCT. Pernell Whitaker was born January 2, 1964. He grew up in the Young Park federal housing project in Norfolk, Virginia. Whitaker, his four sisters, and two brothers shared a three-bedroom apartment with their parents, Raymond and Novella.

Whitaker says that he enjoyed his childhood home. "What matters isn't the size of your house or how much it costs but how much love is under the roof," he explained in *Sports Illustrated.* "Dreams are the same in public housing as they are in a mansion."

FIGHTS FOR SURVIVAL. Growing up Whitaker had to learn to fight on the streets to survive. When he was eight his father talked to him after he came home crying. "A boy had hit him in the head with a stick," Raymond Whitaker recalled in *Sports Illustrated.* "He was bleeding, but it looked worse than it was. I sat him down right then. He was always smaller than the boys his age. I told him he had to take care of himself, because in the Park it's going to happen. Let nobody feel like they can put their hands on you. Fight with everything in you. Then the next time you've got to walk away from it or you'll be fighting every day. And you don't want that."

One day Clyde Taylor—the director of the local recreation center—saw Whitaker involved in a street fight. The young fighter's skills impressed him, and he encouraged Whitaker to get into the ring. In that way Taylor became his first boxing trainer.

Whitaker spent very little time at home after he took up boxing. "Every day it was the same thing," Raymond Whitaker told *Sports Illustrated.* "Pete would box in the gym from four until seven, then play basketball on the hoop at the other end from seven until he came home." His parents made sure Whitaker finished his homework, however, before he went to the gym to train.

PROMISES MOM. Taylor took Whitaker to watch fights at the Navy base in Norfolk. He told his young pupil to look for little things like how boxers moved their feet and how they avoided being hit. Whitaker began his career by fighting others his own

Whitaker (right) attempts to jab James "Buddy" McGirt during a bout at Madison Square Garden in New York.

age, but he soon started to take on sailors from the base. "I fought sailors when I was 13 and 14," Whitaker recalled in *Sports Illustrated*. "I was too good for them after that."

Soon Whitaker was ready to make a promise to his mother. "At first, Pete did a lot of losing," Novella Whitaker, told *Sports Illustrated*. "I'd say, 'Pete, you can't lose 'em all.' Then he started winning. He said, 'Mama, I'm going to be world champion one day.' I said, 'If you believe it, Pete, I believe it.'" Whitaker told his mother that some day he would earn enough money to get her out of the projects.

GOLDEN MOMENT. Before long Whitaker became one of the top amateur (unpaid) boxers in the United States. By the time he turned 20 he had won three world championship trophies. In 1984 Whitaker defeated Joey Belinc to earn a spot on the U.S. Olympic boxing team that would compete at the Summer Olympics in Los Angeles, California. The American team was one of the strongest ever and included such stars as Evander Holyfield, Mark Breland, Meldrick Taylor, and Tyrell Biggs.

Whitaker received a great honor when the U.S. team named him its captain. He hoped to be able to sneak up on the competition. "Lord, I hope I'm not favored in Los Angeles," Whitaker admitted to *Sports Illustrated*. "I just want to be a guy nobody notices as I work my way up."

Many countries allied with the Soviet Union did not participate in the 1984 Olympics, including the powerful Cuban boxing team. This left the United States to dominate the competition, and Whitaker won the gold medal as a 132-pound lightweight. Many observers picked him as the outstanding boxer in the Olympics, but the honor went to fellow American Paul Gonzales, also a gold-medal winner.

TURNS PRO. Whitaker fought a total of 215 fights as an amateur, losing only 14 times. He knocked out his opponent 91 times. Following the Olympics, Whitaker signed to fight professionally with fight manager Lou Duva. Whitaker joined his Olympic teammates Mark Breland, Meldrick Taylor, Evander Holyfield, and Tyrell Biggs—all Olympic medal winners—on a card where he captured his first fight in a match against Farrain Comeaux.

On December 21, 1984, Whitaker married Rovonda (Von) Anthony. The couple bought a house for themselves and their sons, Pernell Jr. and Dominique. Whitaker also bought his parents a new home in Norfolk, out of the projects. "If I had three wishes, they've already been granted," he revealed in *Sports Illustrated*. "I wished to win the gold medal. I wished I could buy my mother a house—a real house, a nice house. And I wished I could have a home and a family of my own."

ROBBED! Whitaker fought his way up the rankings, winning his first 15 professional fights. On March 12, 1988, he fought Jose Luis Ramirez—the World Boxing Council (WBC) lightweight champion—with a chance to capture his first professional title.

Whitaker broke his left hand—the power hand for a left-handed boxer—in the fourth round of the fight. Despite this injury most ringside observers felt the challenger won the fight. The judges, however, saw the fight differently, with two of the three giving the fight to Ramirez. Whitaker was disappointed with the loss and vowed not to let the judges steal a fight from him again.

FIRST TITLE. In February 1989 Whitaker won his first professional championship— the International Boxing Federation (IBF) lightweight title. He won a unanimous decision against Greg Haugen. Whitaker left no doubt this time, ripping repeated hard body shots at Haugen and knocking the champion down for the first time in his career. Two judges had Whitaker winning every round of the fight.

After defeating Haugen, Whitaker got a rematch with Ramirez in August 1989. With his hand healed, he was even more dominating than in their previous bout. "I knew I was in for a long night in the first round," Ramirez admitted to *Sports Illustrated*. "He was so much stronger, so much faster." This time the judges were unanimous that Whitaker was the winner.

Superstar

BEST POUND-FOR-POUND. In 1991 Whitaker defeated Jorge Paez to once again successfully defend his IBF lightweight title. On March 6, 1993, he defeated James "Buddy" McGirt for the World Boxing Council (WBC) welterweight crown. McGirt had won three world titles and was known as a good defensive boxer. Whitaker won a close decision.

The only fighter left to challenge Whitaker as the best pound-for-pound fighter in the world was Julio Cesar Chavez, the legendary champion from Mexico. Chavez had an incredible record of 87-0, with 75 knockouts. He was a powerful body puncher who also had an iron chin. Chavez had won five world titles in three weight divisions during his career.

Whitaker held a 32-1 record with 15 knockouts. He also had won five world titles in three weight classes. Whitaker's style provided a contrast to Chavez. He liked to move around the ring, throwing punches and making his opponent miss.

ROBBED AGAIN. The two great fighters signed to fight on September 10, 1993, at the Alamodome in San Antonio, Texas. The winner of the fight would capture Whitaker's welterweight title, but both fighters knew something more was at stake."This is for the best fighter, pound for pound," Whitaker explained in *Sports Illustrated*. "We may be fighting for my title, but that's not what everyone is talking about. This is like going for the gold again."

The mostly Hispanic crowd at the Alamodome favored Chavez, but Whitaker quickly took the fans out of the fight. He put on a masterful performance, moving around the ring and giving Chavez nothing to hit. Surprisingly, Whitaker also out muscled Chavez on the ropes. As the fight moved into the later rounds, Chavez became more and more frustrated by Whitaker's elusive style.

Boxing experts watching the fight gave Whitaker anywhere from eight to nine of the bout's twelve rounds. Once again, the judges disagreed. Two scored the fight even, while one judge favored Whitaker. The final outcome, therefore, was a draw, or tie.

The judge's decision devastated Whitaker. "I knew this might happen," he said the morning after the fight. "But still it was like a bad dream. Last night it was like someone put a knife in me and twisted it. I want to tell the world that I beat the unbeatable. From now on they're all going to look at me and say, 'There's the guy who beat Julio Cesar Chavez. He has been beaten. Pernell Whitaker beat him up.' Pound for pound, Pernell Whitaker is the best fighter in the world. I'm not just a runner; I can fight. Give me credit. Give me the respect I deserve. Give me this one! Deep down I know I won it. Deep down you know it."

FOUR TITLES. When Whitaker won a decision over Julio Cesar Vasquez to win the World Boxing Association (WBA) junior middleweight title, he became only the fourth boxer in history to win a world title in four different weight classes. The only other boxers to accomplish this feat before Whitaker were Sugar Ray Leonard, Thomas Hearns, and Roberto Duran. Whitaker's titles had come in the following weight classes: lightweight (135 pounds), junior welterweight (140 pounds), welterweight (147 pounds), and junior middleweight (154 pounds).

KEEPS FIGHTING. After his disappointment against Chavez, Whitaker had a hard time getting up for fights. He did not train as hard as he could, even though he kept on winning. Age also began to sap some of the speed that was Whitaker's trademark. "He hasn't had any motivation," his manager, Lou Duva, explained in the *Atlanta Journal-Constitution*. "That's been his downfall. He doesn't know what to do with himself."

Whitaker felt he had nothing left to prove. "Boxing has been completed for Pernell Whitaker," he explained in *Newsday*. "I could've retired and rode off into the sunset and said, 'I'm the best pound-for-pound. I don't have anything else to prove.' But I've been moving on and competing and winning. I fought all my mandatories, all the No. 1 contenders. You never saw me take a joke fight. I fight the best out there. I haven't lost any reason why I'm the best pound-for-pound."

Whitaker's lack of motivation, his poor training habits, and age began to catch up with him. In September 1995 Gary Jacobs of Scotland knocked him down in the eleventh round of their twelve-round fight. Whitaker got off the canvas and knocked Jacobs down twice in the twelfth round and won a unanimous decision. Then in January 1997 he was knocked down twice by Diobelys Hurtado before coming back to win with an eleventh round knockout.

ANOTHER SHOWDOWN. Finally Whitaker found an opponent worthy of him when he agreed to fight Olympic gold medalist and three-time professional champion Oscar De La Hoya in April 1997. He decided to put everything on the line. "The last couple of fights, I wasn't doing a lot of road work," Whitaker admitted to the *Atlanta Journal-Constitution*. "I need my legs under me so I can dazzle him [De La Hoya] with my footwork and slap him around. I'm focused this time on one thing—him. No distractions. This isn't one of those nothing fights I've been having to go through where I went in looking forward to something else. I'm at my peak right now. Everything is at my best. It's like being in the Olympics one more time. It's like going for the gold medal. Peter is focused. Pete is there."

Whitaker realized that the battle with De La Hoya was as important as his fight with Chavez. "This is the fight I'm going to be remembered for," he explained to *USA Today.* "It's not about the money. It's about competition. That's what hypes Pernell Whitaker. This is what brings out the best in Pernell Whitaker. I'm going to give them a performance of a lifetime."

ROBBERY TIMES THREE. The bout was close throughout. Whitaker's skillful defense continually frustrated the stronger De La Hoya, and he knocked his opponent down in the ninth round. The fight went the distance, so once again the judges would decide the great champion's fate. For the third time in his career, Whitaker lost a controversial decision as each judge voted for De La Hoya, giving him Whitaker's welterweight title. De La Hoya already held world championships as a lightweight, junior lightweight, and super lightweight.

"I didn't think I had to knock him out," Whitaker admitted in the *Los Angeles Times.* "I put enough punishment on him, and that speaks for itself. That was the old Pernell Whitaker you saw out there. You guys all said I was 33 years old. And I wanted to come out and prove I had the legs of a 22-year-old. It's sad that we're going to have to do this again and I'm going to have to knock him out. I wasn't expecting anything would happen here [like] what happened in San Antonio [against Chavez]. If Oscar had beaten me, I would be the first to say he is the best fighter in the world. But it's a little sour right now. He didn't come close to hurting me. He couldn't do the things he wanted to do because I was giving him different angles."

De La Hoya gave Whitaker credit. "I said it all along—his style is the most difficult in boxing," he told *Sports Illustrated* after the fight. "He does things in the ring nobody else does. Oh, this guy was smart, very smart. But that experience, that goes with boxing." With the loss to De La Hoya, Whitaker's record dropped to 40-2-1.

OUT OF THE RING. Whitaker lives in Virginia Beach, Virginia. He and his wife Von have three sons, and they also take in other boys to live with them. Whitaker loves playing basketball.

The U.S. Department of Housing and Urban Development (HUD) honored Whitaker as a "hero of public housing" along with seven other honorees, including former president Jimmy Carter. All of the winners were either born or had lived in public or assisted housing. Whitaker wants to be a role model for children living in public housing.

Whitaker described the affect he has on other fighters in an article in *Sports Illustrated:* "Most fighters don't even know what's happened to them. I've taken something from them—their confidence, their fight plan. They can't hit you, the fight is yours. They get self-conscious about punching. After a while they start reaching, just hoping they're going to hit me. I don't care who I'm fighting. I don't care if it's God. If I don't want God to hit me, he's not going to hit me."

THAT'S ENTERTAINMENT!

Whitaker has a reputation for being a showboat. In a bout against Roger Mayweather he ducked a punch and pulled down his opponents trunks. In another fight—against Alfredo Layne—he spun in the air, hitting Layne on his way down.

Boxing experts feel that his goofing around in the ring may have cost Whitaker in the close fights he has lost or tied. He claims that he wants to put on an entertaining show for the fans. "We've got to put our tap shoes on," Whitaker explained to *Sports Illustrated.* "I'm an entertainer."

WHERE TO WRITE:
C/O WORLD BOXING COUNCIL,
GENOVA 33, OFICINA 503,
COLONIA JUAREZ, CUAUHTEMOC, 0600
MEXICO CITY, DF, MEXICO.

Sources

Atlanta Journal-Constitution, April 11, 1997.

Jet, October 17, 1994; September 18, 1995.

Los Angeles Times, April 13, 1997.

Newsday, April 11, 1997.

Sports Illustrated, April 23, 1984; July 14, 1984; November 26, 1984; December 19, 1988; February 27, 1989; August 28, 1989; October 14, 1991; August 9, 1993; September 20, 1993; October 10, 1994; June 10, 1996; April 21, 1997.

Time, November 26, 1984.

USA Today, April 4, 1997.

Additional information provided by the Gannett News Service.

Steve Yzerman

1965–

Steve Yzerman—center for the Detroit Red Wings of the National Hockey League (NHL)—always loved hockey. As a child he daydreamed about skating around the ice carrying the most famous trophy in sports—the Stanley Cup. For 14 years he struggled to make his dream come true, only to fall short in a series of frustrating playoff losses. During the 1996–97 season—just when most hockey experts had given up on Yzerman—his grit and determination helped carry the Red Wings to their first Stanley Cup championship in 42 years.

"He's been the franchise."
—Detroit Red Wings general manager Jimmy Devallano.

Growing Up

LIVES FOR HOCKEY. Steve Yzerman (EYE-zer-man) was born May 9, 1965, in Cranbrook, British Columbia, Canada. He was one of five children of Ronald and Jean Yzerman. The family lived in Nepean, Ontario, a suburb of Ottawa, the capital of Canada. Ronald Yzerman was a high-ranking official in the Canadian social services department.

LED DETROIT RED WINGS TO
FIRST STANLEY CUP
CHAMPIONSHIP IN 42 YEARS
DURING THE 1996–97 SEASON.

WON 1988–89
LESTER B. PEARSON AWARD,
GIVEN BY NHL PLAYERS TO THE
LEAGUE'S OUTSTANDING PLAYER.

SET RECORD FOR MOST
CONSECUTIVE SEASONS SERVING
AS CAPTAIN OF ONE TEAM (13)
DURING THE 1996–97 CAMPAIGN.

YZERMAN QUIETLY LED DETROIT
TO HOCKEY'S ULTIMATE PRIZE.

Yzerman's parents stressed education, and they worried that their son did not take his school work seriously. All he could think about was hockey. "I know it's not good advice to kids, but all I ever thought about was playing hockey," he recalled in the *Detroit Free Press*. "School took a back seat when I started moving up. I just played hockey. I did what I had to do, nothing else." Yzerman's favorite player was Brian Trottier, the star center of the New York Islanders.

Yzerman scored his first goal when he was five years old. He was so small that when he swung his stick he fell over. Yzerman played peewee hockey at the age of seven and dominated a league with children as old as twelve.

Yzerman progressed quickly through Canada's many ranks of midget and peewee hockey. By age 14 he was skating for Cornwell, a highly ranked amateur team that also featured future Chicago Blackhawks goaltender Darren Pang. At the age of 16 Yzerman left home to play for the Peterborough Petes of the Ontario Hockey League (OHL).

DETROIT DRAFT PICK. Yzerman impressed the general manager of the Detroit Red Wings—Jimmy Devellano—when Devellano saw him play for the first time for in Peterborough. "When [Steve] was on the ice, you could tell he had a whole lot of ability," Devellano remembered. "He was a very good skater. He had good balance and good hockey sense."

The Red Wings—who had gone a decade without having a winning record—selected Yzerman with the fourth overall pick in the 1983 NHL Draft. Detroit signed their new player to a seven-year contract, and Yzerman reported to the club at the tender age of 18. At first Detroit thought their top draft pick might need two years of minor-league seasoning, but Yzerman already showed flashes of brilliance. He made the team in training camp.

Yzerman made an instant impression on his new team and the NHL during the 1983–84 season. He scored 39 goals and had 48 assists (87 total points). Yzerman became the youngest-ever player to earn a spot in the NHL All-Star Game. At the end of the season Yzerman finished second in the voting for the Calder Trophy—awarded to the NHL rookie-of-the-year—to goalie Tom Barrasso of the Buffalo Sabres.

FITTING IN. Yzerman had a strong second season (1984–85) with 30 goals and 59 assists. The Red Wings qualified for the playoffs for the first time in his career, but the Chicago Blackhawks swept them in three straight games in the first round.

Despite his early success, Yzerman had a hard time fitting in with his teammates. He was naturally shy and also younger than most of his teammates. "Yzerman was a loner, unable to find his niche with the club," journalist Keith Gave wrote in the *Detroit Free Press*. "He seldom went on a road trip without his Walkman. Through his earphones, he listened to music and sang along to himself. It was an unhappy time."

Yzerman had two close friends on the team—Claude Loiselle and Lane Lambert. When the Red Wings sent both Loiselle and Lambert to the minors, he felt completely alone. "When Claude and Lane got sent down, I lived alone," he revealed to the *Detroit Free Press*. "And I stayed home and did nothing. I didn't fit in anywhere. I didn't feel comfortable. It was a tough position to be in. But I couldn't say anything, because I was one of the major reasons the team didn't do well."

The Red Wings finished last in the NHL during the 1985–86 season with only 17 wins. They scored the fewest goals in the league (266) and gave up the most (415). Yzerman missed part of the year with a broken collar bone and recorded a career-low 14 goals and 28 assists. "Our team wasn't close at all," Yzerman admitted to *Sports Illustrated*. "After practices and games, everybody went their own way, and so did I."

THE CAPTAIN. Before the 1986–87 season the Red Wings hired a new coach, Jacques Demers. Demers recognized immediately that if Detroit was going to succeed—they had

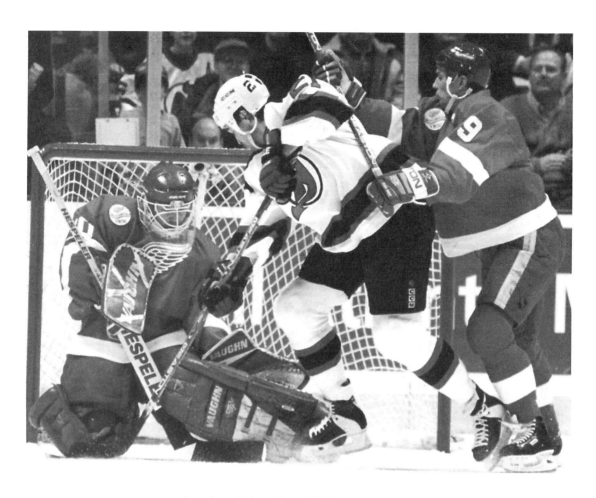

Yzerman checks New Jersey Devils' Randy McKay in front of the Red Wings' net.

missed the playoffs in 16 of the previous 20 seasons—the team needed Yzerman to be a leader. He called Yzerman's parents and his former minor league coach at Peterborough, all of whom told him that the young player responded well to challenges.

After his disappointing season in 1985–86, Yzerman questioned his ability. "All summer I worried about it," he confessed to the *Detroit Free Press.* "I was on the verge of becoming a run-of-the-mill player. Never a day went by when I didn't think, 'Geez, if I'm not careful, in a couple of years I could be out of hockey.' It worried me every day."

Demers made a bold move by appointing his troubled young star as Detroit's captain, the player on the ice who wears a C on his jersey. At 21 years of age Yzerman was the youngest captain in team history. "I remember when Jacques said, 'I want to name him captain,'" Jimmy Devallano told *USA Today*. "I was a bit concerned because I thought he was too young."

Being the captain meant that he had to be the team's leader. The faith his new coach showed in him renewed Yzerman's confidence. Being the captain forced the shy young player to interact with his teammates, most of whom were older than he. Yzerman also gained 15 pounds in the off-season, helping him better handle physical play.

Yzerman rewarded his coach's faith in him by scoring 31 goals and passing off for 59 assists in the 1986–87 season. He led the Wings to a 38-point improvement in the standings and a spot in the playoffs. "We have improved from a year and a half ago," Demers explained to *Sports Illustrated*. "You can't do that without a superstar—and that's what Steve is. He is a meal ticket for a coach."

Demers was pleased with how his superstar responded to his new role. "He's handling the captaincy as well as anyone could," he related to the *Detroit Free Press*. "You can talk about him being a superstar, a rich kid, good-looking and all that. But he's handling it as classy as anybody can handle it. Let me put it this way. Steve Yzerman is a Red Wing."

SERIOUS SLIP. Yzerman had the best season of his career so far in 1987–88. He scored 50 goals and added 52 assists to register his first-ever 100-point campaign. In March 1988 Yzerman scored his fiftieth goal against the Buffalo Sabres.

Later in that same game Yzerman once again drove to the net at great speed, but this time his skate slipped from under him. The slip caused him to slide into the goal post with his right knee. It soon became clear that Yzerman was seriously injured. He had ruptured a ligament in his knee, an injury doctors feared might end his career. Yzerman worked three to four hours every day and returned during the Red Wings' playoff loss in the Campbell Conference Finals to the eventual Stanley Cup champion Edmonton Oilers.

MR. HOCKEY

During his remarkable 26-year, 4-decade NHL career, Gordie Howe of the Red Wings earned the nickname "Mr Hockey." He set league records in goals (801), assists (1,049), and points (1,850) that stood until Wayne Gretzky surpassed them in the 1990s. Howe's record for games played (1,767) may never be broken In addition to his offensive firepower, he was known for his tough, physical play. In October 1997 Howe skated one shift with the Detroit Vipers of the International Hockey League (IHL), becoming the first player to ever appear in a professional game in five different decades.

ONE OF THE BEST. During the next four seasons Yzerman established himself as one of the best players in the NHL. In the 1988–89 season he had 65 goals, 90 assists, and 155 points, all Red Wing single-season team records. Yzerman won the Lester B. Pearson Award that season, given by NHL players to the league's best player. He continued to score at an extraordinary rate during the 1989–90 season, tallying 62 goals (second in the NHL), 65 assists, and 127 points (third in the NHL).

KEEPING HOPE ALIVE. Behind the solid play of their captain, the Red Wings moved slowly toward their ultimate goal—winning the Stanley Cup. Yzerman finished seventh in scoring with 108 points (51 goals and 57 assists) in 1990–91 and eighth with 103 points (45 goals and 58 assists) in 1991–92. During the 1991–92 season the Wings won the Norris Division title with 98 points, but were swept out of the playoffs in the second round by the Chicago Blackhawks.

Yzerman and the Wings flew through the 1992–93 regular season. The Captain scored 58 goals and added 79 assists for 137 points (fourth in the NHL). Detroit finished the season with 103 points, but again lost a tough second-round playoff series against the Toronto Maple Leafs.

UPSET. Before the 1993–94 season the Red Wings hired Scotty Bowman, the winningest head coach in NHL history. Bowman had won six Stanley Cups—five with the Montreal Canadiens and one with the Pittsburgh Penguins. Bowman inherited a team that featured Yzerman, center Sergei Fedorov from Russia, and all-time great defenseman Paul Coffey.

Detroit won the Central Division title in 1993–94 with 100 points—the best mark in the NHL's Western Conference. The Red Wings led the league with 356 goals, despite the fact that Yzerman missed 24 games with injuries. Fedorov finished second in the league with 120 points and won the Hart Trophy—given to the most valuable player in the NHL.

Entering the playoffs the Wings were the favorites to represent the Western Conference in the Stanley Cup Finals. In the first round Detroit faced the San Jose Sharks, an expansion team in only their third year of existence. Most experts predicted a Detroit blow-out, but San Jose had different ideas. The Sharks won a pressure-packed seventh game at Joe Louis Arena, 3-2, to eliminate the highly favored Red Wings.

Yzerman sat in the Red Wings locker room and cried following the game seven defeat. He placed the blame for his team's disappointing showing squarely on his own shoulders. "We failed again, and we need to accept the consequences," Yzerman admitted to *Sports Illustrated*.

TWO-WAY PLAYER. The New York Rangers won the Stanley Cup during the 1993–94 season, ending a 54-year drought without a championship. Their victory now left the Red Wings with the longest streak of Stanley Cup futility. The last time Detroit won the famous trophy was in 1955 and they had not reached the finals since 1966.

Before the 1994–95 season the Red Wings traded defenseman Steve Chaisson to the Calgary Flames for goalie Mike Vernon. Vernon had led the Flames to the Stanley Cup in 1989, and Detroit hoped he could do the same for them. Bowman also installed a new defensive system called the left wing lock. "This team hadn't been built around defense until Scotty got here," Yzerman told *Sports Illustrated*. "Now we're trying to generate scoring chances off our defense."

Bowman challenged his star player. He wanted Yzerman to concentrate more on the defensive end of the ice. "When I first came here [to Detroit], you never saw Steve working in his own end," teammate Mark Howe told *Sports Illustrated*. "His ideal game was, he'd light it up and we'd win 8-6." Yzerman responded to the challenge, working hard to improve his defensive play and becoming a fine two-way player.

FINALS FRUSTRATION. The 1994–95 NHL season was delayed because of a disagreement between the players and team owners over issues like free agency and player salaries. When the sport finally returned in January 1995 the season had been reduced to only 48 games. The Red Wings finished with the league's best record (33-11-4).

The Wings then cruised through the Western Conference playoffs with a 12-2 record. They defeated the Chicago Blackhawks in five games in the conference finals. For the first time in 29 years the Red Wings were in the Stanley Cup Finals.

In the finals Detroit faced the New Jersey Devils. The Devils finished the regular season with 18 fewer points than the Wings, but their neutral zone trap defensive system bottled up Detroit's high-powered offense. "Their defense is good, their system is good," Yzerman explained to *Sports Illustrated*. "You saw the problems we had. They controlled the neutral zone, and we were getting foiled in our own end."

When the Red Wings did have offensive opportunities, New Jersey goalie Martin Brodeur was a brick wall. In a stunning upset, New Jersey won the Stanley Cup Finals in four straight games. Once again Detroit had come up short in the playoffs. "That was a pretty humbling experience," Yzerman admitted to *Sports Illustrated*. "We went from heroes to goats really quick." Yzerman—slowed by a knee injury—scored only one point against the Devils.

RECORD-BREAKING SEASON. The Red Wings considered trading Yzerman to the Ottawa Senators before the 1995–96 season. Because of injuries to his right knee and back, his offensive production had dropped, and Fedorov had taken over as the team's number one center. The trade fell through, and Wings fans showed their support for Yzerman by giving him a stirring standing ovation before Detroit's first home game.

In January 1996 Yzerman scored his five-hundreth goal. He became only the seventh player in NHL history to score 500 goals and play their entire career with one team. "That's the most satisfying part, to know that, at least in some way,

I'll be amongst [great] players, or mentioned alongside them," Yzerman said.

Detroit won a record-setting 62 games in the 1995–96 regular season. (The previous record of 60 wins was set by the Montreal Canadiens during the 1976–77 season.) The Red Wings broke the previous record with a 5-3 victory over the Chicago Blackhawks at Joe Louis Arena, Detroit's home ice. "It was a very emotional night, with the reaction of the crowd," Yzerman—who assisted on three of the Red Wing goals—told the *Los Angeles Times*. "It was a special night."

The Red Wings allowed the fewest goals in the league and scored the third most, led the league in penalty-killing percentage (88.3 percent, the best in the NHL since the Philadelphia Flyers in the 1973–74 season), and had the second-best best percentage for scoring power-play goals. Detroit featured Yzerman, Coffey, and the "Russian Five" unit of Fedorov, Igor Larianov, Slava Kozlov, Slava Fetisov, and Vladimir Konstantinov.

Yzerman took his place as one of the best all-around players in the league. He scored 36 goals and added 59 assists for 95 points. In addition to his offensive skills, Yzerman gained recognition for his defensive play. Writers covering the NHL nominated him as one of three finalists for the Selke Trophy, given annually to the best defensive forward in the league. "He doesn't concern himself with offense as much anymore," Bowman explained to *USA Today*. "Now, the points are coming. But the real key is the team is better, and not everything is on his shoulders." (Ron Francis of the Pittsburgh Penguins won the Selke Trophy.)

BIG GOAL. Most experts picked the Red Wings to cruise to the Stanley Cup. But Detroit struggled to defeat the Winnipeg Jets in six games in the first round, then found themselves down three game to two in the second round versus the St. Louis Blues. The Red Wings faced elimination in game six, to be played in St. Louis.

A determined Yzerman guaranteed a victory in game six. "We'll be back (to Detroit for Game 7)," he said. "It's not going to end Tuesday. We'll be back for Game 7 in Detroit." Yzerman backed up his promise by assisting on a Red Wing goal and playing a great defensive game in a 4-2 Detroit victory.

Game seven of the series was a classic. For only the second time in NHL playoff history the game went into overtime with no goals being scored. (The first time was in a Stanley Cup semifinal game between Detroit and the Toronto Maple Leafs in 1950. Detroit won that game, 1-0.)

The game remained tied through one overtime period, then Yzerman took over. He stole the puck from Wayne Gretzky, skated over the blue line and fired. His laser beam shot found the top corner of the net, just over the shoulder of goalie Jon Casey. "That's a real thrill to score one in overtime in the playoffs," Yzerman declared. "That's my first time, and boy, that's a thrill. Tonight, nobody was concerned. Nobody was worried. We believed somehow we would win. We really enjoyed the game and the whole atmosphere."

UPSET AGAIN. In the Western Conference finals the Red Wings faced the Colorado Avalance—who in previous seasons had played as the Quebec (Canada) Nordiques. The Avalanche were a powerful team featuring centers Joe Sakic and Peter Forsberg and all-time great goalie Patrick Roy. Colorado was healthy and had time to rest up for Detroit because their previous series had not gone the distance.

Colorado won the first two games of the series in Detroit at Joe Louis Arena. Yzerman missed part of game one and all of game two with a thigh-muscle pull. He returned for game three in Colorado and gave the Red Wings a spark. Detroit won that game, 6-4, but dropped game four. They now were one game from elimination.

The Red Wings came home and won game five, 5-2, but now they had to return to Denver for game six. Colorado won that game 4-1, finishing off one of the biggest upsets in NHL history. The Avalanche went on to defeat the Florida Panthers in four straight games to win the Stanley Cup.

The loss to Colorado frustrated Yzerman. "It's just that I get sick and tired of losing, of going home at the end of the season and answering the same questions I answered last year and the year before," he complained to the *Los Angeles Times*. Yzerman had his best-ever playoff performance. He scored 8 goals and added 12 assists for 20 total playoff points.

CHANGED TEAM. At the beginning of the 1996–97 season the Red Wings streak without winning the Stanley Cup had reached 42 years. In an effort to end this drought, Detroit decided to make major changes. Before the season the Red Wings made a trade with the Hartford Whalers, sending center Keith Primeau and defenseman Paul Coffey to the Whalers for Brendan Shanahan, a high-scoring power forward. The team hoped Shanahan would provide Detroit with the size needed to win in the playoffs.

The rivalry between Detroit and the Avalanche reached a boiling point in their final regular meeting. The Red Wings—still angry over an illegal check in the 1996 conference finals by forward Claude Lemieux that injured Detroit player Kris Draper—tried to gain revenge on Colorado.

The game was filled with fights and penalties, including separate match-ups between Wings forward Darren McCarty and Lemieux and the goalies, Mike Vernon and Patrick Roy. Detroit won the game, 6-5, in overtime, but the effect the game had on the Red Wings was even more important. "That game helped make us a team," forward Brendan Shanahan explained in *Sport Illustrated*. "We felt we were growing as a group, but that game gave us—and everyone else—a visual picture. We knew how we felt about sticking up for each other, but that was the opportunity we had to show it."

The Red Wings were unable to match their record-setting regular season performance during the 1996–97 season. They finished with 94 points, second in their division behind the Dallas Stars. Despite this slide, Yzerman was confident that the team's increased size made them a better playoff team. "I felt that despite finishing with 37 points fewer than last year and struggling at times, we were a more irritating team to play against," he explained in the *Sporting News*. "There's more confidence, even for the little guys, when you have more power forwards out there banging. Even the younger guys coming in seem to all be over 6 feet, 1 inch and 200 pounds. We now have a lot of players who are harder to knock off the puck and that does help."

REVENGE. Following a familiar pattern, the Red Wings struggled early in their first-round series against St. Louis. The series was tied at two games apiece when Yzerman exploded. He blasted the team's best players—including himself—and challenged everyone to carry their share of the load. "He said we weren't playing like a team," defenseman Nicklas Lidstrom revealed. "He said the only way for us to win a Cup was to play as a team." Yzerman scored three minutes into game five, a 5-2 Detroit win, and the Red Wings took the series in six games.

Detroit then defeated the Mighty Ducks of Anaheim in four straight games, earning a spot in the Western Conference Finals against the Avalanche. Colorado won game one, 2-1, at home despite being outshot 35-19 by the Red Wings. Detroit came back to win game two, 4-2, evening the series at one game each. Yzerman assisted on one goal and then scored the go ahead goal with 4:00 left in the third period, banking a shot in off the back of Roy's pads. "I just tried to throw it out ahead of him," Yzerman related to *Newsday*. "Even if it doesn't go in, there's a chance that we might get a rebound to somebody going to the net."

The Red Wings returned home and won games three and four to take a 3-1 lead in the best of seven series. Colorado won game five, 6-0, back in Denver, but Detroit earned a trip to the Stanley Cup Finals for the second time in three years with a 3-1 victory in game six. Once again Yzerman had the chance to win the elusive Cup.

FRUSTRATION ENDS. The Wings faced the powerful Philadelphia Flyers in the finals. The Flyers were led by Eric Lindros—the 1995 NHL Most Valuable Player—and his "Legion of Doom" linemates. Detroit started out fast, winning game one in Philadelphia, 4-2. Yzerman scored the game winner, blasting a slap shot past goalie Ron Hextall. When the Red Wings captured game two by an identical 4-2 score, it appeared the 42-year jinx may be about to end.

The packed house at the Joe Louis Arena gave Yzerman a standing ovation when his name was announced for game three. The noise was deafening and shook the arena rafters. "I really wasn't expecting anything like that," Yzerman admitted. "The only way I can describe it is if you have children, and you've been away for a while, and you come home and the dog is barking and the kids run at you and they're all excited. It was like coming home."

With the home crowd behind them, Detroit picked up speed. They won game three, 6-1, and now stood only one game from victory. Yzerman reminded his teammates not to become overconfident. "It doesn't mean anything to win the first three games," Yzerman said. "You've got to go out there and act like champions." The team adopted the phrase "We haven't won anything yet."

The Red Wings won game four, 2-1, to sweep the Flyers. After 42 years of coming up short, Detroit had won the Stanley Cup. Goalie Mike Vernon won the Conn Smythe Trophy as the most valuable player in the NHL playoffs by a mere two votes over Yzerman, who scored three goals in the finals, won nearly every faceoff, and played defense like a man possessed. With the victory Scotty Bowman became the first coach in NHL history to win Stanley Cups with three different teams.

HOISTING THE CUP. Joe Louis Arena erupted as Yzerman took the Stanley Cup from NHL Commissioner Gary Bettman and lifted it over his head. Slowly he circled the ice as the Detroit fans showered him with cheers. "I'm glad the game is over," Yzerman explained in *Sports Illustrated*. "But I wish it had never ended. Since I was five years old, I've watched the Stanley Cup. I have stayed up [late], made a point of watching it being presented in the locker room and always dreamed of the day that maybe I would get there. It's almost like I wanted [the game] back so I could watch the whole thing again and never forget a minute of it."

OFF THE ICE. Yzerman lives with his wife Lisa and their daughter in a suburb of Detroit. He has three brothers—Michael, Gary, and Chris—and one sister—Roni-Jean. Yzerman graduated from high school and took college courses in accounting and finance. His nickname is "Stevie Y." During the off-season Yzerman likes to play golf.

In December 1996 Yzerman signed a four-year, $18 million contract that will enable him to finish his career in Detroit. The contract also provided for a job in the organization after his playing days have ended. "I know I don't want to go anywhere else," Yzerman confessed to the *Detroit Free Press*. "It's very rare, I know, but when you look at a lot of the greats in sports, they all played in one city. I think you lose a little something when you move. You can always move for more money, but I don't believe in that."

Yzerman is a quiet person, but he knows how to motivate his teammates. "Everyone thinks he's so quiet," forward Tim Taylor told *USA Today*. "But Steve Yzerman leads this team. He doesn't lead us by yelling. But when things aren't going well, he lets us know."

The long-time Red Wing captain is second on the all-time team scoring list with 1,340 points. He has led the team in points eight times, in goals six times, and in assists eight times. Yzerman also holds the team season records for goals (65), assists (90), and points (155). Red Wing general manager Jimmy Devallano summed up Yzerman's career when he said: "He's been the franchise."

 WHERE TO WRITE:

C/O DETROIT RED WINGS, JOE LOUIS ARENA,
600 CIVIC CENTER DR.,
DETROIT, MI 48226.

Sources

Atlanta Journal-Constitution, May 17, 1996; May 24, 1996.

Detroit Free Press, February 3, 1987; October 6, 1988; December 9, 1988; December 25, 1988.

Los Angeles Times, February 7, 1996; April 13, 1996; May 16, 1996; May 19, 1996; May 29, 1996; May 30, 1996; November 26, 1996; May 18, 1997.

Maclean's, June 16, 1997.

Newsday, June 7, 1995; June 12, 1995; June 17, 1995; June 20, 1995; June 21, 1995; June 23, 1995; June 25, 1995; April 16, 1996; May 17, 1996; May 22, 1996; September 11, 1996; May 19, 1997.

Sports Illustrated, March 16, 1987; March 20, 1989; January 30, 1995; February 6, 1995; June 5, 1995; June 26, 1995; March 18, 1996; April 29, 1996; June 16, 1997; June 18, 1997.

USA Today, May 7, 1996; May 14, 1996; May 23, 1996; December 13, 1996.

Additional information provided by the Gannett and Knight-Ridder/Tribune news services and the Detroit Red Wings.

Index

Series (ser.) is in *italic;* entries in Series 4
and their page numbers are in **bold.**

Series (ser.) is in *italic;* entries in Series 4 and their page numbers are in **bold.**

Navratilova, Martina *ser. 1,*
413-416
Pierce, Mary *ser. 2,* 379-380,
387
Rubin, Chanda *ser. 3,* 254
Sampras, Pete *ser. 1,* 479
Sanchez Vicario, Arantxa
ser. 1, 485-486
Seles, Monica *ser. 1,* 509-
510, 512
Avery, Steve *ser. 1,* 350; *ser. 2,*
120; *ser. 3,* 262
Awesome Dawesome (See Dawes,
Dominique)
Azinger, Paul *ser. 1,* 144; *ser. 2,*
356

B

Babe Zaharias Female Athlete of
the Year Award
Swoopes, Sheryl *ser. 2,* 472
Baerga, Carlos *ser. 2,* 12-13, 15,
121
Bagwell, Jeff *ser. 3,* 44, 49; *ser. 4,*
1-11, 293
Bailey, Donovan *ser. 3,* 14-23; *ser.
4,* 129, 133-134
Bailey, Jerry *ser. 4,* 102
Baiul, Oksana *ser. 1,* 37-42; *ser. 2,*
29, 224-225; *ser. 3,* 164
Baltimore Orioles *ser. 1,* 468, 470
Ripken, Cal, Jr. *ser. 1,* 454
Banks, Ernie *ser. 1,* 82, 491; *ser. 3,*
246
Barkley, Charles *ser. 1,* 43-49, 260,
357-358, 424, 438, 465; *ser. 2,*
444; *ser. 4,* 126
Barraso, Tom *ser. 1,* 321; *ser. 2,*
115, 179; *ser. 4,* 315
Barrowman, Mike *ser. 2,* 66, 68
Barry, Rick *ser. 3,* 235; *ser. 4,* 178
Baseball All-Star game (See All-
Star game, Baseball)
Baseball no-hitters
Abbott, Jim *ser. 1,* 6
Ryan, Nolan *ser. 1,* 24, 469-
472
Baseball records

Caminiti, Ken *ser. 3,* 47
Johnson, Randy *ser. 2,* 196
Ripken, Cal, Jr. *ser. 1,* 457-
458
Ryan, Nolan *ser. 1,* 469-473
Sandberg, Ryne *ser. 1,* 491-
493
Bash Brothers
McGwire, Mark *ser. 4,* 232
Baylor, Elgin *ser. 1,* 259
Baylor University
Johnson, Michael *ser. 2,* 183
Beamon, Bob *ser. 1,* 329; *ser. 2,*
393, 395
Beard, Amanda *ser. 3,* 24-31
Beattie, Shelly *ser. 2,* 300
Becker, Boris *ser. 1,* 10, 179, 478-
479; *ser. 2,* 384
Belfour, Ed *ser. 4,* 140
Belle, Albert *ser. 2,* 9-16, 121, 345,
510; *ser. 4,* 3
Belmont Stakes
Day, Pat *ser. 4,* 95, 100, 102
Krone, Julie *ser. 1,* 278
Shoemaker, Willie *ser. 1,*
279
Bench, Johnny *ser. 1,* 171, 192
Berger, Wally *ser. 4,* 232
Berg, Patty *ser. 2,* 240
Berning, Susie *ser. 4,* 279
Berra, Yogi *ser. 1,* 82
Bertrand, John *ser. 2,* 301
Bettis, Jerome *ser. 4,* **12-22**
Beuerlein, Steve *ser. 4,* 47-48
Bichette, Dante *ser. 4,* 289
Big Bird (See Johnson, Randy)
Big Daddy (See Bettis, Jerome)
Big Dog (See Robinson, Glenn)
Biggio, Craig *ser. 3,* 44; *ser. 4,* 9
Big Girl in the Middle ser. 4, 263
The Big Hurt (See Thomas, Frank)
Big Unit (See Johnson, Randy)
Birdie *ser. 1,* 142
Bird, Larry *ser. 1,* 50-57, 240, 242,
245, 251, 258, 423, 538; *ser. 2,*
152, 471, 517; *ser. 3,* 235
Black Magic *ser. 2,* 305
Blair, Bonnie *ser. 1,* 58-64, 131
Blake, Peter *ser. 2,* 305

Series (ser.) is in *italic;* entries in Series 4 and their page numbers are in **bold.**

Series (ser.) is in *italic;* entries in Series 4 and their page numbers are in **bold.**

Colorado Silver Bullets *ser. 2*, 39-
47
Richardson, Dot *ser. 3*, 226
Colorado State University
Van Dyken, Amy *ser. 3*, 291
Comaneci, Nadia *ser. 2*, 316-317,
320-321
CONCACAF Qualifying
Championship
Akers, Michelle *ser. 2*, 5
Cone, David *ser. 2*, 195
Conner, Dennis *ser. 2*, 298-299,
302, 304-306
Connors, Jimmy *ser. 1*, 9, 30, 34,
36, 479
Conn Smythe Trophy
Gretzky, Wayne *ser. 1*, 186-
187
Lemieux, Mario *ser. 1*, 321-
322
Messier, Mark *ser. 1*, 377
Roy, Patrick *ser. 2*, 413-414,
416, 419-420
Coombes, Missy *ser. 2*, 44
Cooper, Cynthia *ser. 4*, **67-78**
Cooper, Michael *ser. 2*, 309
Copper Bowl
Bledsoe, Drew *ser. 2*, 19
Cordero, Angel, Jr. *ser. 4*, 104
CoreStates U.S. Professional
Championship
Armstrong, Lance *ser. 3*, 5
Cornell, Shelia *ser. 3*, 80
Coughlin, Tom *ser. 4*, 47
Country (See Favre, Brett)
Courageous ser. 2, 302
Courier, Jim *ser. 1*, 12, 90, 103-
108, 478-479, 508
Court, Margaret *ser. 1*, 178, 412,
416-418, 510
Cousy, Bob *ser. 2*, 447-448
Cowher, Bill *ser. 2*, 540, 542
Cox, Bobby *ser. 2*, 118, 120, 345
Craig, Roger *ser. 1*, 401; *ser. 3*,
300
Crawford, Sam *ser. 1*, 171
Crescent Moon Foundation *ser. 1*,
409
Crockett, Zack *ser. 2*, 94

Cubens (See *Mighty Mary*)
Curl, Rick *ser. 2*, 65
Cuthbert, Jule *ser. 2*, 61
Cy Young Award
Clemens, Roger *ser. 1*, 99-
101
Glavine, Tom *ser. 2*, 115,
118-119, 121
Johnson, Randy *ser. 2*, 189-
190, 195, 198
Maddux, Greg *ser. 1*, 349,
351
Smoltz, John *ser. 3*, 258-
259, 267
Czar of Vaulting (See Bubka,
Sergei)

D

Da Kid (See Garnett, Kevin)
Dallas Cowboys *ser. 1*, 273-274,
329, 398, 451, 463, 547, 585-
586; *ser. 2*, 96, 103, 105, 542;
ser. 3, 276, 302
Aikman, Troy *ser. 1*, 18
Akers, Michelle *ser. 2*, 3
Hill, Calvin *ser. 2*, 156
Irvin, Michael *ser. 2*, 163,
167
Smith, Emmitt *ser. 1*, 517
Dallas Mavericks
Kidd, Jason *ser. 2*, 227, 230
Daly, Chuck *ser. 1*, 538
Daneyko, Ken *ser. 2*, 336
Daniel, Beth *ser. 4*, 278
Dan Marino Foundation *ser. 1*, 374
Dantley, Adrian *ser. 1*, 356, 539
Darnyi, Tamas *ser. 2*, 66
Daulton, Darren *ser. 1*, 119
Davenport, Lindsay *ser. 3*, 252
Davies, Laura *ser. 4*, 299
Davis Cup *ser. 1*, 106-107
Agassi, Andre *ser. 1*, 11
Ashe, Arthur *ser. 1*, 33-35
Chang, Michael *ser. 1*, 94
Sampras, Pete *ser. 1*, 478
Davis, Scott *ser. 3*, 66-67
Davis, Terrell *ser. 4*, 18, 20-21,
50, 53, **78-93**

Series (ser.) is in *italic;* entries in Series 4 and their page numbers are in **bold.**

Miller, Reggie *ser. 2*, 308, 314

Payton, Gary *ser. 3*, 197-198, 205

Richmond, Mitch *ser. 3*, 228-229, 235

Robinson, Glenn *ser. 2*, 411

Drexler, Clyde *ser. 1*, 109-114, 422, 540; *ser. 2*, 153, 517; *ser. 4*, 126

Driver of the Year
Unser, Al, Jr. *ser. 2*, 499

Dr. J (See Erving, Julius)

Dryden, Ken *ser. 2*, 414

Duckworth, Kevin *ser. 2*, 408

Duke University *ser. 1*, 250; *ser. 2*, 410, 516; *ser. 3*, 125
Hill, Grant *ser. 2*, 156, 158

Duluth-Superior Dukes
Borders, Ila *ser. 4*, 36, 41

Dumas, Tony *ser. 2*, 147

Du Maurier Ltd. Classic
King, Betsy *ser. 2*, 239

Duran, Roberto *ser. 4*, 309

Durham, Leon *ser. 2*, 135

Dykstra, Lenny *ser. 1*, 115-120

E

Eagle *ser. 1*, 142

Earnhardt, Dale *ser. 2*, 71-79, 129-130

Easler, Mike *ser. 2*, 508

Eastern Conference finals
Barkley, Charles *ser. 1*, 46
Bird, Larry *ser. 1*, 53, 56
Ewing, Patrick *ser. 1*, 139
Hardaway, Anfernee *ser. 2*, 152
Jordan, Michael *ser. 1*, 257-260
Miller, Reggie *ser. 2*, 311, 313
Pippen, Scottie *ser. 1*, 436-437
Thomas, Isiah *ser. 1*, 538, 540

Eckersley, Dennis *ser. 1*, 567

Eclipse Award

Day, Pat *ser. 4*, 94-95, 98-99, 103

Edberg, Stefan *ser. 1*, 93-94, 106, 478, 479

Edmonton Eskimos
Moon, Warren *ser. 1*, 406

Edmonton Oilers
Gretzky, Wayne *ser. 1*, 184
Messier, Mark *ser. 1*, 376

Edwards, Teresa *ser. 2*, 80-87

Ekhardt, Shawn *ser. 2*, 225

Eldredge, Todd *ser. 2*, 457; *ser. 3*, 61-71, 161; *ser. 4*, 28-30, 112-113

Elliot, Lin *ser. 2*, 482

Elway, John *ser. 1*, 121-126, 270; *ser. 4*, 50

Epstein-Barr syndrome
Akers, Michelle *ser. 2*, 1, 5

Erickson, Craig *ser. 3*, 103

Erp, Charlie *ser. 2*, 349-350

Erving, Julius *ser. 1*, 46; *ser. 2*, 161; *ser. 3*, 122, 229

Esposito, Phil *ser. 1*, 188; *ser. 2*, 400; *ser. 3*, 37

European Figure Skating Championships
Baiul, Oksana *ser. 1*, 39, 41
Bonaly, Surya *ser. 2*, 24-26, 29-30
Witt, Katarina *ser. 1*, 571-573

Evans, Dwight *ser. 4*, 2

Evans, Janet *ser. 1*, 127-132; *ser. 2*, 68; *ser. 3*, 29

Evert, Chris *ser. 1*, 177-178, 412-415, 417-418, 481, 508

Ewing, Patrick *ser. 1*, 133-140, 260, 422, 430, 466; *ser. 2*, 323, 326; *ser. 3*, 193, 195

The Extremists (See Reece, Gabrielle)

F

Fab Five *ser. 2*, 158
Howard, Juwan *ser. 3*, 121-122, 124, 126

Series (ser.) is in *italic;* entries in Series 4 and their page numbers are in **bold.**

Series (ser.) is in *italic;* entries in Series 4 and their page numbers are in **bold.**

378; *ser. 2,* 111-113, 144, 175, 336, 338, 418, 420; *ser. 3,* 37, 131-132, 138; *ser. 4,* 266, 318

Grey Cup
    Moon, Warren *ser. 1,* 407

Griffey, Ken, Jr. *ser. 1,* 191-196, 472; *ser. 2,* 196-197, 216; *ser. 3,* 244-247; *ser. 4,* 220, 236

Griffey, Ken, Sr. *ser. 1,* 191-195

Griffith Joyner, Florence *ser. 1,* 197-203, 266; *ser. 2,* 57, 489

Grissom, Marquis *ser. 4,* 288

Grove, Lefty *ser. 2,* 196

Gugliotta, Tom *ser. 2,* 519

Guthrie, Janet *ser. 1,* 526

Gwynn, Chris *ser. 2,* 140

Gwynn, Tony *ser. 1,* 444, 491; *ser. 2,* 133-140, 376; *ser. 3,* 46

Gypsies
    Lalas, Alexi *ser. 2,* 283

H

Habetz, Alyson *ser. 2,* 40

Habitat for Humanity
    King, Betsy *ser. 2,* 237

Hall of Fame, LPGA
    Lopez, Nancy *ser. 1,* 343

Hamill, Dorothy *ser. 1,* 575-576, 579; *ser. 4,* 24

Hamilton, Scott *ser. 3,* 69

Hammer (See Richmond, Mitch)

Hamm, Mia *ser. 2,* 141-145

Hampton, Rodney *ser. 4,* 83

Hanshin Tigers
    Fielder, Cecil *ser. 1,* 150

Harbaugh, Jim *ser. 2,* 93-94, 104; *ser. 3,* 97-109

Hardaway, Anfernee *ser. 2,* 148-156, 313, 518

Hardaway, Tim *ser. 2,* 408; *ser. 3,* 233

Harding, Tonya *ser. 1,* 41; *ser. 2,* 29, 218-219, 221-225, 246-248, 251; *ser. 4,* 26-27

A Hard Road to Glory ser. 1, 35

Hargrave, Bubbles *ser. 2,* 376

Harkes, John *ser. 3,* 110-120

Harksey (See Harkes, John)

Harmon, Butch *ser. 2,* 355

Harper, Alvin *ser. 2,* 171

Harrigan, Lori *ser. 3,* 78

Hartack, Bill *ser. 4,* 98

Hart, Clyde *ser. 2,* 183

Hart Memorial Trophy
    Fedorov, Sergei *ser. 2,* 107-108, 111
    Gretzky, Wayne *ser. 1,* 185, 320
    Hasek, Dominik *ser. 4,* 138-139, 144
    Hull, Brett *ser. 1,* 215
    Jagr, Jaromir *ser. 2,* 175
    Lemieux, Mario *ser. 1,* 323
    Messier, Mark *ser. 1,* 378, 380

Hasek, Dominik *ser. 4,* **138-146**

Haugen, Greg *ser. 4,* 307

Haynie, Sandra *ser. 2,* 240

Hearns, Thomas *ser. 4,* 309

Hearst, Garrison *ser. 4,* 83

Heath, Jeff *ser. 4,* 293

Heavyweight championship
    Bowe, Riddick *ser. 1,* 87
    Foreman, George *ser. 1,* 164, 167-168
    Holyfield, Evander *ser. 1,* 209-210

Heiden, Eric *ser. 1,* 60

Heisman Trophy
    Detmer, Ty *ser. 1,* 583
    Faulk, Marshall *ser. 2,* 91
    Jackson, Bo *ser. 1,* 226
    Rozier, Mike *ser. 1,* 582
    Sanders, Barry *ser. 1,* 497
    Staubach, Roger *ser. 1,* 463
    Testaverde, Vinny *ser. 1,* 583
    Torretta, Gino *ser. 1,* 583
    Walker, Herschel *ser. 1,* 122
    Ware, Andre *ser. 1,* 517

Henderson, Rickey *ser. 1,* 152; *ser. 3,* 46

Hendrick, Rick *ser. 2,* 127

Henie, Sonja *ser. 1,* 40, 572-573; *ser. 2,* 30

Henry P. Iba Citizen Athlete
    Award

Series (ser.) is in *italic;* entries in Series 4 and their page numbers are
in **bold.**

Gretzky, Wayne *ser. 1,* 184
    Messier, Mark *ser. 1,* 376
Indiana State University *ser. 1,* 240
    Bird, Larry *ser. 1,* 52
Indiana University *ser. 2,* 295
    Bird, Larry *ser. 1,* 51
    Thomas, Isiah *ser. 1,* 536
Induráin, Miguel *ser. 1,* 218-222;
    ser. 3, 10
Infante, Lindy *ser. 3,* 103
International Race of Champions
    Earnhardt, Dale *ser. 2,* 76
    Unser, Al, Jr. *ser. 2,* 497-498
The Intimidator (See Earnhardt,
    Dale)
Ironhead (See Earnhardt, Dale)
Irvan, Ernie *ser. 2,* 78, 128
Irvin, Michael *ser. 1,* 518; *ser. 2,*
    163-173, 543-544; *ser. 3,* 229
Iselin, Hope Goddard *ser. 2,* 300
Isler, J. J. *ser. 2,* 300
Ito, Midori *ser. 2,* 219, 221, 251
Iverson, Allen *ser. 4,* **168-181**

J

Jackson, Bo *ser. 1,* 223-230, 503,
    506, 533, 564
Jackson, Jimmy *ser. 2,* 230
Jackson, Michael *ser. 1,* 243, 574
Jackson, Ray *ser. 2,* 516; *ser. 3,*
    124
Jackson, Reggie *ser. 1,* 442, 455,
    532
Jacksonville Jaguars *ser. 4,* 212
    Brunell, Mark *ser. 4,* 44, 47
Jagr, Jaromir *ser. 2,* 174-181; *ser.*
    3, 95
James, Don *ser. 4,* 45
Jameson, Betty *ser. 2,* 240
Jansen, Dan *ser. 1,* 231-237
Jansen, Jane *ser. 1,* 231-232
Jeffcoat, Jim *ser. 2,* 439
Jenkins, Carol Heiss *ser. 3,* 140
Jenkins, Ferguson *ser. 2,* 120
Jenner, Bruce *ser. 2,* 363
Jesse Owens Award
    Griffith Joyner, Florence *ser.*
        1, 201

Joyner-Kersee, Jackie *ser. 1,*
    266
    Torrence, Gwen *ser. 2,* 491
Jim Pierce Rule *ser. 2,* 384
Jim Thorpe Award
    Woodson, Rod *ser. 2,* 539
Johanson, Stefan *ser. 2,* 501
Johncock, Gordon *ser. 2,* 496
Johnson, Allen *ser. 4,* 136
Johnson, Ben *ser. 3,* 20
Johnson, Bill *ser. 1,* 393; *ser. 4,*
    200
Johnson, Dave *ser. 2,* 363-364
Johnson, Earvin "Magic" *ser. 1,*
    53, 55-56, 111, 238-246, 258,
    356, 365, 423, 437, 464, 537,
    539; *ser. 2,* 147, 152, 161, 216,
    231, 309, 314, 442, 446-447,
    517; *ser. 4,* 118, 176
Johnson, Jimmy *ser. 1,* 16, 517;
    ser. 2, 167-169
Johnson, Larry *ser. 1,* 69, 247-252;
    ser. 2, 327-328; *ser. 3,* 191
Johnson, Michael *ser. 2,* 182-188;
    ser. 3, 20, 22, 235
Johnson, Randy *ser. 2,* 15, 189-
    199; *ser. 3,* 245-246; *ser. 4,* 291
Johnson, Walter *ser. 1,* 470; *ser. 2,*
    196
Johnston, Ed *ser. 2,* 179
Jones, Bobby *ser. 2,* 533
Jones, Chipper *ser. 2,* 346
Jones, Cobi *ser. 3,* 118
Jones, Jerry *ser. 1,* 18, 519; *ser. 2,*
    168-169
Jones, Marion *ser. 4,* 135, **182-**
194
Jones, Roy, Jr. *ser. 2,* 201-209
Jordan, Michael *ser. 1,* 45, 47-48,
    55, 113, 135, 138, 245, 249,
    252-261, 357, 422-423, 431,
    433, 436, 438, 540; *ser. 2,* 37,
    96, 152, 161, 213, 225, 328,
    358, 444, 473, 517, 534; *ser. 3,*
    129, 203-204; *ser. 4,* 177
Joyner, Al *ser. 1,* 200, 263-265
Joyner-Kersee, Jackie *ser. 1,* 200,
    262-267; *ser. 2,* 57, 61, 145;
    ser. 4, 190

Series (ser.) is in *italic;* entries in Series 4 and their page numbers are
in **bold.**

L

Labonte, Terry *ser. 2,* 131
Ladies' Professional Golf
  Association (See LPGA)
Lady Byng Trophy
  Gretzky, Wayne *ser. 1,* 185
  Hull, Brett *ser. 1,* 215
  Kariya, Paul *ser. 3,* 137
Laettner, Christian *ser. 2,* 158
Lafleur, Guy *ser. 4,* 266
LaFontaine, Pat *ser. 4,* 143
Laimbeer, Bill *ser. 1,* 436, 539
Lake, Carnell *ser. 2,* 542
Lake Superior State University *ser. 3,* 134
Lalas, Alexi *ser. 2,* 281-286; *ser. 3,* 118
Landis, Kennesaw Mountain *ser. 2,* 40
Landry, Tom *ser. 1,* 18; *ser. 2,* 167-168
Langston, Mark *ser. 2,* 192, 197
Largent, Steve *ser. 1,* 450
Larionov, Igor *ser. 3,* 36, 40
LaRussa, Tony *ser. 4,* 233-234
Lasorda, Tommy *ser. 2,* 345-346, 372-373
Las Vegas Thunder
  Rheaume, Manon *ser. 2,* 403
Laver, Rod *ser. 1,* 178, 475-476
Leader, Jason *ser. 2,* 508
A League of Their Own ser. 2, 40, 44
Lee, Bruce *ser. 2,* 455
Lee, Spike *ser. 1,* 261
Leetch, Brian *ser. 2,* 115
Leigh, Doug *ser. 2,* 451
Lemieux, Claude *ser. 3,* 91
Lemieux, Mario *ser. 1,* 187, 317-324, 332; *ser. 2,* 113, 174-175, 177-180, 336, 338, 420; *ser. 3,* 37, 95
LeMond, Greg *ser. 1,* 219-220; *ser. 2,* 145; *ser. 3,* 9
Lendl, Ivan *ser. 1,* 92, 178, 476, 479, 482
Leonard, Sugar Ray *ser. 3,* 52; *ser. 4,* 309

Leslie, Lisa *ser. 3,* 148-157; *ser. 4,* 74
Lett, Leon *ser. 2,* 105
Levin, Fred *ser. 2,* 206
Levin, Stanley *ser. 2,* 206
Levy, Marv *ser. 1,* 272, 544; *ser. 2,* 436
Lewis, Carl *ser. 1,* 325-331; *ser. 2,* 187, 389, 392-396; *ser. 3,* 18, 21; *ser. 4,* 130, 135
Liberty ser. 2, 302
Lindh, Hilary *ser. 2,* 464-465; *ser. 4,* **195-204**
Lindros, Eric *ser. 1,* 332-337; *ser. 2,* 180; *ser. 3,* 85, 87, 94; *ser. 4,* 324
Linebacker of the Year
  Seau, Junior *ser. 2,* 429
Lipinski, Tara *ser. 2,* 250; *ser. 3,* 145, 158-164; *ser. 4,* 32-33
Liston, Sonny *ser. 1,* 165
LoboCop (See Lobo, Rebecca)
Lobo, Rebecca *ser. 2,* 287-296; *ser. 4,* 72
Lofton, Kenny *ser. 2,* 13, 345
Lombardi, Ernie *ser. 2,* 376
Long Beach State University
  Davis, Terrell *ser. 4,* 82
Lopez, Javier *ser. 2,* 122
Lopez, Nancy *ser. 1,* 338-345; *ser. 2,* 240; *ser. 4,* 278, 299-300
Los Angeles Dodgers *ser. 1,* 118, 565
  Nomo, Hideo *ser. 2,* 340, 343
  Piazza, Mike *ser. 2,* 369
Los Angeles Express
  Young, Steve *ser. 1,* 582
Los Angeles Galaxy *ser. 3,* 119
Los Angeles Kings *ser. 2,* 418
  Glavine, Tom *ser. 2,* 116
  Gretzky, Wayne *ser. 1,* 187
Los Angeles Lakers *ser. 1,* 54-55, 113, 240, 258, 356, 423, 437, 539; *ser. 2,* 446
  Bryant, Kobe *ser. 4,* 55, 61
  Johnson, Earvin "Magic"
    ser. 1, 240

Series (ser.) is in *italic;* entries in Series 4 and their page numbers are in **bold.**

McDaniel, Xavier *ser. 2,* 214

McDowell, Jack *ser. 2,* 197

McDowell, Sam *ser. 2,* 196

McEnroe, John *ser. 1,* 12, 103, 476, 478-479; *ser. 2,* 523

McGirt, James "Buddy" *ser. 4,* 307

McGriff, Fred *ser. 1,* 27, 150, 350; *ser. 3,* 46

McGwire, Mark *ser. 1,* 171; *ser. 4,* **227-239**

McHale, Kevin *ser. 1,* 53

McLain, Denny *ser. 1,* 100, 351, 532

McMahon, Jim *ser. 1,* 583; *ser. 3,* 99

MC Mass Confusion
    Dolan, Tom *ser. 2,* 70

McNair, Steve *ser. 3,* 173-185

Means, Natrone *ser. 4,* 49

Mears, Rick *ser. 1,* 157, 159-160

Medwick, Joe *ser. 2,* 138; *ser. 4,* 291

Memphis Showboats
    White, Reggie *ser. 1,* 557

Memphis State University
    Hardaway, Anfernee *ser. 2,* 149

Meola, Tony *ser. 3,* 111-112

Merkerson, Alton *ser. 2,* 205-206

Mesa, Jose *ser. 2,* 14

Messier, Mark *ser. 1,* 375-380; *ser. 3,* 38, 94

Metric skating *ser. 1,* 59

Meyers, Ann *ser. 2,* 86

Miami-Dade North Community College
    Piazza, Mike *ser. 2,* 373

Miami Dolphins *ser. 1,* 399, 547
    Marino, Dan *ser. 1,* 370

Miami Heat *ser. 3,* 128
    Mourning, Alonzo *ser. 2,* 322, 328

Michael Irvin Show ser. 2, 173

Michael Jordan Foundation *ser. 1,* 258

Michigan State University *ser. 1,* 240
    Johnson, Earvin "Magic" *ser. 1,* 240

Mighty Ducks of Anaheim
    Selanne, Teemu *ser. 4,* 265, 268

Mighty Mary ser. 2, 297-306
    Beattie, Shelly *ser. 2,* 300
    Dellenbaugh, David *ser. 2,* 304
    Isler, J. J. *ser. 2,* 300
    Riley, Dawn *ser. 2,* 299, 301
    Seaton-Huntington, Anna *ser. 2,* 301
    Swett, Hannah *ser. 2,* 300
    Worthington, Kimo *ser. 2,* 298, 301

Mike Foul (See Powell, Mike)

Mikita, Stan *ser. 1,* 188

Miller, Cheryl *ser. 2,* 307-309, 311; *ser. 3,* 151-152; *ser. 4,* 163, 165

Miller, Reggie *ser. 2,* 152, 307-315

Miller, Shannon *ser. 1,* 381-387; *ser. 2,* 51, 319; *ser. 3,* 282-284

Milutinovic, Bora *ser. 2,* 284

Milwaukee Bucks
    Robinson, Glenn *ser. 2,* 407, 410

Minnesota North Stars *ser. 1,* 321

Minnesota Timberwolves
    Garnett, Kevin *ser. 4,* 117, 122

Minnesota Twins *ser. 1,* 27; *ser. 2,* 119; *ser. 3,* 262
    Puckett, Kirby *ser. 1,* 442
    Winfield, Dave *ser. 1,* 567

Minnesota Vikings
    Moon, Warren *ser. 1,* 410

Mirer, Rick *ser. 2,* 19; *ser. 4,* 14, 46

Mississippi Valley State
    Rice, Jerry *ser. 1,* 447

Missouri Athletic Club Player of the Year
    Harkes, John *ser. 3,* 112

Mitsubishi Electric Corporation
    Edwards, Teresa *ser. 2,* 81, 84

Mize, Johnny *ser. 1,* 152; *ser. 4,* 236

Mize, Larry *ser. 2,* 353

Series (ser.) is in *italic;* entries in Series 4 and their page numbers are in **bold**.

N

Nabisco Dinah Shore Women's
Open
    King, Betsy *ser. 2*, 234, 237-
      238
Naismith Award
    Hardaway, Anfernee *ser. 2*,
      150
    Holdsclaw, Chamique *ser. 4*,
      158-159
    Kidd, Jason *ser. 2*, 230
    Leslie, Lisa *ser. 3*, 152-153
    Mourning, Alonzo *ser. 2*,
      326
    Robinson, Glenn *ser. 2*, 409
    Swoopes, Sheryl *ser. 2*, 471
    Webber, Chris *ser. 2*, 517
Namath, Joe *ser. 1*, 268, 270, 367,
  395
Nance, Jim *ser. 4*, **211**
NASCAR championship
    Earnhardt, Dale *ser. 2*, 71-
      72, 75-77, 129
    Gordon, Jeff *ser. 2*, 77, 124-
      125, 130
    Labonte, Terry *ser. 2*, 131
    Petty, Richard *ser. 2*, 131
    Thomas, Herb *ser. 2*, 131
National AIDS Commission *ser. 1*,
  244
National Association of Baseball
  Leagues *ser. 2*, 39-40
National Baseball Hall of Fame
  and Museum *ser. 2*, 45
    Borders, Ila *ser. 4*, **39**
National Basketball Association
  (See NBA)
National Collegiate Athletic
  Association (See NCAA)
National Footbal Conference (See
  NFL)
National Hockey League (See
  NHL)
National Invitational Tournament
    Bird, Larry *ser. 1*, 52
National Junior Olympics
    Jones, Roy, Jr. *ser. 2*, 204

National Junior Pentathlon
Championship
    Joyner-Kersee, Jackie *ser. 1*,
      264
National Junior Tennis League *ser.
  1*, 35
National League Championship
Series
    Bonds, Barry *ser. 1*, 80
    Dykstra, Lenny *ser. 1*, 117-
      118, 120
    Glavine, Tom *ser. 2*, 118-
      121
    Gwynn, Tony *ser. 2*, 135
    Maddux, Greg *ser. 1*, 348,
      350
    Ryan, Nolan *ser. 1*, 468, 471
    Sandberg, Ryne *ser. 1*, 490-
      491
    Sanders, Deion *ser. 1*, 504-
      505
    Smoltz, John *ser. 3*, 262-
      263, 266
National Sports Festival
    Edwards, Teresa *ser. 2*, 83
Navratilova, Martina *ser. 1*, 176-
  179, 411-418, 508, 510-511;
  ser. 2, 175, 384; *ser. 4*, **147-148**
NBA All-Star game (See All-Star
  game, NBA)
NBA Defensive Player of the Year
    Mutombo, Dikembe *ser. 3*,
      186-187, 193
    Payton, Gary *ser. 3*, 197-
      198, 203
NBA finals
    Barkley, Charles *ser. 1*, 48
    Bird, Larry *ser. 1*, 53-55
    Drexler, Clyde *ser. 1*, 113
    Hardaway, Anfernee *ser. 2*,
      153
    Johnson, Earvin "Magic"
      ser. 1, 54-55, 241-244
    Jordan, Michael *ser. 1*, 258-
      260
    Olajuwon, Hakeem *ser. 1*,
      55, 423
    Payton, Gary *ser. 3*, 204

Series (ser.) is in *italic;* entries in Series 4 and their page numbers are
in **bold.**

Series (ser.) is in *italic;* entries in Series 4 and their page numbers are in **bold.**

Nunno, Steve *ser. 1*, 382, 384
Nurmi, Paavo *ser. 2*, 36
NutraSweet World Professional
     Figure Skating Championships
     Boitano, Brian *ser. 1*, 75

O

Oakland Athletics *ser. 1*, 27, 100,
     567
     McGwire, Mark *ser. 4*, 231
Oakley, Charles *ser. 1*, 137
Oates, Adam *ser. 1*, 216
O'Brien, Dan *ser. 2*, 359-368
O'Donnell, Neil *ser. 3*, 274, 276
Ohio State University *ser. 2*, 471
Okamoto, Ayako *ser. 2*, 237
Okayamo, Yasutak *ser. 4*, 254
Oklahoma State University *ser. 1*,
     496
     Sanders, Barry *ser. 1*, 496
     Thomas, Thurman *ser. 1*,
          543
Olajuwon, Hakeem *ser. 1*, 45, 110,
     135, 255, 419- 425, 430, 466;
     ser. 2, 153, 444; *ser. 3*, 204; *ser.
     4*, 126
Old Dominion University *ser. 4*,
     164
Oldfield, Ed *ser. 2*, 236, 239
Olympics (See Summer Olympics,
     Winter Olympics)
O'Neal, Jermaine *ser. 4*, 63
O'Neal, Shaquille *ser. 1*, 426-432;
     ser. 2, 146, 150, 152, 214, 313,
     326-327
Orange Bowl
     Irvin, Michael *ser. 2*, 167
Oregon State University
     Payton, Gary *ser. 3*, 200
Orlando Magic
     Hardaway, Anfernee *ser. 2*,
          146, 150
     O'Neal, Shaquille *ser. 1*, 430
     Webber, Chris *ser. 2*, 150,
          518
Orr, Bobby *ser. 2*, 335, 420
Orser, Brian *ser. 2*, 451, 457
Osterlund, Rod *ser. 2*, 74

Ottey, Merlene *ser. 2*, 62, 489-491;
     ser. 4, 191
Ott, Mel *ser. 1*, 195
Outland Trophy
     Smith, Bruce *ser. 2*, 435
Owens, Jesse *ser. 1*, 198, 326, 329;
     ser. 2, 187; *ser. 3*, 22; *ser. 4*,
     135, 193

P

Pack-style speedskating *ser. 1*, 59
Palmeiro, Rafael *ser. 1*, 170
Palmer, Arnold *ser. 1*, 340
Palmer, Jim *ser. 1*, 100-101, 173,
     351
Pan-American Games
     Abbott, Jim *ser. 1*, 3
     Edwards, Teresa *ser. 2*, 84-
          85
     Fernandez, Lisa *ser. 3*, 77
     Jordan, Michael *ser. 1*, 255
     Lalas, Alexi *ser. 2*, 282
     Robinson, David *ser. 1*, 464
     Torrence, Gwen *ser. 2*, 488
     Van Dyken, Amy *ser. 3*, 292
Pan-Pacific Games
     Dolan, Tom *ser. 2*, 66, 68
Par *ser. 1*, 142
Parcells, Bill *ser. 2*, 20; *ser. 4*, 209,
     212-213
Parent, Bernie *ser. 2*, 420; *ser. 4*,
     142
Parish, Robert *ser. 1*, 53, 423
Park, Si Hun *ser. 2*, 205
Paterno, Joe *ser. 1*, 270
Paup, Bryce *ser. 2*, 438-439
Pavin, Corey *ser. 2*, 357
Payton, Gary *ser. 3*, 197-207
Payton, Walter *ser. 1*, 494, 521;
     ser. 3, 181, 298; *ser. 4*, 207
Pazienza, Vinnie *ser. 2*, 207
Pearson, David *ser. 2*, 77
Pederson, Barry *ser. 2*, 332
Pedroso, Ivan *ser. 2*, 396-397
Pele *ser. 1*, 361-362; *ser. 2*, 4; *ser.
     3*, 111
Pendleton, Terry *ser. 1*, 80
Penn State University *ser. 1*, 270

Series (ser.) is in *italic;* entries in Series 4 and their page numbers are in **bold.**

Series (ser.) is in *italic;* entries in Series 4 and their page numbers are in **bold.**

Ryan, Nolan *ser. 1,* 2, 24, 97, 116, 345, 467- 473; *ser. 2,* 189, 194, 196

Ryder Cup
Faldo, Nick *ser. 1,* 142, 144

S

Sabatini, Gabriella *ser. 1,* 178-180; *ser. 2,* 384

Sacramento Kings
Richmond, Mitch *ser. 3,* 228, 233

Safe Passage Foundation *ser. 1,* 35

Sakic, Joe *ser. 3,* 94; *ser. 4,* 322

Salaam, Rashaan *ser. 3,* 180, 272; *ser. 4,* 209

Sampras, Pete *ser. 1,* 11, 90, 107, 474-479; *ser. 2,* 523

Sampson, Ralph *ser. 1,* 111, 422, 423

Samuelsson, Ulf *ser. 2,* 334

San Antonio Spurs
Robinson, David *ser. 1,* 463

Sanchez Vicario, Arantxa *ser. 1,* 93, 179, 480-486, 511; *ser. 2,* 379, 386-387, 526; *ser. 3,* 250, 254-255

Sandberg, Ryne *ser. 1,* 348, 487- 493; *ser. 4,* 217

Sanders, Barry *ser. 1,* 466, 494- 499, 545; *ser. 2,* 94, 96, 104, 542; *ser. 4,* 18, 20, 88-89, 211

Sanders, Deion *ser. 1,* 500-506; *ser. 2,* 171, 186, 482; *ser. 3,* 276

San Diego Chargers *ser. 2,* 541; *ser. 3,* 302
Seau, Junior *ser. 2,* 422, 427

San Diego Clippers
Gwynn, Tony *ser. 2,* 134

San Diego Padres *ser. 1,* 490
Alomar, Roberto *ser. 1,* 24
Caminiti, Ken *ser. 3,* 42, 45
Gwynn, Tony *ser. 2,* 133
Winfield, Dave *ser. 1,* 564

San Diego State University
Faulk, Marshall *ser. 2,* 88, 90

Gwynn, Tony *ser. 2,* 134

San Francisco 49ers *ser. 1,* 20-21, 125, 371, 518, 520; *ser. 2,* 170, 430
Montana, Joe *ser. 1,* 397
Rice, Jerry *ser. 1,* 448
Watters, Ricky *ser. 3,* 296, 300
Young, Steve *ser. 1,* 583

San Francisco Giants *ser. 1,* 79, 348, 350, 491; *ser. 4,* 232
Bonds, Barry *ser. 1,* 81

San Jose State University
Caminiti, Ken *ser. 3,* 43

Santee, David *ser. 3,* 69

Santiago, Benito *ser. 1,* 25

Sato, Yuka *ser. 2,* 30

Satriano, Gina *ser. 2,* 43, 45

Sawamura Award
Nomo, Hideo *ser. 2,* 341

Sax, Steve *ser. 2,* 375

Schmidt, Mike *ser. 1,* 82, 532; *ser. 3,* 49; *ser. 4,* 6

Schottenheimer, Marty *ser. 2,* 478, 480

Schrempf, Detlef *ser. 2,* 310

Schroeder, Joyce *ser. 2,* 51

Schuerholz, John *ser. 2,* 118

The Science of Hitting ser. 2, 138

Scioscia, Mike *ser. 2,* 374

Scoring, boxing *ser. 1,* 87

Scoring, figure skating *ser. 2,* 30, 456

Scoring, golf *ser. 1,* 142

Seaton-Huntington, Anna *ser. 2,* 301

Seattle Mariners *ser. 2,* 14
Griffey, Ken, Jr. *ser. 1,* 193
Johnson, Randy *ser. 2,* 189, 192
Martinez, Tino *ser. 4,* 215, 217
Rodriguez, Alex *ser. 3,* 240, 243

Seattle Supersonics *ser. 1,* 48
Kemp, Shawn *ser. 2,* 210, 213
Payton, Gary *ser. 3,* 197, 201

Series (ser.) is in *italic;* entries in Series 4 and their page numbers are in **bold.**

Series (ser.) is in *italic;* entries in Series 4 and their page numbers are in **bold.**

Tyus, Wyomia *ser. 2,* 489

U

UCLA (See University of California, Los Angeles)

Unitas, Johnny *ser. 1,* 268, 367; *ser. 4,* 48

United States Football League *ser. 1,* 271, 557, 582, 585; *ser. 2,* 436

University of Alabama
Thomas, Derrick *ser. 2,* 477

University of Arizona
Sorenstam, Annika *ser. 4,* 275
Van Dyken, Amy *ser. 3,* 290

University of Arkansas *ser. 2,* 160; *ser. 3,* 126

University of California *ser. 2,* 158
Kidd, Jason *ser. 2,* 229

University of California at Irvine
Powell, Mike *ser. 2,* 391

University of California, Los Angeles *ser. 1,* 33, 198, 264; *ser. 2,* 158, 168, 295
Aikman, Troy *ser. 1,* 18
Devers, Gail *ser. 2,* 57
Fernandez, Lisa *ser. 3,* 72-73, 75
Miller, Reggie *ser. 2,* 309
Powell, Mike *ser. 2,* 391
Richardson, Dot *ser. 3,* 220
Strug, Kerri *ser. 3,* 286

University of Central Florida
Akers, Michelle *ser. 2,* 2

University of Cincinnati *ser. 2,* 516; *ser. 3,* 125

University of Colorado
Stewart, Kordell *ser. 3,* 270-271

University of Connecticut
Lobo, Rebecca *ser. 2,* 287-289

University of Florida *ser. 1,* 516
Smith, Emmitt *ser. 1,* 516

University of Georgia *ser. 4,* 162
Davis, Terrell *ser. 4,* 83
Edwards, Teresa *ser. 2,* 82

Torrence, Gwen *ser. 2,* 487

University of Hartford
Bagwell, Jeff *ser. 4,* 1-2

University of Houston *ser. 1,* 135, 327
Drexler, Clyde *ser. 1,* 110
Olajuwon, Hakeem *ser. 1,* 421

University of Idaho
O'Brien, Dan *ser. 2,* 361

University of Kansas *ser. 2,* 158, 310

University of Kentucky *ser. 1,* 135, 138; *ser. 2,* 158, 517; *ser. 3,* 125
Kemp, Shawn *ser. 2,* 211

University of Louisville
Richardson, Dot *ser. 3,* 222

University of Maine
Kariya, Paul *ser. 3,* 133

University of Miami *ser. 1,* 583; *ser. 2,* 167
Irvin, Michael *ser. 2,* 167
Kelly, Jim *ser. 1,* 270
Piazza, Mike *ser. 2,* 373

University of Michigan *ser. 2,* 158; *ser. 3,* 134
Abbott, Jim *ser. 1,* 3
Dolan, Tom *ser. 2,* 66
Harbaugh, Jim *ser. 3,* 98-99
Howard, Juwan *ser. 3,* 121, 125
Webber, Chris *ser. 2,* 512-513, 515

University of Minnesota
Winfield, Dave *ser. 1,* 563

University of Minnesota-Duluth
Hull, Brett *ser. 1,* 214

University of Nevada-Las Vegas
Fielder, Cecil *ser. 1,* 149
Johnson, Larry *ser. 1,* 249

University of North Carolina *ser. 1,* 110, 135, 421, 536; *ser. 2,* 292, 295, 517; *ser. 3,* 125
Hamm, Mia *ser. 2,* 141, 143
Jones, Marion *ser. 4,* 182, 186
Jordan, Michael *ser. 1,* 254

University of Notre Dame
Montana, Joe *ser. 1,* 396

Series (ser.) is in *italic;* entries in Series 4 and their page numbers are in **bold.**

Series (ser.) is in *italic;* entries in Series 4 and their page numbers are in **bold.**

Walker, Herschel *ser. 1,* 19, 122, 585; *ser. 4,* 83

Walker, Larry *ser. 2,* 332; *ser. 4,* **283-294**

Wallace, Rusty *ser. 2,* 76-77, 128

Walsh, Bill *ser. 1,* 397, 399-400, 448-449, 583

Walton, Bill *ser. 1,* 423, 430

Waltrip, Darrell *ser. 2,* 129

Wannstedt, Dave *ser. 3,* 100, 102

Warfield, Paul *ser. 1,* 450

Washington Bullets *ser. 4,* 253
>   Bogues, Tyrone "Muggsy" *ser. 1,* 68
>   Howard, Juwan *ser. 3,* 121, 126
>   Webber, Chris *ser. 2,* 519

Washington Redskins *ser. 1,* 125, 273, 398, 498, 546

Washington State University
>   Bledsoe, Drew *ser. 2,* 18

Washington Wizards *ser. 3,* 128
>   Muresan, Georghe *ser. 4,* 250

Watters, Ricky *ser. 3,* 296-306; *ser. 4,* 14

WBVL Offensive Player of the Year
>   Reece, Gabrielle *ser. 4,* 258-259, 262

Webber, Chris *ser. 2,* 150-151, 157-158, 408, 512- 521; *ser. 3,* 124-127; *ser.4,* 256

Webb, Karrie *ser. 4,* 281, **295-302**

Webb, Spud *ser. 1,* 71

Wells, Georgeann *ser. 3,* 153

Western Conference finals
>   Barkley, Charles *ser. 1,* 48
>   Drexler, Clyde *ser. 1,* 113
>   Johnson, Earvin "Magic" *ser. 1,* 242, 244
>   Malone, Karl *ser. 1,* 356, 358
>   Olajuwon, Hakeem *ser. 1,* 423
>   Payton, Gary *ser. 3,* 204
>   Stockton, John *ser. 2,* 446

Western Illinois University
>   Richardson, Dot *ser. 3,* 220

West Ham United
>   Harkes, John *ser. 3,* 115

West, Jerry *ser. 1,* 259

Wetteland, John *ser. 4,* 289

Whitaker, Pernell *ser. 4,* **303-312**

Whitbread Round-the-World race
>   Riley, Dawn *ser. 2,* 301

White, Reggie *ser. 1,* 556-561, 585; *ser. 2,* 102, 104, 439, 479, 482, 543

Whittier College
>   Borders, Ila *ser. 4,* 39

Whitworth, Kathy *ser. 2,* 240

Wilander, Matts *ser. 1,* 479; *ser. 4,* 275

Wilkens, Dominique *ser. 1,* 259

Wilkens, Lenny *ser. 3,* 236

Williams, Christa *ser. 3,* 78

Williams, Doug *ser. 3,* 181

Williams, John L. *ser. 2,* 430

Williams, Serena *ser. 2,* 523, 525, 527

Williams, Ted *ser. 1,* 195, 531; *ser. 2,* 138-139, 372, 507; *ser. 4,* 291

Williams, Venus *ser. 2,* 522-527; *ser. 4,* 154

Willoughby, Bill *ser. 2,* 213; *ser. 4,* 122

Wills, Maury *ser. 1,* 472

Wilma Rudolph Foundation *ser. 1,* 202

Wilson, Hack *ser. 1,* 152

Wimbledon *ser. 2,* 386
>   Agassi, Andre *ser. 1,* 12-13
>   Ashe, Arthur *ser. 1,* 34
>   Chang, Michael *ser. 1,* 90
>   Courier, Jim *ser. 1,* 107
>   Graf, Steffi *ser. 1,* 177-180
>   Hingis, Martina *ser. 4,* 147-149, 151, 153
>   Navratilova, Martina *ser. 1,* 413-417
>   Pierce, Mary *ser. 2,* 386
>   Rubin, Chanda *ser. 3,* 252
>   Sampras, Pete *ser. 1,* 477
>   Seles, Monica *ser. 1,* 510-511

Series (ser.) is in *italic;* entries in Series 4 and their page numbers are in **bold.**

Series (ser.) is in *italic;* entries in Series 4 and their page numbers are in **bold.**

Z